THE USE AND ABUSE OF HISTORY

By the same Author

*

STUDIES IN LAND AND CREDIT IN ANCIENT ATHENS

THE WORLD OF ODYSSEUS

THE ANCIENT GREEKS

ASPECTS OF ANTIQUITY

ANCIENT SICILY: TO THE ARAB CONQUEST

EARLY GREECE: THE BRONZE AND ARCHAIC AGES

DEMOCRACY ANCIENT AND MODERN

THE ANCIENT ECONOMY

Editor

THE GREEK HISTORIANS

SLAVERY IN CLASSICAL ANTIQUITY

ANCIENT CULTURE AND SOCIETY SERIES

THE USE AND ABUSE OF HISTORY

by

M. I. FINLEY

THE VIKING PRESS / NEW YORK

Copyright © 1971, 1975 by M. I. Finley
All rights reserved
Published in 1975 by The Viking Press, Inc.
625 Madison Avenue, New York, N.Y. 10022
Published simultaneously in Canada by
The Macmillan Company of Canada Limited

"Myth, Memory and History," © Wesleyan University 1965. "Generalizations in Ancient History," © University of Chicago 1963. "The Historical Tradition," © Wesleyan University 1968. "Archaeology and History," © The American Academy of Arts and Sciences 1971, 1972. "The Alienability of Land in Ancient Greece," © Academia, Nakladatelství Československé Akademie Věd 1968. "Sparta," © Mouton & Co. and Ecole Pratique des Hautes Etudes 1968. "Utopianism Ancient and Modern," © Beacon Press 1967. "The Heritage of Isocrates," © University of Edinburgh 1972.

LIBRARY OF CONGRESS CATALOGING IN PUBLICATION DATA

Finley, Moses I
The use and abuse of history.

Includes bibliographical references and index.
1. Greece—Historiography. 2. Rome—Historiography.
I. Title
DE8.F56 1975 938'.007'2 74-30361
ISBN 0-670-74215-5

Printed in U.S.A.

To
ARNALDO MOMIGLIANO

CONTENTS

PREFACE

Despite the diversity of subject reflected in these twelve essays, there is a common concern: the place (or uses) of the past, not only in the academy but also in cultural life, past and present, and in the narrower field of politics and political argument. The echo in my title of the second essay in Nietzsche's *Thoughts Out of Season* is not accidental. Though neither my language nor my thinking is Nietzschean, I agree–and believe it important to argue–that what he called 'monumental history' quickly slides into 'mythical fiction'; that without the 'antiquarian' and the 'critical' methods of studying the past, 'the past itself suffers wrong' and history then 'annihilates and degrades life'.

Some of the essays lean to the programmatic and the didactic, others bring to the fore matters of substance, of particular institutions and societies, while retaining the central concern implicitly. These latter are more technical, but even they do not assume specialized knowledge of the ancient world.

All the essays but one (no. 6) have been published previously. They have all been revised for the present volume, some drastically, and only in my Inaugural Lecture (no. 2) have I retained the language which was appropriate to the occasion. The bibliographical details and acknowledgements are given in an initial footnote to each chapter.

Mr Douglas Matthews has kindly prepared the index.

Jesus College, Cambridge M.I.F.
June 1974

I

MYTH, MEMORY AND HISTORY*

THE Fathers of History were Greeks. Historians of antiquity are very proud of that, so much so that they prefer not to remember that some of the best minds in antiquity were not all impressed by this achievement. History as a discipline has always been a great favourite with the coiners of *bons mots*–it is false, it is dangerous, it is bunk. Historians can comfortably ignore the jibes and doubts of Walpole or Henry Ford, or even Goethe, but Aristotle is another matter; Aristotle, after all, founded a number of sciences and made all the others his own, too, in one fashion or another–except history and economics. He did not jibe at history, he rejected it, in the famous dictum in the ninth chapter of his *Poetics*:

'Poetry is more philosophical and more weighty than history, for poetry speaks rather of the universal, history of the particular. By the universal I mean that such or such a kind of man will say or do such or such things from probability or necessity; that is the aim of poetry, adding proper names to the characters. By the particular I mean what Alcibiades did and what he suffered.'

No wonder the ninth chapter has been perhaps the worst victim of all in the familiar 'grousing about what are thought to be Aristotle's omissions' in the *Poetics*.[1] It has been called 'inadequate'; it has been explained away by clever exegesis, as if Aristotle were one of the pre-Socratic philosophers of whom only a few cryptic sentences survive, which can be made to fit a thousand different theories; or it has been politely dismissed as not dealing with history at all. This last argument has a dangerous element of truth in it. It is not only chapter nine which does not deal with history; Aristotle never does. Apart from two incidental references in the *Poetics*, and a recommendation in the *Rhetoric* (1360a33–37) that political leaders should

* A shorter version of this essay, published in *History and Theory* 4 (1965) 281–302, was delivered as a lecture at the Warburg Institute on 28 October 1964. I am grateful to G. S. Kirk and E. R. Leach for criticisms and suggestions.

Copyright © 1965 by Wesleyan University, and reprinted by permission of Wesleyan University Press.

widen their experience by reading books of travel and history, he fails to mention the subject again in all the vast corpus of his extant works. Nothing could speak more emphatically than that massive silence. Evidence from the past, the past as a source of paradigms, is one thing; history as a systematic study, as a discipline, is another.[2] It is not weighty enough, not philosophical enough, not even in comparison with poetry. It cannot be analysed, reduced to principles, systematized. It tells us merely what Alcibiades did or suffered. It establishes no truths. It has no serious function.

One can go much further. All Greek philosophers, to the last of the neo-Platonists, were evidently agreed in their indifference to history (as discipline). At least that is what their silence suggests, a silence broken only by the most fleeting of whispers. Aristotle's pupil Theophrastus is reported to have written a work called *On History*, and so, too, the latter's younger friend Praxiphanes, another Peripatetic. Beyond their titles, nothing is known of either work. Speculation about their content is idle. We must simply record the total disappearance of both works, the fact that they are never quoted by Diogenes Laertius in his *Lives of the Philosophers*, for example, or by the commentators on Aristotle.*

What philosophy would not have, rhetoric took possession of. It is a sobering thought that the only ancient work to have come down to us which pretends to be a systematic essay on historiography is Lucian's *How to Write History*, written soon after A.D. 165. And that is nothing but a concoction of the rules and maxims which had become the commonplaces of a rhetorical education, a shallow and essentially worthless pot-boiler.[3] Its one point of interest for us is that five hundred years after Aristotle, Lucian was still setting history against poetry. Historians themselves had long since accepted the need to compete for favour with poetry – by surrendering and writing works which Polybius dismissed with the sneering label, 'tragic history'.[4] Not every historian, but too many, and, what is crucial, even the stoutest of the resisters failed to break down either the indifference of the philosophers or the taste of the ordinary readers.

Why poetry? The answer, of course, is that by poetry Aristotle and the others meant epic poetry, late lyric poetry such as Pindar's, and tragedy, which portrayed the great figures and the great events

* I have not forgotten Posidonius, the one apparent exception to what I have said about Greek philosophers and history. But not even this author of a (lost) large-scale historical work in the rhetorical tradition made the slightest contribution to historical method, let alone to philosophy of history. The considerable importance of Posidonius' work in extending Graeco-Roman knowledge of other peoples and nations, particularly those the Romans were conquering in the west, does not weaken my general proposition about ancient philosophers and history.

of the past. The issue was not whether or not, or to what extent, such poetry was historically reliable, in the sense in which we ask that kind of question of the ancient epics today, but the deeper question of universality, of truth about life in general. The issue, in short, was that between myth and history. By 'myth' I mean what is commonly meant, in ordinary usage, by both 'myth' and 'legend', and not the more metaphorical senses, as in the phrase, 'the racist myth', or in the well-known extensions of the term by such modern thinkers as Sorel or Cassirer.[5] I mean such myths as that of Prometheus and Heracles and the Trojan War.

The atmosphere in which the Fathers of History set to work was saturated with myth. Without myth, indeed, they could never have begun their work. The past is an intractable, incomprehensible mass of uncounted and uncountable data. It can be rendered intelligible only if some selection is made, around some focus or foci. In all the endless debate that has been generated by Ranke's *wie es eigentlich gewesen* ('how things really were'), a first question is often neglected: what 'things' merit or require consideration in order to establish how they 'really were'? Long before anyone dreamed of history, myth gave an answer. That was its function, or rather one of its functions; to make the past intelligible and meaningful by selection, by focusing on a few bits of the past which thereby acquired permanence, relevance, universal significance.[6]

When Herodotus was in his prime, the distant past was very much alive in men's consciousness, more so than the recent centuries or generations: Oedipus and Agamemnon and Theseus were more real to fifth-century Athenians than any pre-fifth-century historical figure save Solon, and he was elevated to their ranks by being transformed into a mythical figure. Annually the mythical heroes re-appeared at the great religious festivals in tragedy and choral ode, and they re-created for their audiences the unbroken web of all life, stretching back over the generations of men to the gods; for the heroes of the past, and even many heroes of the present, were divinely descended. All this was serious and true, literally true. It was the basis of their religion, for example. There is a fine passage by Robertson Smith which sums the picture up:

'In ancient Greece . . . certain things were done at a temple, and people were agreed that it would be impious not to do them. But if you had asked why they were done, you would probably have had several mutually contradictory explanations from different persons, and no one would have thought it a matter of the least religious importance which of these you chose to adopt. Indeed, the explanations offered would not have been of a kind to stir any strong feeling;

for in most cases they would have been merely different stories as to the circumstances under which the rite first came to be established, by the command or by the direct example of the god. The rite, in short, was connected not with a dogma but with a myth.'[7]

Greeks did not love epic and tragedy, however, solely because they needed to be reminded about the origins of their rites, important as that function was for the individual–and even more for the community, which was rooted in divine patronage and ancestry. Myth was their great teacher in all matters of the spirit. There they learned morality and conduct; the virtues of nobility and the golden mean or the menace of *hybris*; and they learned about race and culture and even politics. Were not both Solon and Pisistratus accused of falsifying the text of the *Iliad*, interpolating two lines in order to have Homeric authority for the seizure of Salamis from the Megarians?*

With this background it is not surprising that history should have been discussed and judged in antiquity, should have been measured, against poetry. Fundamentally, one kind of retelling of the past was being measured against another. For there must be no misunderstanding about one thing: everyone accepted the epic tradition as grounded in hard fact. Even Thucydides. He tells us that right off, as soon as he finishes introducing himself. The Peloponnesian War, he argues, is more worthy of narration than any which preceded, 'for it was the greatest movement thus far among the Hellenes and among a portion of the barbarian world', greater, specifically, than even the Trojan War. He argues this at some length, and among the 'historical' personages whom he introduces in his opening pages there appear Hellen son of Deucalion (the eponymous ancestor of the Hellenes), Minos, king of Crete, and Agamemnon and Pelops. Details are uncertain, he says, both about the remote past and about the period before the Peloponnesian War–a most significant coupling–but the general outlines are clear and reliable.[8] Homer exaggerated, because he was a poet and properly employed a poet's licence, and Thucydides, unlike the vulgar majority, allowed for this in his introduction. Thucydides himself, we remember, warns his readers that his own work will not cater to the demand for exaggeration and poetic adornment; it will relate the facts free from romance. But neither Thucydides nor Plato nor Aristotle nor anyone else proceeded to outright scepticism about what a modern writer might call the historical kernel in the epic, and surely not to outright denial.

Yet, whatever else it may have been, the epic was *not history*. It

* The lines are 2.557–58: 'Ajax brought twelve ships from Salamis, and bringing, he stationed them alongside the ranks of the Athenians.'

was narrative, detailed and precise, with minute descriptions of fighting and sailing and feasting and burials and sacrifices, all very real and very vivid; it may even contain, buried away, some kernels of historical fact–but it was not history. Like all myth, it was timeless. Dates and a coherent dating scheme are as essential to history as exact measurement is to physics.[9] Myth also presented concrete facts, but these facts were completely detached: they were linked neither with what went before nor with what came after. The *Iliad* begins with the wrath of Achilles over an affront to his honour and ends with the death of Hector. The *Odyssey*, as background to the travels of Odysseus, mentions the ending of the Trojan War and the return of some of the heroes. But it all happened 'once upon a time', flowing out of nothing (for the rape of Helen is merely another isolated fact, totally unhistorical in any significant sense) and leading to nothing. Even within the narrative the account is fundamentally timeless, despite the many fixed numbers (of days or years). 'These numbers, most of them typical numbers which recur for all possible quantities, are in general not binding; they are not the bases for calculations or synchronizations. They merely indicate, broadly, magnitude or scale, and in their stylized pseudo-precision they symbolize long duration. To all intents and purposes there is no interest in chronology, whether relative or absolute.'[10] Many years later the Greek tragedians maintained the same indifference: Oedipus, Iphigenia, Orestes all did things or suffered things which were believed to be historical facts, but what occurred floated dimly in the far-away past, unconnected by time or pattern with other events.

Timelessness is reflected in still another way, in the individual characters. Death is one main topic of their lives (along with honour from which it is inseparable), and fate is often the chief propelling power. In that sense they live in time, but in no other way. It ought not escape any reader of the *Odyssey* that when the hero returns after twenty years, he and Penelope are exactly what they were half a generation earlier. It escaped Samuel Butler, to be sure, when he wrote: 'There is no love-business in the *Odyssey* except the return of a bald elderly married man to his elderly wife and grown-up son after an absence of twenty years, and furious at having been robbed of so much money in the meantime. But this can hardly be called love-business; it is at the utmost domesticity.'[11]

The poet does not say that Odysseus was bald and elderly; Butler says it, and this is presumably what he called reading the Homeric lines 'intelligently' by reading 'between them'. It goes against common sense and 'intelligence' for Odysseus not to be bald and elderly by the time of his return. The flaw–and Samuel Butler is only a convenient whipping-boy for a frequent practice–is to apply modern historical thinking in the guise of common sense to a mythical, non-historical tale. Historical husbands and wives grow old, but the plain fact is that neither Odysseus nor Penelope has changed one bit; they have neither developed nor deteriorated, nor does anyone else in the epic. Such men and women cannot be figures in history: they are too simple, too self-enclosed, too rigid and stable, too detached from their backgrounds. They are as timeless as the story itself.

Perhaps the most decisive example comes not from Homer but from his near contemporary Hesiod.* The opening of the *Works and Days* contains one of the most famous of all primitivistic tales, the account of man's decline from a golden age of the past in several stages, each symbolized by another metal: after gold comes silver, then bronze or copper, and finally iron (the present age). But Hesiod's vision is not one of progressive deterioration, of evolution in reverse. Each race of men (Hesiod speaks of races, *genê*, not of ages) does not evolve into the next; it is destroyed and replaced by a new creation. Each race exists neither in time nor in place. The races of man are as timeless as the Trojan War: for the future as well as the past. And so Hesiod can lament: 'would that I were not among the men of the fifth generation, but either had died before *or been born afterwards*' (lines 174–75).[12]

It is possible that the myth of the four metallic ages or races was an eastern one in origin, Hellenized by Hesiod. But there was also a fifth age or race, and that was surely Greek through and through, the age of heroes injected between the bronze and the iron. 'But when earth had covered this [bronze] generation also, Zeus the son of Cronos made yet another, the fourth, upon the fruitful earth, which was nobler and more righteous, a god-like race of hero-men who are called demi-gods, the race before our own, throughout the boundless earth.' This is patchwork, unavoidable because the myths of the heroes were too deeply fixed in the mind, too indispensable to be passed by. Patchwork is the rule in myth, and it gives no trouble. Only the historically minded see the rough stitches and the faulty joins and are bothered by them, as is abundantly evident in Herodotus. But Hesiod was not historically minded. Here on the one hand were the four races and here on the other hand was the race of heroes. They were data, and his task was to assemble them. He did it in the easiest way possible, thanks to the total absence of the time

* It is convenient (and in this context, harmless) to speak of Homer and Hesiod each in the singular, ignoring the complex problem of the authorship of 'their' poems.

element. There were no chronological problems, no dates to be synchronized, no development to trace or explain. The race of heroes had no beginning in history: it was simply made by Zeus. And it had no ending, no transition to the next, contemporary stage. Some of the heroes were destroyed before the gates of Thebes and in the Trojan War. 'But to the others father Zeus the son of Cronos gave a living and an abode apart from men, and made them dwell at the ends of the earth. And they live untouched by sorrow in the islands of the blessed along the shore of deep swirling Ocean.'[13]

There is a sense, of course, in which the myth of the ages is not a proper myth. It is too abstract. Hesiod's poem deals, in its first part, with the problem of evil, and no more despairing indictment of the injustice of the world has ever been written. Why, he asks, why is the world so full of evil? His first answer is mythical in its most traditional sense; he tells the story of Prometheus and Pandora: that is the answer, a typically mythical answer, the kind of answer Greeks continued to give to explain rites and beliefs all through their history. But now, he continues without pause, I will tell you another tale, and his second one, the alternative to the Pandora myth, is the account of the races of man. Clearly there is a new kind of thinking here, inchoate, poetic and not systematic, not followed through and not even properly linked with the rest of the long poem, but nonetheless pointing to an entirely new line of intellectual endeavour and pointing away from myth and epic. 'What was at the beginning?' a historian of Greek philosophy wrote of Hesiod, 'is the question of history precisely at the point where it turns into philosophy. . . . The question Hesiod poses is no longer about the historical past, but about the beginning of what exists, the question of philosophical origins. . . .'[14] But 'history' is wholly out of place here. Hesiod is foreshadowing the step from *mythos* to *logos*, and that step was not mediated by history. It bypassed history altogether. It moved from the timelessness of myth to the timelessness of metaphysics.

More than two centuries went by before the (more recent) past was bound into any sort of chronology. That was the work of Herodotus. Writing in the third quarter of the fifth century, Herodotus conjectured that Homer lived four hundred years earlier (about 850 B.C.) and that the Trojan War took place another four hundred years before that (about 1250 B.C.). Many events were known to have occurred during that long interval, such as the return of the Heraclids to Sparta, the various (and chronologically incompatible) deeds of Theseus, or the legislation of Lycurgus. These Herodotus was totally unable to fit into his chronological scheme. The fault was not his, but a consequence of the fact that the data were timeless, and therefore unhistorical. The measure of his genius lies in the simple point that he appreciated these limitations (if not to the extent of disbelief in the 'fact' of Orestes and Theseus and the rest) and therefore he made no effort to assign dates to the undatable myths. Herodotus' historical chronology, in so far as there is one, is more accurate than has usually been allowed, equally so in his refusal to ruin it by incorporating the mythical events.[15] The latter frequently recur in his work, but as something detached, as something which happened once upon a time, unlike, say, the career of Solon or the reign of Polycrates in Samos. Polycrates, says Herodotus (3.122), seems to have been the first Greek to think of a maritime empire, 'leaving aside Minos' and others like him, the first, in other words, 'in what is called the time of men'–which we should express as the first in historical, as distinct from mythical, times.[16] What Herodotus was able to do was to establish some kind of time-sequence for perhaps two centuries of the past, roughly from the middle of the seventh century B.C. on. All that came before remained as it had been when he began his work, epic tales and myths believed to be true, at least in essence, but incorrigibly timeless.

The plain fact is that the classical Greeks knew little about their history before 650 B.C. (or even 550 B.C.), and that what they thought they knew was a jumble of fact and fiction, some miscellaneous facts and much fiction about the essentials and about most of the details. One need only consider Thucydides' introduction, which I have already mentioned, in which he justified his own effort by offering in twenty-one chapters (a dozen pages) a most remarkable interpretation of early Greek history. From chapter fourteen he was on pretty firm ground, established by Herodotus (whose book he had studied with great care) with the indispensable help of Egyptian, Persian and other Near Eastern records. But in the first part he had nothing to go on other than Homer and other 'old poets', tradition, contemporary evidence, and a very powerful and disciplined mind. The result is a sweeping theory, namely, that Hellenic power and greatness emerged only in consequence of the systematic development of navigation and commerce, which were followed by an accumulation of resources, stable community organization, imperialism (to use an anachronistic word), and finally the greatest of all Greek power struggles, the Peloponnesian War. This theory may be right, in whole or in part, or it may be wrong–I am not concerned with that question here. What is crucial is that it is a theory derived from prolonged meditation about the world in which Thucydides lived, not from a study of history. True, there is something here which is history in a conceptual sense: Thucydides has made the bold suggestion that there was a continuity and a development in Greece from the most ancient (mythical) times to his own. I do not underestimate this new conception, but its actual working out by Thucydides in his opening pages is not history in any meaningful sense of that word. Instead he has given us what amounts to a general sociological theory, a theory about power and progress, applied retrospectively to the past, and applied, one must add, with caution and hesitation, for, as Thucydides explains at the outset, one cannot achieve certainty about ancient times, one can merely say that this is what all the 'signs' point to.

Among the signs are astonishingly few concrete events: the first thalassocracy 'known to tradition' (that of King Minos), the Trojan War, a few migrations, change in habits of dress and in the practice of carrying arms, the extension from Sparta to the Olympic games of the practice of competing entirely naked in athletics, and a few other scraps – until the age of tyrants and Persian annals. There are only four dates: the migration of the Boeotians to Boeotia sixty years after the Trojan War and of the Dorians into the Peloponnese twenty years after that; the construction of four triremes (an important new invention) by the Corinthian Ameinocles for the Samians three hundred years before the end of the Peloponnesian War (i.e., about 700 B.C.); and forty years later the first recorded naval battle, between Corinth and Corcyra. Thucydides does not date the Trojan War, but if he accepted Herodotus' chronology, then he has no dated event between 1170 and 700 B.C., a period equal in length to that between the accession of Henry VII and our own day. Everything that fell between could only be fixed as 'later' or 'much later'. Moreover, we have no independent check on his two late dates, and we can dismiss his two early ones as still in the realm of myth, whatever the truth about the movements of Boeotians and Dorians.

But we do have some control over the general picture of material progress and migration, and the result is negative (quite apart from the possible validity of the sea-power theory itself). Twice in this section Thucydides argues explicitly from what we should call archaeological evidence, once from the ruins of Mycenae and the other time from the bones and artifacts uncovered when Delos was purified in 426/5 B.C. (in Thucydides' own lifetime) by opening all the graves and transferring their contents to the adjacent island of Rhenaea. The arguments are clever and cogent, but are they valid? On the contrary, they reveal a gross ignorance and misunderstanding of the past on several points of major significance. Thucydides was clearly unaware (as were all other Greek writers, so far as we know) of the catastrophic destruction of Mycenaean civilization near the end of the second millennium B.C. and of the profound discontinuity between Mycenaean civilization and Greek civilization proper; he 'did not recognise Geometric . . . pottery as being particularly Greek and dated it at least three hundred years too early'; he 'either did not know of what we call the Bronze Age or else dated its end too early'. In sum, in his view, 'Agamemnon's Mycenae and fifth-century Mycenae could be thought of as one city, repaired and casually rebuilt but essentially the same'.[17]

These mistakes, coupled with the absence of all dates and of virtually all fixed events between 1170 and 700, destroy any possibility of a proper history of early Greece. I do not mean that Thucydides tried to write one, even in capsule form, and failed: on the contrary, he did not try because he did not believe it possible or necessary. I mean, rather, that from such a start no Greek could write one, and the proof is in the pathetic failure of those men in later centuries who tried to write annals and universal histories from the Trojan War (or from the creation of the world) to their own day. They lacked the information, and there was no way they could get it. Of this we can be confident, as we can confidently correct Thucydides' mistakes about the fall of Mycenae or the origin and date of Geometric vases. More than that, we know much more (and much more accurately) about the political trends and the growth of cities and the development of trade and money and so on through the whole list of institutional and social phenomena. And yet, we too are wholly incapable of writing a history of this period. That is our inescapable heritage from the Greeks. We can, for example, discourse with considerable subtlety and sophistication–and with inherent probability–about the decline of monarchy and the rise of the aristocratic *polis*, but we cannot narrate that story, not even in fragmentary fashion, for any single community; we are gradually assembling much information about the physical appearance of early Ionian cities and we can date their development to close limits, but we have no significant knowledge about the political life within them; we can lay out the vases in most elaborate series, but we know nothing about the potters or the pottery industry. And we never shall. In short, like Thucydides, we can formulate sociological theories, and unlike him, we can write art history (largely restricted to pure externals). But we, too, cannot write a history of early Greece.

The reason is very simple: there are no documents, nothing which records events or reports who did things, what things, and why. Before the year 700 B.C. (a round number which I use as a signpost, not as a precise date) such documents never existed, not even in the most transient form, on papyrus or wax. After 700 a body of Greek writing began to emerge, steadily increasing in volume and variety as the classical world of the fifth and fourth centuries B.C. drew nearer. Little survives, some quotations in later writers and fragmentary collections recovered in the present century on Egyptian papyri of Hellenistic and Roman times. It is not beyond hope that more will be found in the future which will add to our stock of information, much as the new fragments of the poet Alcaeus have taught us things about the political struggles within the aristocracy of Lesbos round the year 600, and about the tyranny of Pittacus which had been as mysterious in its details as it was famous in legend. Were every lost line written between 700 and 500 to be recovered, including the texts of laws and decrees as well as poems and philosophical writings, a generation of historians would be kept busy sorting and organizing and interpreting the new material – and we should still be unable to write a history of these two centuries, let alone of the earlier centuries.

That gloomy prediction follows inevitably from the nature of the material. For complicated reasons – which I do not believe we are in a position to formulate fully – the composition of epic poetry came to a rather abrupt end. Poets turned their backs on the past, both on the literary forms of the past and on the past as subject-matter, and they began to write about themselves and their friends, their loves and hates, their feelings, their joys and their pleasures. For two centuries all the poetry was personal; it might be flippant or anacreontic, it might be amatory (Sapphic or otherwise), or it might be serious, moralistic and philosophical – but always it dealt with personal problems and with generalities, not with narration nor with politics or society in their concrete institutional expressions.*

I hate the lanky officer, stiff-standing, legs apart,
Whose cut of hair and whisker is his principal renown;
I prefer the little fellow with his bigness in his heart,
And let his legs be bandy, if they never let him down.

These lines of Archilochus[18] reveal a new, un-heroic, un-Homeric set of values. Others offer biographical bits – 'We, the down-and-outs of Hellas, flocked to Thasos in a troop' – often with important social implications (in this instance, the appearance of the mercenary soldier). They are precious bits, given the sparseness of our knowledge of these centuries, but they cannot be converted, not even if

* One might consider some of Solon's poems as exceptions, but they are so lacking in concreteness, even about his own reforms, that they argue for my generalization, not against.

they were counted in the tens of thousands, into a consistent and continuous story of how the Greek cities emerged, grew, took shape, struggled and lived. Nor do the philosophical writers add another dimension. And that is all there was.

No one before the fifth century tried to organize, either for his own time or for earlier generations, the essential stuff of history. There were lists–of the kings of Sparta and the archons of Athens and the victors in the various games. They could provide a chronology, if we knew what happened in the archonship of X or the reign of Y; but we do not know, except in a few isolated instances about a few isolated events. Law codes and individual rulings were recorded somehow, but there were no proper archives, and they soon disappeared from sight for the most part. This combination of negatives –the absence of annals (like those of the kings of Assyria), the indifference of poets and philosophers, and the loss of public documents– is irrevocable. Unless a generation is captured on paper and the framework of its history fixed, either contemporaneously or soon thereafter, the future historian is for ever blocked. He can reinterpret, shift the emphases, add and deduct data, but he cannot create the framework *e nihilo*. That is why we can write the history of the Persian wars, thanks to Herodotus, and the history of the Peloponnesian War, thanks to Thucydides, but not the history of the intervening fifty years, not for all the writers of tragedy and comedy and all the inscriptions and material objects unearthed by modern archaeologists.[19]

Contemporary archaeology is a highly refined, highly professional and technical procedure. Carbon-14 dating and similar techniques will one day produce firm evidence undreamed of in the world of Thucydides. Yet it would be a great mistake to explain our superior knowledge of Mycenae solely by reference to scientific advances. Technically, Schliemann and Sir Arthur Evans had little at their disposal which was not available to fifth-century Athenians. The ancient Greeks already possessed the skills and the manpower with which to discover the shaft-graves of Mycenae and the palace of Cnossus, and they had the intelligence to link the buried stones–had they dug them up–with the myths of Agamemnon and Minos, respectively. What they lacked was the interest: that is where the enormous gap lies between their civilization and ours, between their view of the past and ours. A reverse example comes from their use of literary evidence. Thucydides and his contemporaries knew the full corpus of lyric and elegiac poetry, but they made less use, and less skilful use, of this material for historical analysis than we make of the few scraps which have survived in our time. Again neither technique nor intelligence is a useful criterion; only interest will explain the difference.

Some kind of interest in the past is, of course, universal. That statement helps very little, however, though it is repeated often enough in books about history and the writing of history, as if it were an important point worth making.[20] In so far as it is not just a tautology–man by nature has memory, including memory of things told to him by older generations, and therefore he has an 'interest' in the past–it has no meaning which is not either wrong or confusing. Interest in the sense of curiosity or desire for knowledge is, in ordinary usage, a term of individual psychology, descriptive of a state of mind or feeling, not sufficient as an explanation of individual behaviour, totally useless when extended to a society. Interest must itself be defined and accounted for: what part of the past and how much of it? Interest to what purpose, to fulfil what function? The past has been studied didactically and morally, as an exemplar of man's essential sinfulness, for example, or as a guide to future political action; it has performed the social-psychological function of giving a society cohesion and purpose, of strengthening morale and encouraging patriotism; it can be and has been put to romantic uses. And so on. Each of these interests requires a different kind of approach and a different kind of study (within limits)–in short, a different kind of knowledge.

None of the interests I have just enumerated requires a systematic account of the past. The question which is implicit in so much modern writing on the history of history–how could the Greeks (or anyone else) remain content with a past which was filled with so many blank spaces and which was, essentially, timeless?–rests on a false conception of time in human psychology. We are in thrall to the highly sophisticated, highly abstract scientific conception of time as a measurable continuum, a conception which is largely meaningless for ordinary human purposes. Time past consists of a number of individual events (including biological transformations and sensual satisfactions); time future consists of anticipated events or satisfactions. Duration of time, if it is a consideration at all, which is not always the case, is not experienced as a measurable quantity but as an associative or emotional quality: time drags, for example.[21] Individual memory illustrates this exactly. We do not recall a past event, whether we are consciously searching our memories for one or one comes to mind without deliberation, by working our way from the present through the past. Memory leaps instantaneously to the desired point and it then dates by association. There is a certain consciousness of duration, to be sure, but that is satisfied by 'long ago' or 'the other day', or by an association which implies 'long ago', for example, 'when I was still a schoolboy'.

This is familiar and obvious, and it is as true of group experience as of personal experience. Claud Cockburn records a revealing meeting with three Ladino-speaking Jews in Sofia shortly after the Second World War. He had approached the three men in the railway station, not knowing who or what they were. After attempting conversation in several languages without success, he tried Spanish.

'They understood, and replied in what was certainly intelligible as a form of Spanish–though a very strange form. . . . I remarked that it was rather odd to find Spanish here [in Sofia]. They explained. They were not Spaniards, but, one of them said, "Our family used to live in Spain before they moved to Turkey. Now we are moving to Bulgaria." Thinking that perhaps they had been "displaced" from Spain by the upheaval of the civil war, I asked how long it had been since their family lived there. He said it was approximately five hundred years. . . . He spoke of these events as though they had occurred a couple of years ago.'[22]

Essentially the 'historical' references of these Ladino-speaking Jews were like the 'mythical' references of most Greeks, with one difference the significance of which is more potential than actual. When pressed, the former translated 'our family used to live in Spain' into 'it was approximately five hundred years ago'. They were able to do that thanks to the modern calendar, with its dating by years from a fixed initial point. The Greeks eventually acquired that technique, too, when dating by Olympiads was introduced, but that remained for them an artificial convention, invented and used by a small number of antiquarian-minded intellectuals, never introduced into daily life. And that brings us back to the matter of interest. The only people in antiquity who were somehow 'modern' in this respect were the Hebrews, and the interest which lay behind, and which provoked, their detailed account of the past as a continuum was, of course, a religious one, the story of the unfolding of God's will from the Creation to the final triumph in the future. The Greeks had no such interest, religious or otherwise; whatever the function in the present of Agamemnon, it did not require locating him along a time continuum; it did not matter whether he lived two hundred years ago or four hundred or a thousand.

Effectively, Greek thinking divided the past into two parts, two compartments, the heroic age and the post-heroic (or the time of the gods and the time of men). The first was the part fixed, defined and described by the myth-makers, who worked in the centuries which are, to us, prehistoric in the strict sense. They created and transmitted myths orally, bringing together purely cult material (the origins of which can be speculated about, but not documented), genuine historical events (including personal details about the noble families), and much purely imaginary material. Their orientation was towards the past; at first, presumably, towards the more recent past, but, as time went on, increasingly–and to a considerable extent, deliberately–to more remote times. The interest, however, was not historical in the sense of an objective inquiry into the facts of the Trojan War (or any other period of history). That is obvious, but it needs saying.[23] Even when we put aside aesthetic considerations, the pleasures evoked by the beauty of the lines and the chanting, or the not inconsiderable satisfactions aroused by a story simply because it is a good story, the remaining interests lay far outside the realm of inquiry and science. Pan-Hellenic or regional consciousness and pride, aristocratic rule, and especially their right to rule, their pre-eminent qualifications and virtues, an understanding of the gods, the meaning of cult practices–these and other, comparable, ends were served by the continual repetition of the old tales. And by their constant re-working, for new conditions were always intruding.

In this first phase, then, when oral tradition was built up and kept alive, the product was a mythical past created out of disparate elements, differing in their character and their (factual) accuracy, and having their (factual) origin in widely scattered periods of time. 'Tradition' did not merely transmit the past, it created it. In a shape which sometimes looks like history, and has been widely accepted as history both by the Greeks and (with qualifications) by many modern students, the bards fashioned a timeless mythology.[24] Then a new phase set in, symbolized by the eventual writing down of the epics and other mythological documents. In a world which lacked any kind of central authority, political or ecclesiastical, and which was filled with separate and often clashing political and regional interests, this step helped fixed the texts of the tales, creating an authoritative version. Important as that was, however, it need not, by itself, have been decisive. The myth-making process did not stop in the eighth century; it never wholly stopped. Apart from the mythicizing of men like Solon, myth-making continued because Greek religion continued to develop new rites, introduce new gods, and combine old elements into new forms, each step requiring an appropriate adjustment in the inherited mythology. Likewise, the great dispersion of Greeks from about 750 to about 600 B.C., carrying them to southern Italy, Sicily, and to many other places along the Mediterranean and Black Sea shores, demanded further changes to suit new political alignments between cities and regions and to incorporate traditions of the (non-Greek) peoples among whom they settled. All this later myth-making activity, however, was secondary: the 'mythical charter' of Hellenic self-consciousness was now fully fashioned.[25] Interests moved in new directions.

The second phase was therefore one in which interest in the distant, and important, past, though fully alive, expressed itself in retention and repetition of the mythical charter. Along with the writing down of the epics went the disappearance of the bards as a class. They were replaced by rhapsodes, men like Plato's Ion who were professionals too, but reciters–actors–not creators. The creative intellects, as I have already said, turned to entirely new fields, to personal and contemporary poetry and to philosophy. The heroic past needed no further attention, other than the passive one of seeing to it that everyone was reminded of it, in the accepted version, on all appropriate occasions, and that each succeeding generation retained this knowledge and made use of it in the same ways.

How and by whom, we must then ask, were traditions about the post-heroic centuries preserved and transmitted? How, for example, did the memory survive of the sea-battle between Corinth and Corcyra or of the construction by a Corinthian of four warships for the Samians, which Thucydides reports and to which he even assigns precise dates? Thucydides himself could have read about these things in Herodotus or in some other writer. But someone put them down on paper for a first time two hundred or more years after the event (and there were many other traditional facts of a still earlier date, requiring oral transmission for still more centuries). The first man to write them down (and in some instances that may well have been someone as late as Thucydides) had no documents or archives to draw on–that cannot be stressed too often. He had to capture something which had been transmitted orally.

Oral tradition is an old favourite in books dealing with distant ages, or even with fairly recent ages, for which there are few (or no) written records. And there are few notions which historians of the Greek Dark Age are less prepared to examine critically enough, enveloping themselves in the warm glow thrown off by the word 'tradition'. Now there is the tradition which shapes a large part of our lives, perpetuating customs, habits of behaviour, rites, ethical norms and beliefs. There is nothing mysterious about tradition in this sense; it is transmitted from one generation to the next, partly by the ordinary process of living in society, without any conscious effort on anyone's part, partly by men whose function it is to do so: priests, schoolmasters, parents, judges, party leaders, censors, neighbours. There is also nothing reliable about this sort of tradition; that is to say, its explanations and narrations are, as anyone can judge by a minimum of observation, rarely quite accurate, and sometimes altogether false. Reliability is, of course, irrelevant; so long as the tradition is accepted, it works, and it must work if the society is not to fall apart.

But 'tradition' detached from living practices and institutions–a tradition about a war two hundred years back, for example–is not the same thing at all; only a semantic confusion seems to place it in the same category. Wherever tradition can be studied among living people, the evidence is not only that it does not exist apart from a connection with a practice or belief, but also that other kinds of memory, irrelevant memories, so to speak, are short-lived, going back to the third generation, to the grandfather's generation, and, with the rarest of exceptions, no further. This is true even of genealogies, unless they are recorded in writing; it may be taken as a rule that orally transmitted genealogies, unless some very powerful interest intervenes (such as charismatic kingship), are often distorted, disputed or wholly fictitious beyond the fourth generation, and often even beyond the third. There is a nice Greek illustration: the Homeric heroes recite their genealogies frequently and in detail, and without exception a few steps take them from human ancestors to gods or goddesses.

The analogy with individual memory is again useful. It, too, normally stops at the third generation, with things told by grandparents, by parents about their parents, by elderly nurses. It, too, is controlled by relevance. All memory is selective, and though the reason why something remains (apart from something actively and deliberately learned, like a school lesson) more often than not escapes us, that is a defect in our knowledge, not a manifestation of random, purposeless behaviour. But then the analogy breaks down, for 'group memory' is never subconsciously motivated in the sense of being, or seeming to be, automatic and uncontrolled, unsought for as personal memory so often appears. Group memory, after all, is no more than the transmittal to many people of the memory of one man or a few men, repeated many times over; and the act of transmittal, of communication and therefore of preservation of the memory, is not spontaneous and unconscious but deliberate, intended to serve a purpose known to the man who performs it. He may misjudge his motives, he may not formulate them clearly, he probably does not go through a long prior process of reflection, but invariably he is acting, doing something, bringing about an effect he desires or wills. Unless such conscious, deliberate activity occurs, eventually the memory of any event will die; whereas individual memories can lie dormant for decades and then come to life without warning or conscious action.

Oral tradition, therefore, is not a tool the historian can count on 'in the nature of things'. He must always ask *Cui bono?* In my judgment, for the post-heroic period well into the fifth century, the survival of the sort of tradition I have been discussing must be credited largely to the noble families in the various communities, including royal families where they existed, and, what amounts to the same thing in a special variation, to the priests of such shrines as Delphi, Eleusis and Delos. They alone, in most circumstances at least, had both the interest to 'remember' events and incidents which mattered to them (for whatever reason), and the status to impress that memory, whether true or false, so as to convert it into a public tradition. It goes without saying that neither the interest nor the process was historical–perhaps I should say 'historiographical'–in any significant sense. The objective was an immediate and practical one, whether it was fully conscious or not, and that was the enhancement of prestige or the warranty of power or the justification of an institution.

Several conclusions follow. In the first place, the losses, the numbers of facts which were completely and irrevocably forgotten by everyone, were enormous, in a never ending process. Much depended on the fortunes of the individual families, as to whether their particular memories became public memories, and then as to the duration and purity of the tradition in succeeding generations.

Second, the surviving material has the appearance of a random scatter. For example, Thucydides writes (1.13.2) that the 'Corinthians, they say, were the first to pursue the naval art in a modern sort of way, and Corinth was the first place in Greece where triremes were constructed'. No names are mentioned, but in the following sentence Thucydides adds the irrelevant fact that a Corinthian named Ameinocles built four triremes for Samos, presumably the first on that island. Why this curious choice? As far as our evidence goes, no name of the inventor of triremes had come down in the tradition, but Ameinocles did (no doubt among the Samians). We cannot possibly explain this particular survival pattern, nor can we in most of the other instances, for the explanation rests in contemporary circumstances about which we know absolutely nothing. That is why I speak of the *appearance* of a random scatter, of a large number of individual facts most of which bear no visible connection with one another, as if pure chance, the throw of dice, determined whether they were to be remembered or not. They did not even have a close chronological connection until one was imposed upon them. Thucydides' dates for Ameinocles and for the battle between Corinth and Corcyra are his own calculation, not the tradition as he received it. And, though we cannot check either date, there are strong reasons for believing that they are much too early, assuming that the two events are facts, not fictions. Given the paucity and the scatter of the tradition, it would be sheer luck if he or anyone else were able to construct an accurate chronological relationship.

Third, individual elements of the tradition were conflated, modified and sometimes invented. Family rivalries, conflicts between communities and regions, changes in power relationships, new values and beliefs–all these historical developments shaped tradition. They had a relatively free hand with what was happening currently, but often they could not afford to ignore traditions they themselves had inherited. Where a vital interest was affected, it was imperative that corrections be made. Even in a world which makes considerable use of writing, this process is not too difficult; for example, falsification of archaic Athenian political developments was characteristic of the political pamphleteering and party conflict in Athens in the last years of the Peloponnesian War and the next two or three decades. So effective was this falsification that neither fourth-century Athenians nor modern historians have been able to unscramble the pictures which were drawn. And when tradition is entirely oral, conflation and falsification are that much simpler to bring about. They cannot, indeed, be prevented.[26]

Truth, however, as I have already said, truth in the Rankean sense of 'how things really were', was neither an important consideration nor a claim one could substantiate. Acceptance and belief were what counted, and the Greeks had all the knowledge of the past they needed without the help of historians. The poets took care of the heroic past; for the rest, specific traditions, largely oral, were sufficient. In Athens, the Solonic codification, the tyrannicides, Marathon were the stock allusions of political orators and pamphleteers, and everyone knew all that anyone needed to know about them. Occasional efforts by historians to correct factual errors in the tradition met with no response, as Thucydides' angry remarks about the tyrannicides reveal.[27] Harmodius and Aristogeiton were essential to the Athenian mythical charter, which the truth would have damaged and weakened. Even in the fourth century, after Herodotus and Thucydides, Athenian orators still clung to their traditional myths and their popular history, utterly indifferent to the new knowledge and the new conceptions. Demosthenes could be as precise as anyone about current affairs, citing customs house records and treaties and court proceedings to support his facts and figures, but about the past he was as ignorant, perhaps deliberately so, as his hearers, restricting himself to the same commonplace references–and inaccuracies–as his opponents, and his audience.[28]

It is both an intellectualist and a modernist fallacy to think that this is what requires explanation. On the contrary, the difficult question is why anyone–specifically, why Herodotus and Thucydides–broke so radically from the customary attitudes and 'invented' the idea of history.[29] The conventional answer begins with the Ionian philosophers and their scepticism, and that contains a half-truth. The Ionians and their successors provided two necessary conditions, their scepticism about the myths and their notion of 'inquiry'. These were, however, not a sufficient reason, as I have already said in discussing Hesiod. Scepticism about myth led the Ionians to inquiry about the cosmos, to metaphysics, not to historiography. We must still ask why Herodotus applied the word *historia*, which simply means 'inquiry', to an inquiry into the past. His own answer is given right at the beginning of his work: to preserve the fame of the great and wonderful actions of the Greeks and barbarians and to inquire into the reasons why they fought each other.

The reasons why they fought each other: that is not a new question. After all, myth gave the reasons why the Greeks and Trojans fought each other, and reasons why many other events occurred. What is new in Herodotus is not only the systematic inquiry he pursued in seeking answers, which produced an historical narrative, but the extent to which his explanations are human and secular, and, in particular, political. In the next generation Thucydides then carried those novelties very much further, as he insisted on continuous narrative with a strict chronology, on a rigorously secular analysis, and on an equally rigorous emphasis on political behaviour. The new impulse came from the classical *polis*, and in particular the Athenian *polis*, which for the first time, at least in western history, introduced politics as a human activity and then elevated it to the most fundamental social activity. A new look at the past was required. That is to say, not that no other impetus could have produced the idea of history,[30] but that among the Greeks this was the decisive condition (in combination with the scepticism and habit of inquiry already mentioned).

The new look had to be secular, non-mythical, and political–but did it have to be historical in the sense of a survey over a long period of continuous time? More precisely, for how long a period, for how much of the past? If one considers the histories of Herodotus and Thucydides without prejudice, the obvious–though not the most familiar–answer is that not much of the past was really relevant. Herodotus wandered about a great deal in the past, the mythical as well as the historical, the Egyptian as well as the Greek, but for reasons which were more often than not irrelevant to that part of his inquiry which was properly historical. Thucydides rejected that kind of digression, that 'romancing', so completely that his work contains no continuous past history at all. When Thucydides decided in 431 B.C. that the Greek world was entering the greatest war ever and that he would devote his life to recording it, that war was still in the future. Ultimately, he wrote an introduction, drawing some generalizations about the Trojan War and the emergence of the classical world, and filling a little of the gap between Herodotus' narrative and the onset of the Peloponnesian War. But that was no more than an introduction, conceptually historical, as I have already said, but not history. Everything else was contemporary.

Thereafter serious Greek historical writing was about contemporary history. In a brilliantly phrased paragraph, Collingwood said: The Greek historian 'cannot, like Gibbon, begin by wishing to write a great historical work and go on to ask himself what he shall write about. . . . Instead of the historian choosing the subject, the subject chooses the historian; I mean that history is written only because memorable things have happened which call for a chronicler among the contemporaries of the people who have seen them. One might almost say that in ancient Greece there were no historians in the sense in which there were artists and philosophers; there were no people who devoted their lives to the study of history; the historian was only the autobiographer of his generation and autobiography is not a profession.'[31]

This may be too simple, too one-sided; it is not simply false. Thucydides found himself caught up in contradictory pulls, which he was never able to resolve. He accepted the need to narrate events in sequence, but on the other hand he wished to extract from the events the essence of politics and political behaviour, the nature and consequences of power. That, if he could achieve it, would be a 'possession for ever', among other reasons because human nature is a constant and therefore recurrence is the pattern. But if so, what is the point to a linear account over long periods of time? One can really know only one's own time, and that is sufficient anyway. The past can yield nothing more than paradigmatic support for the conclusions one has drawn from the present; the past, in other words, may still be treated in the timeless fashion of myth. There is a relevant passage in Sir Isaiah Berlin's *The Hedgehog and the Fox*, which is about Tolstoy but in which one could substitute the name of Thucydides and go a long way (though not the whole way) without sacrificing accuracy.

'Tolstoy's interest in history began early in his life. It seems to have arisen not from interest in the past as such, but from the desire to penetrate to first causes, to understand how and why things happen as they do and not otherwise . . . from a tendency to doubt and place under suspicion and, if need be, reject whatever does not fully answer the question, to go to the root of every matter, at whatever cost. . . . And with this went an incurable love of the concrete, the empirical, the verifiable, and an instinctive distrust of the abstract, the impalpable, the supernatural–in short an early tendency to a scientific and positivist approach, unfriendly to romanticism, abstract formulations, metaphysics. Always and in every situation he looked for "hard" facts. . . . He was tormented by the ultimate problems which face young men in every generation . . . but the answers provided by theologians and metaphysicians struck him as absurd. . . . History, only history, only the sum of the concrete events in time and space . . . this alone contained the truth, the material out of which genuine answers . . . might be constructed.'[32]

So one wrote *War and Peace*, the other the *Peloponnesian War*. I am not being frivolous when I put it that way. History 'contained the truth', and for Thucydides that meant that it was unnecessary to invent as the poets did. But it was also impossible merely to record what had happened. It was necessary to compose speeches which would lay bare the appropriate arguments (appropriate in Thucydides' judgment) on both sides of an issue. It was even necessary to write a sophistical treatise on might and right, the Melian Dialogue. The narrative alone proved a failure in the end: it told only what Alcibiades did and what he suffered. Those were facts, not truths.

After Thucydides every serious historian wrestled with the same difficulties, and usually preferred to wrestle with them in the field of contemporary history. The idea of a historical narrative, of a continuum of events in time, had come to stay. But what purpose was it to serve? That question was never answered satisfactorily. The idea had arisen, and had been nurtured, that society was bound to its past, and up to a point could be understood from its past, in ways which differed from the old ways of myth. That idea was thwarted, however, by the absence of an idea of progress, by the idealization of the eternal and immutable against the changing and transient ('a rigorously anti-historical metaphysics' in Collingwood's phrase), by cyclical views of history, by primitivistic doctrines. On the intellectual level everything was against the idea of history. Only the

Tolstoyan types struggled on, stimulated by each extraordinary situation or development to try again: Timaeus and the fierce struggles in Sicily over tyranny, Polybius and the establishment of Rome's world-empire; or, among the Romans, Sallust and the disintegration of the Roman Republic, Tacitus and the emergence of despotic absolutism. Like Thucydides, each of these men was ultimately seeking to understand and explain his own, contemporary world.

Their appeal and influence are hard to measure. It is significant, however, how quickly historians abandoned the austerity of Thucydides for the emotional appeals of the poets, how history became 'tragic history', even in Polybius who denied it so vehemently. It is also significant that the philosophers rejected the whole enterprise. As for the people at large, there is no reason to think that they ever moved beyond the old myths and the occasional bits of mythologized history. Why should they have, after all? As Hans Meyerhoff said in a different, but somewhat related, context: 'Previous generations *knew* much less about the past than we do, but perhaps *felt* a much greater sense of identity and continuity with it. . . .'[33] Myth achieved that, and there was nothing in the society which required its abandonment or replacement. Perhaps that was a flaw in the *polis*–but that is a different subject.

2

THE ANCESTRAL CONSTITUTION*

IN a political pamphlet, the *Areopagiticus*, probably written not long before 350 B.C., Isocrates, the influential Athenian rhetorician, grumbled (7.15–16) that, 'though we sit around in the shops denouncing the current situation, saying that never under our democracy have we been worse governed', we act as if we are more satisfied with our present democracy 'than with the one inherited from our ancestors'. I shall argue, he continued, that 'the only way to rescue ourselves from our present evils and head off future dangers is if we are willing to restore the democracy instituted by Solon, who was the most demotic of legislators, and re-established by Cleisthenes, who drove out the tyrants and led the people back to power'.

Two thousand years later the House of Commons complained that Charles I 'had a wicked design to subvert the ancient and fundamental laws and liberties of this nation'.[1] In our own century, a New York lawyer delivered the following effusion: 'Our great and sacred Constitution, serene and inviolable, stretches its beneficent powers over our land–over its lakes and rivers and forests, over every mother's son of us, like the outstretched arm of God himself. . . . O Marvelous Constitution! Magic Parchment! Transforming word! Maker, Monitor, Guardian of Mankind!'[2] Mr Henry Estabrook's rhetoric was not exhausted by these few words, as you will have guessed, but one brief sample is sufficient for my point.

This rhetoric may lack the rotundity of Isocrates, nevertheless it is on its level a manifestation of one political argument that has been deployed in widely different historical situations. Not a sophisticated

* The Inaugural Lecture I delivered on 4 May 1971 was an abridged version of this original text. I made a few revisions prior to publication by Cambridge University Press, following suggestions of A. Andrewes and John Dunn, who kindly read the manuscript. I have made no changes in the style.

Copyright © 1971 by M. I. Finley, and reprinted by permission of Cambridge University Press.

argument, to be sure–one will find no mention of it in Brian Barry's recent book on political argument; and an argument that is easily caricatured, as in Cornford's 'nothing should ever be done for the first time'.[3] But a high level of sophistication is not a necessary condition for effectiveness. The appeal to the 'ancestral constitution' satisfies the canon that it must '*seem* rational and persuasive', that both its proponents and those they persuaded could, if pressed, defend themselves 'by some rules of logic and evidence that they would themselves accept'.[4] It is therefore a legitimate historical exercise to examine the argument seriously, as I now propose to do in three periods of sharp political conflict, once approaching and twice reaching civil war.

The first occurred in Athens at the end of the fifth century B.C. Athens had been a democracy for a century, ever since that form of government was established by Cleisthenes in 508 B.C., and it had gradually stretched the notion of a direct democracy (as distinct from a representative system) about as far as was possible outside Utopia. The sovereign assembly met frequently throughout the year, and its membership consisted of whichever adult male citizens (who had attained the age of eighteen) chanced or chose to be present at any particular meeting. The council of 500, virtually all administrative offices and the juries were selected by lot and were paid a small daily wage while on duty. Most posts were restricted to a tenure of one year, so that a very large proportion of the male population had some direct experience in government in addition to attendance in the assembly or membership on a jury. Political leadership, it is true, remained with the wealthy, and for a long time even more narrowly with the old aristocratic families, but this was not thought to be a breach in the democracy, nor was it in practice.

Not everyone in Athens was enamoured of the system, but opposition was effectively silenced by its success, as Athens became the largest, richest and most powerful state in the Greek world. Then came the long war with Sparta, beginning in 431, and still there was little evidence of anti-democratic activity for nearly two decades, until the Sicilian disaster of 413, which appeared to end any chance of an Athenian victory. The despairing mood that ensued gave the latent opposition an opportunity, and they soon seized it. Early in 411 there was an oligarchic coup; the assembly, its composition distorted by the absence of a large proportion of the poorer citizens on active naval service, its wits assailed by organized conspirators employing a classic mixture of terror and propaganda, voted the democracy out of existence. A commission of thirty was instructed to create new instruments of government on certain lines, which included a property qualification for office-holding and abandonment of pay for most offices. Meantime power was given to a council of 400, appointed (not elected) by a procedure which guaranteed that the key conspirators controlled its membership. Within a few months it became apparent that the ruling junta were not proceeding as they had promised, and they were unseated in a brief flurry of street fighting. For another few months Athens had a government based on property qualification, about which we know nothing, and then the democracy was quietly restored.

Our contemporary evidence is almost entirely restricted to some forty 'chapters' in Thucydides (8.54–97). From his account we know only that the decisive propaganda on behalf of the coup was the argument that the war against Sparta could no longer be won except with Persian financial support, the condition for which was the replacement of democracy by oligarchy, and that the leaders of the coup were divided between a hard core who never intended to surrender tyrannical power and another group, led by Theramenes, who genuinely sought a more broadly based government, in which full citizenship would be confined to those eligible by wealth for military service. However, the chance preservation of three brief documents reveals the existence of another political argument, which Thucydides ignored as he regularly ignored all arguments which, in his judgment, did not express the 'real' issues.

At the assembly that set up the drafting commission of thirty, Cleitophon moved the following amendment to the decree, 'that the elected commissioners should also investigate (search out) the ancestral laws (*nomoi*) laid down by Cleisthenes when he instituted the democracy'.[5] Cleitophon was not a major figure in Athenian life, but he was a man of some standing, both in politics, in which he was associated with Theramenes,[6] and in the intellectual circles that gravitated towards and round the Sophists. Cleitophon makes two appearances in the Platonic corpus, once briefly and insignificantly in the first book of the *Republic* and again in the pathetic and very short pseudo-dialogue that goes under the name of *Cleitophon*, certainly not written by Plato. Both times he is identified as a friend and follower of the Sophist Thrasymachus, and by chance the only substantial surviving fragment of Thrasymachus bears directly on our theme. No more than thirty lines long, it pretends to be a speech in the Athenian assembly which it could not have been, since Thrasymachus was not an Athenian citizen. And yet its authenticity is not to be doubted, and it has to be dated on internal evidence to precisely the time we are considering.[7]

'I wish', the fragment begins, 'I had lived in those olden times when the young men could remain silent because affairs did not require public discussion and the old men were administering the state correctly.' Now we are in a mess, and yet the factions are arguing over an issue that is no issue. 'There is an uproar over the ancestral constitution (*patrios politeia*), which is in fact easy to understand and which all citizens have in common.'

Thrasymachus was not referring to learned discussion in intellectual circles, but to public political argument, in the market-place and in the assembly itself. Cleitophon's amendment was thus not an isolated quirky intellectual's idea but a formal proposal to turn widespread talk into action, whether Thucydides thought it a 'real' issue or not, and we must ask what Cleitophon (and presumably Theramenes) was after.

Our task is not made easier by the language employed. We conventionally translate *nomos* as 'law', *politeia* as 'constitution', *psephisma* as 'decree' and *patrios* as 'ancestral', and though each rendering can be defended, each can also be misleading, for two reasons. The first is that each word has a cluster of meanings: when Thucydides has Alcibiades say that the oligarchic conspirators had abolished the 'ancestral laws' of Athens (8.76.6), he may have been unconsciously reflecting the debate he consciously ignored, but he did not mean what Cleitophon meant. His 'ancestral laws' were the laws in force on the day the fatal vote took place in the assembly, and that use of *patrios* is well attested: it can mean 'traditional' in the specific sense of 'what we have been doing for some time now'.[8]

You will also have noted that both Alcibiades (or Thucydides) and Cleitophon spoke of ancestral *nomoi*, Thrasymachus of the ancestral *politeia*. No distinction is to be inferred, and there lies the second weakness in our translations. Another contemporary began one of his model forensic speeches in this way: 'When the facts are agreed, a case is decided in advance by the law (*nomos*) or decrees (*psephismata*) which rule the whole *politeia*',[9] and here *politeia* is not 'constitution' but 'way of life'. Of course Athenians at the end of the fifth century B.C. were intellectually capable of distinguishing among the laws which defined the powers of the assembly, council and magistrates, the laws which laid down penalties for assault and theft, the laws establishing the calendar of festivals and sacrifices, and the decrees declaring war against Sparta or extending honours to a distinguished foreigner.* However, they had not yet begun to

* I have written 'laws' for more general rules, 'decrees' for decisions of the assembly pertaining to a single action, only because that linguistic distinction comes more 'naturally' to us. I do not mean to suggest that such a distinction was made *in the language* by fifth-century Athenians.

work out a conceptual framework for either jurisprudence or political science, let alone political theory. And on the particular distinctions we are now concerned with, they never advanced very far. It is therefore an anachronism to impose on Cleitophon, say, a distinction between constitutional law and some other kind of law.[10] When Cleitophon proposed an investigation into the laws of Cleisthenes, he was obviously referring to what *we* should call the constitution and not to laws about contracts or inheritance or assault and battery. The issue was, How shall Athens be governed? By whom? If he said *nomoi*, not *politeia*, no one in his audience misunderstood him, and probably no one even noticed.

But why did he bother at all? We can only surmise, and the direction towards which to turn may be signposted by another question. Why should a large section, probably a majority, of Athenian citizens have agreed to abandon permanently the democratic system under which they had been brought up and from which they had greatly benefited? 'Win the war' was no doubt a powerful appeal, but the patriotic and militant Athenian sailors then based on the island of Samos rejected it as a transparent trick. Theoretical arguments about the superiority of one system of government over another would have convinced no one but those already convinced. The men I have called the hard core were unconcerned; they were happy to seize power by terror and hold it by force. Not the Theramenes group, however, and, lacking other (or better) arguments, they grasped a limited psychological one.

The Athenian heroic past was almost exclusively a mythical one; few genuinely historical figures were heroized, fewer still were relevant in the present crisis: one could not appeal, for example, to the tyrannicides Harmodius and Aristogeiton. Not even the historically decisive Cleisthenes had become a folk-hero, but at least he was known as the man who had instituted the democracy. Therefore, Cleitophon proposed, let us turn back to the father of democracy, under whose laws, he might have added, we Athenians had our finest hour when we saved Greece from the barbarians, the invading Persians, at Marathon and Salamis. By turning that far back, we shall still remain a democracy, the ancestral one, the one that served us so well before men like Ephialtes and Pericles distorted its pristine form through such demagogic devices as pay for office. Not much of an appeal to the 'naval mob', certainly, but ideologically attractive to the largish group in the middle who disliked government by 'demagogues' but shuddered at the word 'oligarchy'.

The attempt at oligarchy was, as we have seen, a rapid failure, but one practical consequence followed from the debate. After the fall of the Four Hundred, it was decided to examine the ramshackle accumulation of laws and decrees, and to publish a tidied-up code of binding law over the whole field, of which a (to us) surprisingly large part consisted of the sacred calendar.[11] The commission given this assignment in 410 B.C. had not finished its work when Athens finally lost the war in 404, partly because of the magnitude of the task in a state that had no central record office–hence Cleitophon's choice of words when he moved that the laws of Cleisthenes be investigated or searched out; partly because the commission seems to have behaved disreputably, in ways that are obscure to us. The end of the war disrupted the work of codification, but it revived the political conflicts of 411, with one faction again demanding a narrow oligarchy, another resisting on behalf of democracy, and a third, in which Theramenes and Cleitophon reappear, proposing the return to the ancestral constitution.[12] The decision, however, was not left to Athenians: the victorious Spartans sent in a garrison and imposed a junta, even tighter and far more brutal than the Four Hundred of 411, a junta who later came to be called the Thirty Tyrants.

Thanks to a division within the Spartan leadership, the Athenian democrats were soon able to fight their way back into control of their city. No sooner was the democracy restored in 403 than it was decided to complete the codification proposed in 410. The decree begins as follows: 'The Athenians shall be governed in the ancestral way [*patrios* is here converted into a plural noun, *ta patria*], using the laws, weights and measures of Solon and also the regulations of Draco, which had previously been in force.'[13] Clearly *patrios* here is ancestral in the sense we have previously noticed in Thucydides, to mean merely the way Athens was governed before the Thirty Tyrants took charge, further defined as 'the laws of Solon and the regulations of Draco'; not in any archaic sense of going back to codifications of 594 and 621 B.C., respectively, but in an elliptical sense.[14] By 'the laws of Solon and Draco' the decree meant the law of Athens as it stood in 403, some of it indeed going back to the ancient lawgivers but much of it either revised or wholly new legislation promulgated in the two centuries since Solon. Such ellipsis may strain the imagination, but even more striking examples are available from texts composed after the completion of the codification. After the year 403/2 no earlier law was valid unless it had been incorporated into the code: yet advocates went on cheerfully citing in the courts what they called 'a law of Solon', even when it was blatantly impossible for the enactment to have been very ancient.

Draco introduces a further complication which I must put aside, except to note that one of the first actions of the legislative commission, in 409 or 408, was to republish Draconic laws on homicide.[15] Solon occupied a different rank: he was one of the Seven Sages and the most charismatic of all historical Athenians of the olden days. Although the decree of 403 is the earliest surviving reference to him in the debate over the ancestral constitution, I am confident that this is mere chance, given the scarcity of available texts. What is not chance, surely, is Solon's appearance in an official document in the context of the restored democracy. Let us speculate a moment. The Therameneans, we know, attempted to claim ancestral authority for oligarchy in the name of democracy. The democrats, I suggest, promptly countered by invoking an even older and more heroic ancestor, Solon himself.[16] The play on words helped. The metaphorically ancestral constitution of the present was coalesced with the literally ancestral constitution going back two hundred years. In so far as the argument mattered at all, the democrats had played a trump card. Then, once the political crisis was resolved, the argument lost significance in practical affairs. However, it had created a stir among intellectuals, and what they did with it in the following century is a subject I shall look at later. Here I shall just record one final flurry. In 322 B.C., following the death of Alexander the Great, the Macedonians subdued an Athenian rebellion and included among the peace terms the condition that 'the ancestral constitution based on a property qualification' be restored.[17] The qualifying clause prevented any further games with words.

From Cleitophon we turn to Sir Edward Coke. The seventeenth-century constitutional crisis was of course a different one, between king and parliament, but the basic issue can be reduced to the same questions: How shall England be governed? By whom? And again there was an appeal not only to contemporary interests, but, with great force, to the authority of the distant past. The lead was given by the common lawyers, with Coke in command. Starting from their professional stress on immemorial custom and usage, interpreted and applied by the courts, they found it a short step to the 'fundamental laws' and the pre-Conquest 'ancient constitution', the political frame within which, they insisted, the common law functioned 'immune from the king's prerogative action'.[18] So attractive did the historical argument prove that it was quickly to become perhaps the most favoured single argument among the pamphleteers, whether lawyers or not. There was even an English Solon available in Edward the Confessor, and it was unnecessary to forge the *leges Edwardi Confessoris*; that had already been accomplished in the later Middle Ages, and Coke, for example, cited them repeatedly in his

Institutes.[19] The paradox, as Professor Pocock noted, was that the great common lawyer thus turned for his highest authority to apocryphal *statutes* and succeeded 'in some peculiar way in regarding their existence as proof of the antiquity of the unwritten law which they do not contain'.[20]

The story is now so well known that I can restrict myself to three aspects, selected primarily to pinpoint parallels with the Athenian situation:

(1) There is the element of bogus history: not only were the laws of Edward the Confessor a fiction but the whole account of the institutions before and after the Conquest was false, as was the account of Magna Carta. 'Coke was no historian', wrote Professor Douglas with rare understatement, 'but he was ever ready to seek the origin of the Common Law in Saxon antiquity.'[21] Maitland spoke in less veiled terms: 'It is true that, as regards very old times, little that was of real value came from the imperious dogmatist who dominated the jurisprudence of his time. When he was on unfamiliar ground Sir Edward Coke was, of all mankind, the most credulous. There was no fable, no forgery, that he would not endorse; and a good many medieval legends and medieval lies passed into currency with his name upon their backs.'[22]

(2) Although there is much vagueness about such terms as 'constitution', a relatively late comer anyway, and 'fundamental law', nevertheless, when Francis Bacon, for example, wrote in 1596 that Edward I 'bent himself to endow his state with sundry notable and fundamental laws, upon which the government since hath principally rested', his language, reminiscent of some of the Greek authors I have quoted, was as unambiguous as theirs, despite the absence of the word 'constitution'.[23]

(3) There is the same refusal of the other side to surrender the past. James I took a dim view, and rightly so in the event, when the Society of Antiquaries was re-founded in 1614,[24] but the crown lawyers were in fact able to summon better history in the king's defence: 'the Prerogative of the Crown is the first Table of that Fundamental Law'[25] was easy to document a long way into the past. History proved a weak defensive weapon; the royalists lost the real battle, and the victorious parliamentarians were promptly attacked by the radicals, with the charge that the common law itself was an oppressive instrument, the creation of the Norman conquest. The word 'Norman' is employed pejoratively in numerous pamphleteering passages by the Levellers; even poor Coke was tarred with the label. The Levellers appealed to natural right and reason, profoundly non-historical authorities, but they, too, would not forego

the past, and a curious hybrid emerged. The Englishman's law, wrote Robert Norwood in 1653, was both enacted by the Parliament of 'King Ethelree' and 'rooted by Heaven itself in the hearts of Englishmen'. Seven years earlier, John Lilburne, in *The Just Man's Justification*, used language we have already encountered several times: we must abolish the 'Norman innovation' of courts at Westminster and restore 'the ancient frame of government in this Kingdome before the Conquerors dayes'.[26]

We need not pursue the curious byways of the quarrel over the Norman Yoke thereafter.[27] For all its boisterousness (and its continuing reliance on largely fictitious history), it did not possess the sting, as a political argument, of Coke's ancient constitution, because the political situation had altered. After the Glorious Revolution, indeed, 'the Conquest theory ceased to be a threat and became a joke',[28] though it produced a few serious historical inquiries and a flurry of controversy in the press between 1730 and 1735.[29]

My third case-study is an American one, recent enough still to be called contemporary. The United States of course possesses *the* ancestral constitution, written down, well documented, and sanctified ever since John Marshall converted the Supreme Court into the arbiter of public policy. Interpretation of the constitution has been a continuing topic of political debate for more than a century and a half, but that is a different activity from the one I am discussing. For this, Americans replaced the ancestral constitution by the Founding Fathers, and reliance on their sanction is no new phenomenon, for reasons to which I shall return. During the presidential election of 1900, Sir Denis Brogan's favourite comic character, Mr Dooley, commented that both candidates were 'ancestor worshippers like th' Chinese'.[30] But it was in the struggle over the New Deal that a crescendo was reached, a struggle, it is important to recall, that included a constitutional crisis, over the Supreme Court, which strengthens the parallel with the two situations we have already examined.

The almost unanimous choice for paramount Father was Thomas Jefferson, and that is puzzling. He was, to be sure, the patron of the Democratic Party and the author of the Declaration of Independence, the opening sentences of which every schoolboy learns by heart. However, he had not been (and never became) a folk hero–George Washington brooked no rival earlier than Abraham Lincoln –he had not been a distinguished president, he placed his faith in a society of agrarian homesteaders free from a strong centralized authority. 'Cultivators of the earth are the most valuable citizens,' he wrote from Paris in 1785. 'I consider the class of artificers as the panders of vice and the instruments by which the liberties of a country are generally overturned.'[31] Yet now he became the ancestral spirit of an interventionist national government trying to resolve an industrial crisis in a highly urbanized country–an inversion of roles reminiscent of the respective appeals, each to the 'wrong' view of history, by the Bolingbroke and Walpole camps in the 1730s.[32] Franklin Roosevelt contributed personally to the new mythmaking. In 1925 he had written his only book review, of Claude Bowers' *Jefferson and Hamilton: The Struggle for Democracy in America.* Once in office, he had a large and systematic dossier of Jefferson quotations compiled, which he plundered liberally for his speeches, and every 13 April a personal aide laid a wreath at Jefferson's tomb.[33]

Jefferson's shade may well have been pleased. He himself, from similar motives, 'painstakingly collected every scrap of evidence to reconstruct the history' of his 'Saxon ancestors', as he called them.[34] However, historians were not alone in promptly pointing out that on the substantive questions of the nature and role of government, Jefferson's antithesis, the élitist Alexander Hamilton, was the more appropriate Father. Some Republicans did indeed turn to him, but for several reasons he was an ineffectual and even dangerous ancestor.[35] So they played the game we have already encountered: they claimed Jefferson from Roosevelt and the Democrats. By the time of the presidential election of 1936, when Roosevelt ran for his second term, the clashing appeals achieved a comic-opera effect, though the tone was solemnly earnest. In an article written early in that year Professor Brogan summed it up: 'Mr Dooley asserted, it is true, that "ye can't vote th' cimitries". American politicians are not so sure, and all this year there will be a determined effort to cast the vote of that [one] founding father.'[36]

Obviously the American argument from the ancestral past had to differ from the other two we have looked at because it was already too well documented and studied a past. Selective quotation therefore replaced forgery as the operational device. There are other differences: I need waste no time in pointing out that, institutionally and structurally, fifth-century Athens, seventeenth-century England and twentieth-century America diverged widely. On the other hand, significant common elements can be isolated, and the very fact of their recurrence in political argument among such diverse and temporally separated societies (nor are these three the only available examples)[37] suggests that something fundamental about social behaviour is involved, something that cannot be smugly labelled 'rhetoric' or 'propaganda' and left at that. (Rhetoric and propaganda can never be 'left at that' anyway.)

There are at least four common elements to consider:

(1) It was assumed, rather than justified, that the argument from antiquity is a valid one in a debate about current politics. There were sceptics, of course, Mr Dooley, for example: 'I have a great respect for the sages, and I believe in namin' streets an' public schools afther thim.'[38] However, those who joined in the debate, on both sides, disputed about the facts of the past, as they said these were, not about the legitimacy or even the limits of the appeal itself. They knew what they wished to find in the past, they sought it, and they found it.

(2) The distant past was concretized and personalized, exactly as it had been in the myths and legends of archaic societies. The sanctioning ancestor was normally *an* ancestor, Solon or Edward the Confessor or Thomas Jefferson, or whoever, not just the past in general or even a specified period in the past. This was equally true of the seventeenth-century common lawyers, for all their rhetoric about 'the immemorial past': like fourth-century Athenian advocates, who never cited 'the law' or 'custom' in the abstract,[39] neither Coke nor Sir Matthew Hale failed to specify which code, which statute, which king defined for the English any of their timeless liberties.[40] We may no longer be able to understand in all instances why the choice fell on whom it did, as with the eighteenth-century discovery of King Alfred,[41] but we must acknowledge the psychological insight revealed by the procedure. Our own public opinion experts have solemnly advanced 'the proposition that "who" says something to someone significantly influences the response to what is said'.[42] Burke never heard of a poll, or a mass interview, but he already knew that. In the long fragment now known as *An Essay towards an Abridgement of English History*, he wrote that Alfred 'is generally honoured as the founder of our laws and Constitution', and then added in a footnote that, though historians, 'copying after one another', falsely attribute this and that reform to Alfred, 'these reports, however ill imagined, are a strong proof of the high veneration in which this excellent prince has always been held; as it has been thought that the attributing of these regulations to him would endear them to the nation'.[43] Once the candidate for veneration had been selected, furthermore, everyone wished to share him, usually in preference to offering an alternative. Sometimes there was little or no choice: it is not difficult to appreciate why no one wanted the sanction of William the Conqueror in a constitutional crisis. But sometimes the absence of alternatives eludes our understanding.

(3) Viewed objectively, that is to say, from the standpoint of an outside observer who is not involved (in so far as that is ever humanly possible) in the controversy itself, the debates were over genuine issues, over constitutional or other questions in which there were definable differences in interests and goals, and which could therefore be argued about rationally. Yet we have seen that even those who stressed the rational and moral arguments most strongly could at the same time rarely resist adding an appeal to the past. An important recent testimony comes from Dr Staughton Lynd, a leader of the American intellectual New Left and a good historian in his own right. 'Despite the alleged antihistoricism of the New Left,' he wrote, 'the need for a collective past is felt with particular keenness today by young people. Many rebellious young Americans have profoundly mixed feelings when they confront our country's history.' Nevertheless, 'there is a diffuse sense that the rhetoric of the Revolution and the Civil War spoke then and speaks now to hopes widespread among mankind.'[44]

(4) I do not believe I am straining when I detect a certain kinship between Dr Lynd's rebellious young Americans and Mr Estabrook's 'O Marvellous Constitution! Maker, Monitor, Guardian of Mankind!' 'The past has always been the handmaid of authority,' Professor Plumb has recently remonstrated with biting eloquence.[45] A good servant, one must add: the appeal to, and argument from, the ancestral past habitually crosses lines, whether of class, educational level or political disposition. It has been sounded in the Athenian popular assembly, the English Parliament and the American Congress, in Fourth of July orations and Roosevelt's fireside chats, in the press, in popular pamphlets, in more learned disquisitions. It is, in short, ideology in its classic form. It can be linked with conservatism, as in Burke, but it need not be; both in seventeenth-century England and in America of the 1930s, the appeal was first raised by the party seeking more or less radical change, with the 'conservatives' then chiming in.

And what have modern historians made of all this? The plain answer is–very little. In our more general histories and in the narratives of the respective periods, the deployment of arguments from the ancestral past is scarcely noticed. In Bury's *History of Greece* there is only a brief, inaccurate reference to the *patrios politeia* appeal in 411 B.C., and Hammond, in his *History of Greece*, has a single sentence reporting Cleitophon's amendment of 411 and another on the 403 motion, without comment. Thomas Jefferson's name does not appear in the index of Leuchtenberg's *Franklin D. Roosevelt and the New Deal* or of Schlesinger's minutely detailed three-volume *Age of Roosevelt.*

One must turn to specialized monographs and articles, concerned with aspects of the history of historiography or scholarship or political thought, or written just because a new subject was required for a doctoral dissertation, or because an archive was newly opened to research. Even the best of these, furthermore–and some are very good indeed in achieving their objectives–evade the difficulties of explanation. One way or another, the legitimacy of the appeal is accepted as if it were one of Euclid's axioms. To say that 'never perhaps have statesmen . . . turned more instinctively to the past' for 'a solution to the problems of the present' is just not helpful.[46] 'Americans have never found it necessary to apologize for their return, again and again, to the Founding Fathers for wisdom and inspiration' is correct but again not helpful; to continue that a proper appraisal of Hamilton will provide 'clear guidance . . . as we confront our own perplexities' is not even correct, strictly speaking.[47]

Two reasons for this failure (not too strong a word) suggest themselves. The first is that, however one explains the phenomenon, historians have not concerned themselves much with the psychology of the people who are their subject, with what the French call *structures mentales*, by no means identical with the 'conscious level–the manifest content of ideas and beliefs'.[48] The history of religion seems to be an exception, in connection with such activities as asceticism or conversion, and I do not understand why psychological factors are permitted there but not in political behaviour. (There is, of course, the work, under Freudian influence, examining individual creative geniuses in depth, especially in literature, art and music, but that kind of 'psychohistory'–Erik Erikson's term for his own studies of Luther and Gandhi–has little bearing on our problem.)

The second reason is that we are all Thucydideans; by a kind of tacit collective decision, historians have given themselves licence not to report political arguments they themselves demean as 'romance' (Thucydides' *to mythodes*) or as irrational or as irrelevant to the realities of politics. We like to think of ourselves as hard-headed realists, and we project this image not only on to the actors but also on to those being acted upon. Paradoxically, historians are at the same time not averse to welcoming bogus history in political debate as better than no history at all. The Master of Balliol finds a kind of logic in the Norman Yoke theory: if we take the 'broader patriotic appeal into account', it 'was not quite so absurd as some twentieth-century historians have assumed'.[49] Professor Malone concludes from Roosevelt's standing Thomas Jefferson on his head that 'it begins to appear that Mr Roosevelt had read his history with greater discrimination' than had his predecessors.[50]

Particular explanations for the recurrence of this class of argument are not hard to find. I myself suggested earlier that, in Athens, it was comforting to be able to accept oligarchy in the name of Cleisthenes, father of democracy. The peculiar English development of the common law has been powerfully advocated as the key to the seventeenth-century appeal. Alternatively Mr Hill has written that 'Men dared not yet appeal to reason and utility alone; authority must be challenged by counter-authority',[51] but that does not tell us why the counter-authority lay in six-hundred-year-old Anglo-Saxon precedent. No doubt when life becomes intolerable for large sections of the population, a measure of relief is obtained by dreaming about, and believing in, a time when things were different and better, customarily a time in the distant past, for obvious reasons. However, dreaming produces nothing more concrete than Utopian visions of a Golden Age, irrecoverable save by a miracle or act of divine grace, whereas our concern is precisely with moments when specific political action is being demanded.[52]

I suggest that the roots lie deeper, in the very nature of man, who alone possesses both memory and the prescience of inevitable death, leading unconsciously to a desire, a need, for something that will create a feeling of continuity and permanence. Modern psychopathology has demonstrated how a breakdown in the 'temporal horizon' leads to disorientation and disorder of the personality.[53] Hans Meyerhoff made the attractive suggestion that one of the ways in which Sophocles' *Oedipus Tyrannus* may be read is 'as the tragedy of a man who is suddenly and brutally destroyed because the continuity of time in his life is irremediably disrupted. A terrible gap is opened up: on the one hand, there is his past as lived and remembered since the defeat of the sphinx, the liberation of Thebes, and the winning of throne and wife; on the other hand, there is the past of his childhood and youth, forgotten, repressed, or simply falsified, and subsequently brought to light. Oedipus, therefore, may be said to have no self-identity.'[54]

The tragedy of Oedipus is of course not only a personal one; it implicates his family, as does much Greek tragedy; his *oikos*, as the Greeks would say, and an *oikos* stretched backwards and forwards in time.[55] For our purposes, two aspects are important. The *oikos* was the repository and transmitter of 'memories' of the past; without the memories of the aristocratic houses Herodotus could not have begun to write his history.[56] And these same houses dominated Athenian politics at least to the death of Pericles, reinforcing their authority both by ancient tradition and by religious sanction. The two sanctions were, in fact, intertwined.

Here we enter treacherous ground, and I must be careful. In societies simpler than the classical Greek, and especially in stateless societies, ancestor cults are directly linked, often in quite subtle ways, not only with the health and prosperity of the living descendants but also with the maintenance of social norms, with power inside the lineage and with the transmission of its property.[57] By the time the Greeks provide us with useful documentation, ancestor cult in the strict sense appears to have been replaced among them by cults of the household, especially of Zeus Herkeios, and of the heroes, a technical term in post-Homeric times most easily defined by quoting the poet Hesiod (*Works and Days* 159–60), 'a god-like race of hero-men who are called demi-gods'. The historical link between the two cults, of ancestors and of heroes, is well established.[58] In so far as heroes were patrons of cities and of political sub-groupings, ancestor worship in the strict sense had given way to a metaphoric version, analogous to the worship of saints, in general and in particular (as individual patrons). However, each of the aristocratic houses of classical Greece, even in democratic Athens, also had its hero, from whom the members were descended, and that is where matters become difficult. What did the Alcmaeonids, who counted among their members both Cleisthenes and Pericles, 'really' believe about Alcmaeon and their 'descent' from him? Or Pericles' great aristocratic rival, Cimon, who produced a pedigree straight back to Ajax?[59]

With pedigrees we at least know where we stand. Whether of a royal family or of an aristocratic house, a pedigree, in Dr Goody's phrasing, 'is a charter to office and to other rights; the longer the pedigree, the more imposing and the more effective it is as a device for legitimizing both the office and the officeholder'.[60] Divine origin, even divine right, helps but is not indispensable; a generalized, not necessarily explicit, reference to God's will seems to serve almost as well. Pedigrees, furthermore, put us on the road back from individual and family-group psychology to the state or nation, which is our subject. I do not believe the kinship symbolism – the *ancestral* constitution, the Founding *Fathers* – to be accidental or meaningless. It is striking and often repeated in Burke; I shall restrict myself to a few sentences and clauses from a single passage in the *Reflections*: 'People will not look forward to posterity, who never look backward to their ancestors. Besides, the people of England well know, that the idea of inheritance furnishes a sure principle of conservation, and a sure principle of transmission. . . . In this choice of inheritance we have given to our frame of polity the image of a relation in blood; binding up the constitution of our country with our dearest domestic ties; adopting our fundamental laws into the bosom of our family affections.... Always acting as if in the presence of canonized forefathers....'[61]

I am of course not suggesting that biological kinship, or fictitious or symbolic kinship, is the only notion binding a society to its past, or that in times of crises one always appeals to one's own past. The French Revolution, as Marx said in the opening of the *Eighteenth Brumaire*, 'draped itself alternately as the Roman Republic and the Roman Empire'. However, we all have personal experience of the way in which, in a variety of groups, bonds within the group are reinforced by the sense of continuity that comes from a shared knowledge (or pretended knowledge) of key figures and incidents in its past. And so too with the political unit. If historians are unable to comment beyond a few superficial or platitudinous remarks, or are driven to rather free speculation, in so far as that is not the consequence of their own disinterest, the responsibility lies with the comparable disinterest of social psychologists in this aspect of social behaviour and values. At least, I have not succeeded in finding a serious account of the matter.

It will be said in reply that there is nothing for the social psychologist to examine because the contemporary Western world has detached itself from its past, it has become a world of technical go-ahead in practical life and of incessant *nouvelles vagues* in culture. That was said to me in private conversation: when I countered with Jefferson and the New Deal, the further reply was that the United States is peculiar. And so it is. In an essay entitled 'The Search for a Usable Past', Henry Steele Commager pointed to the two key elements.[62] The United States became a state before it was a nation, unequipped with 'history, tradition and memory'. The lack was quickly dealt with in the first half of the nineteenth century, chiefly by New England literati. Then came the repeated waves of immigrants, who had to be incorporated psychologically, and that was achieved by constant repetition of 'easily grasped common denominators' selected from the now well-established 'usable past'.

But the Soviet Union is also peculiar. The creation of a revolution that consciously and explicitly accepted its roots in the past, in the Marxist sense, and therefore stressed its dialectical break from the past, the Soviet Union by the late 30s paradoxically rediscovered its (Russian) ancestral heroes, Kutuzov, Peter the Great, even Ivan the Terrible. Israel, too, is peculiar–I need not go on, beyond mentioning the conversion of Masada into a national shrine.

The point at which we are let down most badly is in trying to assess the effectiveness of a political argument based on the ancestral past. How much did it weigh on public opinion, the opinion of whichever public mattered at the time; in reinforcing or diverting opinion, as an appeal distinct from, and for some contrary to, arguments from reason and utility? I do not believe the tools of analysis exist with which to cope with such a question about a past age, but experts in contemporary public opinion might have provided us with a model, and I have been unable to find one. The model would not be automatically workable: such factors as the radical leap in the life-span and changes in the nature and role of the family would constitute important variables.[63] Nevertheless, even a defective model would be better than none at all. Meantime, we are restricted to an examination of the place of the argument in the history of ideas, specifically in political theory and in historiography.

With the restoration of democracy in Athens at the end of the fifth century B.C., oligarchy ceased to be a practical issue. However, the intellectual opposition to democracy remained, and in those circles (except for Plato and his close disciples) the appeal to the ancestral constitution retained vitality. Everyone now agreed that it was Solon who founded the modern Athenian state; hence Plutarch was to write his biography whereas Cleisthenes gradually dropped from sight. But what kind of state? A 'mixed' constitution, said the pamphleteers who preferred oligarchy (much as they denied it), with Isocrates as their chief spokesman, unflagging in his call for a return to the good old days.[64] The democrats of course disagreed, and Demosthenes, for one, never even bothered to argue the case.

One looks in vain in all this writing for political theory in the proper sense. Political sentiments, dispositions, arguments, concepts perhaps–that is the highest claim one may make. Greek political theory began with the Sophists, who are too shadowy for close analysis in this context. But with Plato, the position is in no doubt. He was about eighteen when Cleitophon moved the amendment that opened the debate, he had close personal connections with some of the chief actors, he had an acute ear for what was going on, and when the time came, he dismissed the whole 'historical' discussion with magnificent contempt. Solon is mentioned some eighteen times in the Platonic corpus; Theseus appears six times, but never either Draco or Cleisthenes, and that is already a clue to the irrelevance of constitutional history.[65] The references to Solon are casual but friendly: he is one of the old sages, a good lawgiver like Lycurgus of

Sparta, the man who transmitted the Atlantis myth, a gnomic poet to be quoted. No serious argument ever rests on these casual remarks; they are simply part of the Platonic style of discourse, with its constant citation of the activities and references familiar to every ordinary Athenian.

In the *Republic*, needless to say, there could be no place for the ancestral constitution, nor any reason to talk about it. In the *Laws*, Plato does show some respect for *ta patria* as such, but not in any way relevant to our subject: at issue are painting and music (II 656E), the nurture of infants from conception (VII 793A–D), and the like. That Plato reveals an 'archaic' bent is no doubt true, but his philosophy never rested on 'ancestral' arguments, and in the *Politikos* or *Statesman* he delivered his crushing dismissal. Having established that statesmanship is a science (*episteme*) and that the only test of a true or correct constitution is whether or not it is scientifically established and administered (not whether it is oligarchic or timocratic or democratic or anything equally irrelevant), the Eleatic Stranger goes on (293B–299A) to demonstrate the 'hard doctrine' that formal legislation would then be unnecessary, indeed, a bad thing. This he does by an outrageous resort to the familiar Platonic analogy of the doctor and the pilot, climaxed in a hilarious parody of contemporary Athenian legislative practice. A bill is moved in the assembly, inviting all persons, no matter how unqualified, to lay down detailed rules for the practice of medicine and navigation; specifying that the rules shall be committed to writing; commanding that 'for all time' no other rules may be followed; providing for the selection of (unqualified) officials to navigate ships and cure the sick according to the code, and for popular control over these 'magistrates' by the usual methods.

Neither Solon nor the ancestral constitution is mentioned in these pages, but the passage is carefully dotted with pointers that no literate Athenian would have missed. The new laws are to be inscribed on *kyrbeis* and *stelai*, and everyone knew that Solon's laws were inscribed on *kyrbeis*, modern ones on *stelai*; repeatedly and regularly it is said that the assembly and the jurors are to be chosen either from the whole *demos* or from the rich alone, and it was well known how the 'Therameneans' insisted that the Solonic constitution was timocratic. Professor Skemp must be right in his comment: 'Plato's answer is, The rot goes deeper . . . and affects "Solonian" democracy as much as any other.'[66] That is always Plato's answer: of all existing constitutions, even the best are mere imitations of the true constitution; the debate over the ancestral constitution is a waste of time or worse; constitutions cannot be judged by reference to this or that past hero or constitution. The echo of Thrasymachus is a pretty irony.

Aristotle's radically different method led him to the same fundamental conclusion, though he did not say so expressly and though there are aspects of his work which superficially seem to suggest otherwise. One can be misled by Aristotle's temperament: he was a dazzling virtuoso and could not always resist a virtuoso display, as in the long section of the *Politics* (1313a34ff.) laying out systematically the ways in which tyranny could be preserved, or in the brief section (1273b35–74a21) correcting the factual errors of 'those' who hold that Solon 'had established the ancestral democracy'. In politics as in biology, Aristotle amassed data tirelessly and he sought political data in the past as in the present, but also abroad as at home. The reading of history enabled him to extend the range and number of experiences available for study; it had no virtue of itself. The approach, in Professor Guthrie's words, 'was in truth not genetic at all, but analytic'.[67] The 'ancestral constitution' of Athens interested him because it was a *constitution* that others were discussing, not because it was *ancestral*. Writing about proposals to bring about equality of property, he says (*Politics* 1266b16–19): 'among the ancients . . ., for example, there was the legislation of Solon, and elsewhere there is a law prohibiting a man from acquiring as much as he wishes; similarly there are laws prohibiting the sale of property; for example, there is a law in Locris . . .'. The mixture of tenses, the indifference to time, place and even circumstance are typical of the method.

This is paradigmatic history, not to be confused either with historiography or with political argument based on the past and tradition.[68] Paradigms served to exemplify principles which were worked out by rational means (and also to reveal that Aristotle, unlike Plato, always kept the possible as well as the ideal in view). As for any claim that historiography is an *episteme*, a discipline, never has it been dismissed more peremptorily than in the notorious ninth chapter of the *Poetics*: 'Poetry is more philosophical and more weighty than history for poetry speaks rather of the universal, history of the particular. By the universal I mean that such and such a kind of man will say or do such or such things from probability or necessity; that is the aim of poetry, adding proper names to the characters. By the particular I mean what Alcibiades did and what he suffered.'

After Aristotle, Greek political thought, in so far as one may still speak of it at all, turned away from the realities of the city-state and of politics; hence nothing would be gained by pursuing the inquiry in that quarter. Rome is another matter, but I have refrained from including Rome among my case-histories because that would have required a full study by itself. I might just note that in Cicero's unconsummated marriage between the natural reason or natural law of the Middle Stoa and Roman *mos maiorum*, with his not surprising discovery that the Roman 'ancestral constitution' was the embodiment of natural reason, it was the Stoic concepts that kept his *De republica* alive for later generations, not the bogus history.

When we turn to political theory in England, the impact of the seventeenth-century debate is so negligible that extended discussion becomes unnecessary. Hobbes was very learned, and, like Aristotle, could not resist an opportunity to correct historical errors. Exactly like Aristotle, too, he accepted no more than paradigmatic value in history, which, he said in *Behemoth*, can provide only 'examples of fact', not 'argument of right'.[69] That Locke did not think otherwise about the ancestral argument requires no demonstration. Burke alone need occupy us.

Burke is not easy. He was not a systematic thinker;[70] much of his enormous literary output was written for one or another political occasion, in which he was emotionally involved and in which he was trying to advance his party and its cause. No political thinker is a more obvious target for Mr Dunn's recent demand that the history of ideas be treated 'as the history of an *activity*'.[71] A small number of simple sentiments reappear with fair consistency, but precisely what they imply is not self-evident, as is shown by the internal disagreements among the neo-conservative American group centring round the *Burke Newsletter* (since 1966 known as *Studies in Burke and His Time*). A measure of subjectivism is hard to avoid, especially in selecting the right quotation, and I do not pretend that I can myself do otherwise.

I begin by observing that most of the Burke texts adduced in modern discussions about our particular subject are taken from the *Reflections on the Revolution in France*, and by suggesting that it is not entirely irrelevant to remember that this was a political polemic of a bitterness and eloquence rarely if ever paralleled, that Burke's personal stake in the outcome of the debate over Whig policy towards France was very great, and that he was fully conscious of all the implications. The fury of the attack comes as something of a surprise; there is nothing in Burke's correspondence or public activity before the beginning of 1790 to suggest that he was about to burst forth with his lengthy manifesto calling for a pan-European counter-revolution;[72] nothing in Burke's career, with its marks of antipathy to France, to prepare us for his activity in trying to help organize the counter-revolution or for the adulation of Louis XVI, most obsequious in the sequel to the *Reflections*, the odious *Appeal from the New to the Old Whigs*.[73] What was responsible? A reading of the correspondence indicates that three themes, which recur regularly, lie at the root: the large-scale confiscation of property, the attack on the clergy, and fear amounting to panic lest the Revolution spread to England, especially through the activity of Dr Richard Price and his group of Dissenters.[74]

About this there can be little dispute, or about the outcome, the formulation in the *Reflections* of the quintessential doctrine of conservatism.[75] But there is an important question of accent. In what has already become a classic article, Professor Pocock argued that Burke was deliberately placing himself within the common-law tradition, that 'a doctrine of traditionalism, very much akin to Burke's own, grew out of the concept of the ancient constitution', that, in the *Reflections*, Burke 'in fact reverted to the position he formerly rebuked [Sir Matthew] Hale for adopting'.[76] That there are passages in the *Reflections* and elsewhere which Pocock has legitimately quoted to support his claim is certainly the case. But has he the accent right? I think not, for two main reasons (quite apart from the point that an equally impressive collection of quotations can be assembled to press the claim that the protection of property was uppermost in Burke's mind).[77]

First, although Burke never abandoned his belief that the seventeenth-century common lawyers had relied on bogus history, that a proper history of English law could and ought to be written,[78] his own appeals to the ancient constitution and immemorial custom in the *Reflections* are vague and timeless, except in so far as he persistently pins his case on the Revolution of 1688. That difference in stress from the arguments we have been examining, with their reference to specific ancestors and specific ancestral events, seems to me to be substantially significant.

My second reason is that Burke was arguing, after all, that the *French* Revolution was a bad thing because it swept aside *French* traditions and customs, including above all the rights of property and the power and property of the clergy, but not including, I need hardly say, anything remotely resembling the English common law. Burke, in short, was laying down universal conservative principles. Addressing an English audience of a particular stamp, he employed some of the rhetoric familiar to them. For the history of political theory, what is of interest is that Burke alone among the major figures did not simply dismiss the argument from the ancestral constitution, he transcended it, and that is in its way a dismissal, too.

It is pointless to pursue this question with my third case-study, given the problematical status of political theory at the present time; nor, for different but equally obvious reasons, will the Jefferson-New-Deal syndrome help us with the problem of the rise of historiography, to which I now turn. Fifth-century Greece is of course central to any discussion of that question, but seventeenth-century England still has something to contribute, thanks to the medieval hiatus. I call this a 'problem' deliberately, because I do not believe it to be self-evident how historiography arose from the awareness of the past that all human societies reveal in some form. By historiography I mean a systematic, critical inquiry into some part or aspect of the past, critical not only in the sense of critical evaluation of evidence, but also in the larger sense of a conscious, rational examination of one's subject, its dimensions and implications, as free as one can make oneself of the automatic acceptance of received views, approaches, habits of mind.[79]

The Greeks knew all they had to know about the past before Herodotus was born, knew through their myths, legends and orally transmitted tales what was essential for the various functions the more distant past fulfilled in the present. And even after Herodotus not many Greeks thought they had qualitatively better knowledge because of what he had done, no matter how much they may have been entertained. Thucydides, after all, immediately made two fundamental criticisms: history, he implied, was about politics, and that could be studied only in the present, not in the past.

Near the end of Thucydides' life a prolific writer, Hellanicus of Lesbos, published a *Chronicle of Athens* from the beginning to his own day.[80] The mythical period was not distinguished in treatment from the historical, and the surviving fragments indicate that he ranged widely over Athenian antiquities. His impetus did not come from politics or political debates, and it is decisive for us that no Athenian tried to supersede him for half a century, during precisely the half-century when the political pamphleteering was in full swing, with its polemic about the ancestral constitution. No one was moved to say, I shall try to settle this controversy about the past by a systematic inquiry into the evidence, not even after Herodotus and Thucydides had each in his own way fathered history, and others were continuing to write history.[81] In the *Areopagiticus* (7.19), Isocrates asked his readers to follow him attentively so that they could choose 'from exact knowledge' between the good ancestral democracy of Solon and the corrupt one under which they were now living. The exact knowledge then turns out to be pages of sententious rhetoric about how the young used to be trained properly and about other such matters, interspersed with very few precise and even fewer accurate statements about the Solonic constitution. Why did no one counter him by historical inquiry?

My rhetorical question becomes acute when we observe that just about the time Isocrates produced the *Areopagiticus*, someone named Cleidemus finally replaced Hellanicus with a *Chronicle of Athens* by an Athenian; that Cleidemus was emulated in the course of a century by five others (collectively known ever since antiquity as the Atthidographers); that, though these works look like history and are not devoid of scholarship, they lack the essential ingredient, critical inquiry.[82] The Atthidographers, Felix Jacoby explained, 'write . . . on the basis of their own experience (as did the great historians); where this experience ceases they write on the basis of predecessors' narratives, and where such a narrative does not exist, on the basis of the general conception accepted in their circles about the development of the Attic State'.[83] Isocrates gives us a fair idea of that general conception. Inevitably the ancestral constitution was included in the chronicle, but it was neither the major stimulus nor the central theme; nor did such disagreements as there were among them about the facts of Solon or Cleisthenes rest on anything more substantial than their personal political views. For genuine inquiry, Athens (and the Greeks generally) had to turn to Aristotle and his school, and their interest, as we have seen, though critical, was not historiographical (nor should we exaggerate, because of *our* interest and because of the accident that only the *Constitution of Athens* has survived of the 158 such compilations produced by the school, the amount of attention Aristotle was able or wished to give to Athenian constitutional history). In Athens, in sum, the political debate over the ancestral constitution made no significant contribution to the history of historiography.

Neither did the seventeenth-century debate in England, except negatively, unless one holds bogus history and endless talk about the past to be historiography none the less. This is all the more striking because the seventeenth century was a great century in English antiquarian research, little of which had any visible connection with the law or lawyers. Of the tiny number of figures of the time writing legal history, Matthew Hale did not publish his *History*, Henry Spelman was briefly at Lincoln's Inn but never practised the law, and Robert Brady, Master of Caius, was Professor of Physic. Otherwise, clerics like George Hickes, Thomas Gale or Henry Wharton, or professional antiquaries supported by such institutions as libraries and the Heralds' College or by private patrons–William Dugdale, Humphrey Wanley, Thomas Hearne, for example–were primarily interested not in legal history but in church antiquities, the Anglo-

Saxon language, local history.[84] The Reformation was a far more significant stimulus to serious research into the documents of the past than the ancestral-constitution debate; that was not the first time in the history of the Christian Church when schism, or the threat of schism, had this consequence.[85]

Paradoxically, the insistence on the unbroken continuity of the common law left the history of English law in limbo. The young Burke complained in the eighteenth century, Bagehot repeated the complaint in 1867 and again in 1872,[86] Maitland in 1904. Reviewing Felix Liebermann's great work in the *Quarterly Review*, Maitland welcomed it warmly but added a sad note: 'the Anglo-Saxon laws, which henceforward we shall know as "Die Gesetze der Angelsachsen"'.[87] The contrast with the early appearance and unbroken continuity of legal history on the continent has been frequently noticed; the source of the difference will be found in the European struggle between competing legal systems with the revival of Roman law. Nor is that the end of the negative influence of the ancestral-constitution debate: Mr Skinner has recently and forcefully called attention to the fact that the 'partisan dismissal of the Norman Conquest was to become enshrined as the *accepted scholarly tradition.* The error was manifest, yet it has only been eradicated by the most polemical revisions of modern scholarship' (my italics).[88]

If I am right in this negative evaluation when one might have expected the reverse, it then becomes necessary to ask what function (in the descriptive, not the normative, sense) critical history, professional history, does perform. Stated differently, given the existence in all human societies of some image of their past, of some identification with it, who wishes to abandon the traditional–mythical, if I may–past for a new non-mythical past, and why? We have seen that those engaged in political controversy in which the ancestral constitution was invoked did not, and that is not a peculiar case.

In a famous, angry and, strictly speaking, irrelevant digression, Thucydides (6.54–9) demolished the official view of the tyrannicides of 514 B.C., in order 'to show that the Athenians are no more accurate than the others about their own tyrants and the facts of their own history'.[89] (By 'the others' he probably meant Hellanicus' recently published *Chronicle of Athens*.) Thucydides was historically correct, as Herodotus had been on this particular point, but he made little impact on either the popular or the official view. In this or any other respect: historical allusions by the fourth-century orators were vague, inaccurate, easy and familiar. Isocrates was perhaps the worst offender, but not the only one: Demosthenes was 'extremely careful not to claim for himself more knowledge than he expects his hearers to possess'.[90]

One must have sympathy with Demosthenes. The traditions he and his fellow-orators were invoking–and I speak of tradition only in this more restricted sense–were more than a common past or common memory, they were 'a common *interpretation* of the past'.[91] What Thucydides was demanding of the Athenians was that they abandon a common interpretation of the tyrannicides, an interpretation that had become for them the myth of their collective hostility to tyranny and their collective passionate devotion to freedom, *their* 'Whig view of history'. In its place he offered unpleasant facts: that the tyrannicides were motivated by nothing higher than a squalid homosexual love affair, that the liberators of Athens from tyranny were the Spartans, not the Athenians themselves–*their* 'Norman yoke'. Demosthenes might have said, with a most distinguished Regius Professor of History in this University, 'we must congratulate ourselves that our . . . forefathers . . . did not resurrect and fasten upon us the authentic Middle Ages'.[92]

A critical inquiry, professional historiography, is thus a potential danger to the 'sublime and powerful unhistoricity' of tradition.[93] It is also terribly complicated: it piles up data, documents, events beyond number, it impedes what Professor Barnes happily called 'structural amnesia',[94] it offers too many partial explanations (when it does not refuse to explain altogether), it may undermine a common interpretation of the past and therefore the social bonds that are fortified by a common identification with the past.[95] It threatens to render the past unusable. Not the least of the complications is in the very idea of an historical process. Individual memory works with concrete occurrences and a variety of associations among them. The sense of personal identity and continuity does not require more than that. Nor do the myths of the past. 'In popular usage,' Marc Bloch noted, 'an origin is a beginning which explains. Worse still, a beginning which is a complete explanation.'[96] Simplicity is equally the key to the popular success of Oswald Spengler and Arnold Toynbee, for all the bulk of their writing; each in his own way produced 'a universal, unified world history organized around a simple general principle or law–the principle of cycles in Spengler, and a mixture of the cyclical principle with the law of challenge and response in Toynbee'.[97]

Much as professional historians may dislike it, that success is an important fact of our time. Some have found refuge in mandarinism–Professor Oakeshott with his distinction between the practical and the historical past, who will not allow us to read history backwards or to use the word 'cause' in our discourse;[98] Professor Elton in so far as he asserts that the 'main service' of the historian's activity 'lies in its essence', though he then qualifies by adding that 'it would certainly be untrue to suppose that history can teach no practical lessons';[99] Ernst Cassirer who provides us with a good analogy from a comparable field: 'It is beyond the power of philosophy to destroy the political myths. A myth is in a sense invulnerable. . . . But philosophy can do us another important service. It can make us understand the adversary';[100] and many others, not all of whom have been so explicit about their view of the matter. I do not wish to underestimate or denigrate the search for the truth for its own sake or what Professor Elton calls the 'cultural role' of the historian–'he contributes to the complex of non-practical activities which make up the culture of a society'.[101] I do not even insist that the latter be high culture; there is a place for history as entertainment, as gossip and trivia. But if one rejects the Oakeshott distinction, the question earnestly imposes itself whether we are in fact accomplishing much. In his Inaugural, Lord Acton announced that ever since the Renaissance 'the historian has obtained an increasing ascendancy' over men.[102] The inquiry into the ancestral constitution raises doubts. The time has perhaps come, in the considerable introspective activity now being carried on among (and about) historians, to add to the questions, What is history? What is historical explanation? a third, What is the effect of the study of history? I might rephrase it, *Cui bono*? Who listens? Why not?

Mr Vice-Chancellor, my ancestral piety, at any rate, can scarcely be faulted. Without straining in the least, I have invoked by name twenty-five Cambridge men, a few admittedly still too young to qualify as proper ancestors. I close with the twenty-sixth, Hugo Jones, whose premature death a year ago was such a bitter loss to Cambridge and to the international world of historical learning. I will not dwell on the personal loss, after fifteen years of close co-operation and friendship. Today's lecture would perhaps not have interested him much: he always preferred to study institutions rather than ideas about them. But he would surely have agreed that ancient history is a practical subject.

3

GENERALIZATIONS IN ANCIENT HISTORY*

I

THIS essay has a pervasively critical tone, which is neither accidental nor 'unconscious'. Its subject is methodological–the nature and problem of generalizations–not historical. It is not concerned with the content, the truth or falsity, of any particular generalization in ancient history; it is concerned with the way ancient historians go about their work, what they say or do not say, what they assume or overlook. I have deliberately adopted the expository device of the polemic, but I have not sought out atypical, heterodox studies, nor have I looked for Aunt Sallys and easy targets. Silly generalizations can be found; ancient history is no more immune from bad work than is any other discipline. I have tried to choose my few examples from typical and responsible writing by well-known historians. The choices are arbitrary, but only in the sense that the illustrations are those which happen to be more familiar to me because of my special interests. It is not suggested that the particular subjects and areas selected for illustration are better (or worse) instances of what is being done than any others or that the examples cannot be readily countered by others with different tendencies and approaches. I do believe, however, that the problem of generalization is not often studied with sufficient rigour by ancient

* When this essay was commissioned in 1960 by the Committee on Historical Analysis of the (American) Social Science Research Council, I was supplied with the text of an essay on the same subject already prepared by C. G. Starr, and my brief was to give my views 'with Starr's paper in mind'. Our two contributions were eventually published as the opening chapters of *Generalization in the Writing of History*, ed. Louis Gottschalk (Chicago 1963). In revising mine considerably for republication, I have not thought it necessary to eliminate from my text the references to those points on which I disagreed with Starr, references which were intended not as a personal debate but as a commentary, admittedly sharp, on a widely shared view. I am grateful to Quentin Skinner for valuable suggestions.

Copyright © 1963 by the University of Chicago, and reprinted by permission of the University of Chicago Press.

historians and that loose, inadequate, and even erroneous conceptions are common enough to warrant a polemical discussion.

It is generally agreed that ancient historians rarely discuss questions of method (other than questions of technique in ancillary disciplines such as archaeology or textual criticism). It would be difficult, for example, and perhaps impossible to compile even a short anthology in the field comparable to Pieter Geyl's *Debates with Historians*.[1] Max Weber and Eduard Meyer once debated problems of method and Mommsen's centenary stimulated some analysis, but who has studied the underlying assumptions and methods of Rostovtzeff or Glotz, of Tenney Frank or Beloch or Bury?* Admittedly many historians think the subject is better off without such discussion. Historians, one hears all the time, should get on with their proper business, the investigation of the concrete experiences of the past, and leave the 'philosophy of history' (which is a barren, abstract and pretty useless activity anyway) to the philosophers. Unfortunately the historian is no mere chronicler, and he cannot do his work at all without assumptions and judgments, without generalizations, in other words. In so far as he is unwilling to discuss generalizations explicitly–which means that he does not reflect on them–he runs grave risks.

The first weakness is a misconception of the nature and extent of the problem of generalization. 'The perversity of human nature is such that we do generalize', Starr writes. How much should the historian generalize? How little? That is the question he poses, and 'perversity' (even if meant ironically) suggests, as does much of his discussion, that the issue is a moral one or, at least, that there is a free, personal choice to generalize or not to generalize. 'Generalizations . . . are commonly the summation by the historian of those views of historical explanation and causation which he has exhibited less obviously in the selection and arrangement of his facts.' Unlike 'factual statements', generalizations 'seem dangerously pliable to the subjective drive of the particular mind which produces them'.[2]

No doubt there is an element of truth in these remarks. And no doubt they would receive widespread assent–they are familiar enough to anyone who has read on the subject. But they start the discussion at the wrong end. Some generalizations are the summation after long study of a historian's views about one or more

* The obvious answer to my rhetorical question is Arnaldo Momigliano, on whose work see below in this chapter and more extensively in chapter 4. Note should also be taken of the seminar conducted in recent years by Karl Christ at the University of Marburg on leading modern historians of the ancient world; see his *Von Gibbon zu Rostovtzeff* (Darmstadt 1972).

aspects of human behaviour, in the form of general propositions, hypotheses, laws. However, those are neither the only generalizations nor the most common: most historical studies in fact have no reason to conclude in that way. It is the other kinds–the initial generalizations, the (often) unexpressed generalizations that are postulated in attempts at historical explanation and equally in conventional narratives that appear to avoid general statements–which tend to escape consideration, and they, at least, cannot be usefully analysed in terms of 'shall' and 'ought', of human frailty, subjectivity and perversity. The proper question is, then, not how much or how little generalization but what kinds and levels of generalization.

II

I begin with the most elementary of the tools of the historian, with the common terms and concepts of his discourse. In themselves they are not generalizations but abbreviated descriptions or labels, classifications. However, they are rarely employed 'neutrally': their deployment presupposes general propositions or they are allowed to slide, illegitimately, into an explanatory role.

Consider the word 'Greek', whether as noun or as adjective. It is literally impossible to make any statement including 'Greek' which excludes some sort of generalization. Furthermore, it is impossible to make such a statement which would be true without greater or less qualification (excepting such truisms as 'All Greeks must eat'). In the first place, there is no meaningful definition of 'Greek' which does not differentiate in time, between a Mycenaean Greek and a contemporary Greek, to give the most extreme example. Second, applied to the ancient world any definition must face the fact of mixed populations, part Greek, part something else. Third, any meaningful statement, even when restricted to 'pure' Greeks at a fixed moment of time, must allow for variations in ideas or practices, whether by region or by class or for some other reason.

All this is commonplace, yet it has to be stressed at the outset because, for example, when some historians of ancient philosophy find it necessary to mention the (possibly) 'Semitic' ancestry of Zeno, founder of Stoicism (the 'Greekness' of whose culture is beyond dispute), they imply (and some do more than imply) a relationship between 'race' and philosophizing which serves as an explanation of the radical turn Zeno gave to Greek philosophy. Effectively the same process underlines such a statement as, 'The basic conceptions of Greek family law were already worked out in the Homeric age.'*

* See chapter 8 below.

A 'mere' classificatory term has been translated into a general proposition, treated as an axiom.

The same situation prevails with such specifically Greek institutional terms as *polis* ('city-state') or 'metic' (free non-citizen), which I shall not discuss. The case is more complicated, however, with a special category of terms, those which transcend ancient history altogether: trade, investment, class, empire, democracy, nation, slavery, and so on.* One example will serve as a pointer. In a paper on slavery in the Graeco-Roman world, Lauffer wrote as follows:

'The word *Sklave*, *esclave*, *schiavo*, which stems from the Middle Ages and originally marked Slavic war captives from eastern Europe, can be transferred to antiquity only in an anachronistic way, and that means with misunderstanding. Furthermore, the word brings to mind the Negro slavery of North America and the colonial areas in the most recent centuries, which makes its transfer to the relationships of antiquity even more difficult. The ancient "slave" is an entirely different social type.'[3]

Few (if any) of the ancient historians present at the discussion of Lauffer's paper looked with favour on this radical suggestion to abandon the word 'slave', and, in fact, it is an evasion of the difficulties, not a solution. If a label is seriously misleading, perhaps it can be replaced by a neutral one. The obvious choice for the Greek historian is the Greek word *doulos*, which can have no non-Greek associations. But this is pretence. All words have associations, and they cannot be removed by fiat. Even nonsense syllables or algebraic symbols, which can be presumed to start life without associations, necessarily acquire them if they are used in a substantive context. *Doulos* as an isolated word may have no meaning to a modern historian, but as soon as he reads and thinks about *douloi* in Athens he cannot, being human, avoid making connections with servitude, and hence with slaves. He may persist with absolute rigour in calling them *douloi*, never slaves, but all that he will accomplish by this artificial procedure will be to prevent his more general statements from being properly explicit, from being examined systematically (by himself or his readers). Lauffer has enunciated a sweeping negative conclusion about ancient slavery, not a safer working method.

And where does this process logically end? 'The ancient "slave" is an entirely different social type' presupposes that the ancient slave *is* a social type. But the Greeks regularly used the word *doulos* (and the abstract noun *douleia*) to cover a range of statuses. Even if we ignore the more metaphorical uses–'the allies became *douloi* of the

* On nation see chapter 7 below.

Athenians'–there remains the famous crux of the Spartan helots. Contemporary Greeks had no qualms about calling them *douloi*. Most historians today object: they will not allow the translation 'slaves' for the helots while employing it for the *douloi* of Athens and, curiously and most inconsistently, for the debt-bondsmen of pre-Solonic Attica or early Rome. Significant differences among these ancient status categories are undeniable. Therefore, one should argue on the Lauffer line of reasoning, the ancient slave is not a single social type at all, any more than slave in general. One should insist on breaking the concept down still further, on using different words for helot, debt-bondsman, and so on.

This process, carried far enough, would make all historical discourse impossible: even the sparest annalist would find himself in trouble, for he could safely say no more than that individual X performed action Y in a given place on a given day. At least that would be a consistent procedure. What often happens in current practice has neither that virtue nor any other. Instead of grappling with the difficulties which Lauffer noticed–and they are serious ones–students of antiquity often run from them to the illusory safety of the term 'serf', which they apply most commonly to Spartan helots but sometimes even to the pre-Solonic debt-bondsmen in Attica and to other groups who were not chattels in a strict sense. It should be immediately evident that this procedure merely transfers the problem from one rubric to another, from 'slave' to 'serf'. It solves nothing. The conclusion is demonstrable that at present, on this particular topic, the use of classificatory labels and concepts is in an unsatisfactory state, in which the inconsistent terminology reflects a deeper confusion in the interpretation of the institutions themselves.[4]

Analogous weaknesses are evident in another kind of classification, into periods. Current practice is not altogether uniform. 'Classical' and 'Hellenistic' have become standard terms in Greek history, but there is less unanimity for the earlier periods, for which various labels are used, drawn almost entirely from art and archaeology, such as 'archaic', 'Geometric', even 'sub-Geometric' and 'proto-Geometric'. Roman history, on the other hand, is traditionally divided according to political systems–kingdom, republic, empire (with subdivisions: early and late, principate and dominate). There are obvious reasons why the practice differs between Greek and Roman history. There are equally obvious difficulties with, and justifications for, the practice of periodization, but they are substantially the same in medieval and modern history. I can do no more here than exemplify the prevailing situation in ancient history.

The validity of the scheme of periods (or their essentials, which is the same thing) is rarely discussed. The traditional Roman scheme, in particular, is customarily accepted without examination, as if it were self-evident. I do not wish to challenge it here, but I must point out that it presumes a very big generalization, namely, that the form of political organization is the pivotal institution; the form, furthermore, in its crudest sense of monarchy or not-monarchy. As soon as one concerns oneself with other aspects of Roman history, this generalization is put to the test and difficulties arise. For example, there is still uncertainty among the experts on the right way to divide the history of Roman law into periods, apart from the break between classical and post-classical law which is said to have occurred in the third century of our era. In so far as this lack of agreement is but another instance of the usual difficulties with all periodization in history, it requires no comment. But there is also a difficulty peculiar to this situation, and that is the apparent lack of synchronization between legal history and political history. What does one do?

As a test case, I choose H. F. Jolowicz's excellent *Historical Introduction to the Study of Roman Law*, a standard work since 1932.[5] In the opening chapter, entitled 'Periods in the History of Rome and in the History of Her Law', Jolowicz sketches and characterizes the periods in six pages, first 'in history' (a rubric that should be pondered) and then 'in the history of the law'. The latter he divides in this way: (1) the period of conjecture to the XII Tables, (2) from the XII Tables to the end of the Republic, (3) the first century of the Empire, (4) the classical period, from Hadrian to the Severi, (5) the post-classical period down to the reign of Justinian, and (6) the reign of Justinian.

In principle this is a poor classification, since the basis oscillates between the state of our knowledge and the state of the law. It is also poor in substance, because it employs the Procrustean device of forcing legal history into political periods. Despite Jolowicz's statement regarding period 2 that 'it is impossible to find any obvious break in this long stretch of some four hundred years', his book leaves no doubt that a break must be made (this is most obvious from his chapters on the sources of law and on legal procedure). As for periods 3 and 4, he himself destroys them as soon as he creates them. 'The change from republic to empire,' he writes, 'did not make any immediate difference to private law'–so much for one end; as for the other, 'this period [3] indeed merges into' period 4. And all that is claimed to have happened in the course of period 3 is this: 'Bringing peace after about a century of turmoil, the new order was favourable to legal development. It is also perhaps true to say that now, opportunities for political distinction being necessarily few, the law remained the chief avenue for men who aspired to a public career.'

There is the usual caution: 'If it is difficult to divide general history into periods without introducing a false idea that a people develops by starts rather than continuously, it is still more difficult with legal history, for there are seldom any violent breaks.' Nevertheless, not only does Jolowicz make the attempt in the introductory chapter, but he then organizes his entire book accordingly. To do otherwise would be impossible. That is why it is important to stress (a) that the organization is set down in the most casual way, without any significant explanation or justification, without serious presentation of the criteria or implications; (b) that two possibly distinct developments are merged arbitrarily, with the political one in the prior position, again without any attempt at justification; and (c) that in the course of these six pages a number of sweeping generalizations are introduced, which are not essential to the periodization, which embrace law in general, not merely Roman law, and which are stated *ex cathedra*. Among these are (1) it is 'a false idea that a people develops by starts rather than continuously'; (2) peace, not 'turmoil', is 'favourable to legal development'; (3) because there were few 'opportunities for political distinction'–'necessarily' so because the Republic had been replaced by the Empire–'the law remained [why "remained"?] the chief avenue for men who aspired to a public career'. None of these propositions is self-evident. Indeed, the one about peace is thrown into doubt on the following page when Jolowicz notes that the next time there was a 'restoration of order' following an 'era of confusion', that is to say, with the accession of Diocletian, it 'did not revive legal literature'. No explanation is suggested.* There is one, however, again laid down *ex cathedra*, in Fritz Schulz's *History of Roman Legal Science*, namely, the complete 'victory of bureaucracy'.[6] Schulz gives some bibliography to justify the label 'classical' but none to justify his substantive proposition about the effect of bureaucracy on classical (which he also calls 'aristocratic') jurisprudence.†

* The problem is touched on in the final section of the book, but even there one cannot find a clear explanation, and surely none which throws light on the apparent contradiction within the opening chapter itself.

† In this discussion I have not been concerned with the particular choice of labels. The implications of a word like 'classical' are interesting, but what I have written would not be affected in the least if the word were replaced by something else, by dates for example (fifth and fourth centuries B.C. in Greek history).

III

These considerations at last bring me to the kind of generalization on which attention is usually concentrated – to general statements about, or implicit in accounts of, the *interrelations* of events and, beyond that, to *causes*, to answers to the question, Why?

If the historian does nothing else, he arranges events in a temporal sequence. If he did no more, if he were a chronicler in the narrowest sense, there would be no problem other than getting the dates right. But he always does much more, even when he is working within a very restricted field. When Thucydides selected the incidents at Corcyra and Potidaea for a detailed narrative rather than any of the other events which occurred in the years 433–432 B.C., his choice was dictated by a decision he had made about causes. He said so explicitly, and he underscored his decision by passing over the Megarian decrees in a few words and by refusing even to mention a contemporary belief that Pericles deliberately provoked the Peloponnesian War in order to detract attention from his personal peculations. Thucydides need not have talked about the problem of causes at all; the excision of a few sentences and phrases in his text would have converted his account into a strict narrative, leaving the question of causation, in any explicit formulation, to the reader. That is what historians frequently do. Yet there is no fundamental difference in the two procedures, however different they may appear in the end-product, aesthetically or psychologically. The choice of events which are to be arranged in a temporal sequence, which are to be interrelated, necessarily rests on a judgment of an inherent connection among them, whether that judgment is or is not expressed in so many words: a judgment, furthermore, that flows from the historian's understanding of 'relationships to longer enduring factors which are not themselves links in the sequential chain of events which constitute the "story" '.[7]

The next step in the argument carries us to a point which has usually escaped notice in the relevant discussions. War has always been a central theme in western historiography – its causes, main events and results. The Peloponnesian War alone has perhaps been the subject of as many books and articles as any other single topic in ancient history. What Thucydides began has never ended. It is therefore a startling paradox to be reminded, as Momigliano tried to remind us a few years ago, that there is 'a great deal of truth' in Cornford's old, neglected thesis that Thucydides was 'not interested in causes'.

'The Greeks came to accept war as a natural fact like birth and death about which nothing could be done. They were interested in causes of *wars*, not in causes of *war* as such. Yes, the golden age had been free from wars, but then that was the golden age. In ordinary life you could postpone *a* war, but you could not avoid *war*. . . .

'I think there would be some truth in saying that historical writing from the Renaissance to the beginnings of this century has been much more successful in dealing with causes of political revolutions than with causes of external wars, just because it has been so largely under the influence of Greek and Roman historiography.'[8]

The heritage of Greek historiography is a distinction between causes and pretexts, between remote and immediate causes, between '*isolated episodes of past history*' (my italics) and other episodes which were nearer at hand and therefore more obviously linked with a particular war. The twentieth century, Momigliano continued, has finally broken with the 'classical interpretation of war' in order to seek 'all-pervading economic, social, religious and psychological factors'. Yet, with the century more than half over, he was compelled to close his paper by enumerating ten major topics, connected with ancient warfare, which had not been systematically investigated: the idea of a just war, 'the propensity to attribute strictly personal reasons–sometimes silly ones–to declarations of war', the role of public opinion, the idea of war guilt, and so on.

Even if Momigliano was right in his cautiously stated view that the inadequacy of western historiography in this field can be explained by the influence of Greek and Roman historiography–I do not discuss that–a crucial point emerges. Hardly a month goes by without another article on the causes of this or that ancient war, and still no one (or scarcely anyone) turns to the 'all-pervading factors'.[9] The matter of generalization lies at the root of this neglect. A thorough study of, say, the role of public opinion must end with conclusions, generalizations, and it may even begin with them. The causes of a single war, on the other hand, customarily are studied in isolated episodes, and it is assumed that therefore the subject is a concrete study of particular events, the historian's proper business, because it is essentially free from generalizations, given the usual warnings about prejudice, about every man's being a product of his own time, and the like. I suggest that there is a fundamental fallacy here, that behind the carefully 'objective' correlating of events in a linear, sequential series, in which no connections are made other than those dictated by 'common sense', there lurk generalizations as sweeping as those which are sedulously avoided, sometimes the biggest of them all, that war is 'a natural fact like birth and death'. These generalizations are no less sweeping for being unexpressed and undiscussed; they are merely less defensible, less likely to rest on Greek or Roman economic, social, religious and psychological factors, more likely to rest on present-day factors as the individual historian accepts them (by habit, not by reflection) in his role as an individual in his own society (not in his role as a reflecting historian); and, therefore, they are less objective than the avowed generalizations which he dismisses as subjective and unverifiable.

The alternative which is presented, usually by implication but often enough, expecially in book reviews, by sharp assertion, between generalization and no-generalization (or 'little generalization') turns out not to be that at all. Every attempt, no matter how cautious, to order the unique events of history in some fashion–by classification or by interrelation–entails as much generalization as any attempt frankly to state general propositions about public opinion and war or the effects of slavery or the decline of the Roman Empire. Epistemological and metaphysical considerations apart, every historian is plunged into explanations, into generalizations, the moment he goes beyond mere naming or counting or dating. The illusion that he can draw distinctions of the kind I have been challenging serves merely to stultify him. It does not make him more objective, more circumspect, more of a historian (and surely not a better historian).

IV

Nothing I have said so far bears specifically on ancient history, as distinct from any other history, medieval or modern, eastern or western. Does the study of ancient history have special qualities or characteristics which give some kind of twist to the problem of generalization or require special approaches?

Starr says that 'the peculiar qualities of ancient history . . . probably lead scholars in this field to generalize more often than would be required in fields where factual evidence is more abundant and less digested'. Neither Starr nor anyone else has assembled any statistical evidence on the point, and it would therefore be futile to try to defend or challenge the statement on the question whether it is a fact that ancient historians generalize more often than modern historians. But I believe it needs to be challenged on its reasoning. That ancient historians have a smaller body of source material than most historians and that they must rely much more on belles-lettres and archaeological finds and proportionately less on documents cannot be denied. It follows that they are more concerned with textual criticism and with material objects, that they often have less control over the reliability of a source, that they must often depend on a single statement by a single author, that there are greater gaps in the chain of data–in short, that they must more often guess and hesitate and qualify and end with a *non liquet*. But what have any of these things to do with the *frequency* of generalizations as distinct from the greater or lesser probability of their being right? Do ancient historians draw more generalizations about slavery, for example, than do historians of the American South? On the contrary, I think they tend to draw fewer, and sometimes worse ones, precisely because of the limitations imposed by the evidence.

One should not confuse extrapolation and inference with generalization. In dealing with such factors as population or prices, the ancient historian lacks the material for a series. Therefore he extrapolates more freely, but that does not mean that he generalizes more freely. On the contrary–again, as with slavery–the tendency is to throw up one's hands in despair at the lack of evidence. Or consider this example of inference: We know that in Attica at the beginning of the sixth century B.C. there was a deep agrarian crisis, which Solon sought to abate, whereas in the fifth century the small-farmer class was numerous and, if not prosperous, at least relatively secure; some historians believe that Solon failed and they therefore infer that the tyrant Pisistratus redistributed a fair amount of land, although not a single existing source says so. Whether right or wrong (and I think wrong), this inference is no more than a kind of extrapolation, working from one isolated episode to another, much like a discussion of the causes of the Peloponnesian War. Probably ancient historians are forced to this kind of reasoning oftener than others. But such an inference is not a generalization; in so far as it rests on generalizations, the situation is no different from what I have already discussed. There is nothing peculiar to ancient history in the reasoning process.

Only in one respect, perhaps, does the ancient historian face a rather special, though not unique, problem. Gaps in the evidence send him (should send him more often than they do, I may say) to other societies and periods for guidance. This is a legitimate procedure even for historians with much more abundant material, and it raises the familiar problems inherent in all comparative social analysis. Those I shall not discuss, but I think there is something rather special in the field of ancient history, namely, that the concepts and underlying assumptions are derived in very large part from more or less recent experience. How much writing about ancient economics, for example, assumes without discussion that trade and money have characteristics and impacts which are universally the same, except for differences in quantity or scale? The answer will be obvious to anyone who has read the modern literature on, say, Aristotle's brief discussion of exchange in the fifth book of the *Nicomachean Ethics.*[10]

Thirty years ago Johannes Hasebroek, influenced by Max Weber, urged a reconsideration of the accepted assumptions about ancient economics. His work had serious defects, but he was neither corrected nor answered on the central issues; he was crushed and dismissed, sunk with hardly a trace. The remarks by A. W. Gomme are typical:

'Hasebroek has to admit of course that Athens imported most of the corn and almost all her timber. He often makes a point that these were necessities; and somehow or other persuades himself that there is some essential difference between trade in necessities, in articles of primary consumption, and other trade. . . . We might go indeed further: one of Hasebroek's main arguments is that the policy of ancient states was never determined by commercial considerations–neither foreign nor internal policy; yet a country dependent on supplies of *necessities* from abroad would, one might suppose, be more likely to take trade into consideration than one which traded in non-essential goods. . . . The Greeks were well aware that imports and exports must in the long run, somehow, balance.'[11]

If there is any doubt about the source of Gomme's economic ideas, it is removed a few pages later when he offers a longish argument, derived in the end from Adam Smith, to support the certainly erroneous contention that the Greeks 'were perfectly familiar with the principle of subdivision of labour'. Gomme's argument is exactly the kind of modern argument his one source, Xenophon, was not making. The few ancient writers who mention division of labour at all do so in a context and from a point of view which are essentially different from Adam Smith's. They were interested in the quality of manufacture, not in quantity or efficiency. Indeed, the very notion of 'efficiency' is one of the best examples of a modern concept which, though taken as self-evident, turns out to be missing (in such contexts) throughout antiquity.[12]

If I am right, if it is the case that much of the subsurface generalization in ancient history comes from outside, so to speak, then the ancient historian is placed under a particular burden, one which is made still heavier by a contingent factor. Ancient history is unique in western history (but has parallels in Middle and Far Eastern history) in that its professional practitioners are by long tradition often men who are not in the first instance historians but men trained in language and literature who call themselves classicists (or

Hellenists) and classical philologists, epigraphists and papyrologists. In raising this point, I make no suggestion that there is something arcane about history or even that it requires technical training in the same sense in which the natural sciences do. The implications lie in two other directions.

First, there is an unmistakable tendency for classicists, steeped as they are in the literature of Greece and Rome, to follow the lead of ancient writers, and particularly of ancient historical writers. The example of the causes of wars has already been given. Another is the characteristic remark by Starr that since one must 'rely . . . mostly upon Thucydides for an account of the Peloponnesian War, . . . independent generalization will be difficult'. I agree that classicists find it difficult, but I believe that the reason is not the one given but rather a mind-set, a deeply rooted value-judgment which, consciously nor not, inhibits and even prohibits 'independent generalization' (that is, a different explanation). Hindsight is more than a subject for bad jokes; it is shorthand for the truth that further experience may, and often does, provide understanding which contemporaries missed, in other words, for new and better generalizations.

Second, classicists by definition do not have the habit of thinking about history and historical problems other than those on which they happen to be working, do not, by and large, even read history in a serious way outside the ancient field. Their general historical views, like their economic ideas, are in a sense fixed in their schooldays, and those make up their basic assumptions, their subsurface generalizations, from which they proceed to classify and order events and institutions of the ancient world. Their independent study is restricted to the superstructure and is not often checked by re-examination of the substructure which came from the outside. It was not without justification that E. R. Dodds wrote in the preface to *The Greeks and the Irrational*:

'To my fellow-professionals I perhaps owe some defence of the use which I have made in several places of recent anthropological and psychological observations and theories. . . . I see here good reason to be cautious in applying to the Greeks generalizations based on non-Greek evidence, but none for the withdrawal of Greek scholarship into a self-imposed isolation. Still less are classical scholars justified in continuing to operate–as many of them do–with obsolete anthropological concepts.'[13]

To the objection that Dodds is talking about something else, about the relationship between history and other disciplines, I reply that for many classicists history is in effect another discipline. No doubt few will go so far as to offer an apologia like this: 'I realize that the subject matter of this book belongs to a field of research more appropriate for a trained jurist than for a general student of Hellenic antiquity. . . . Nevertheless, in studying Athenian private law the novice has one advantage which is denied to the professional. He can approach the subject free from all preconceived notions derived from other legal systems.'[14] But, apart from the astonishing conception of human knowledge which is implied (things learned are condemned as misleading preconceptions), this statement does reflect much actual practice. What is 'a general student of Hellenic antiquities'? No historian of France (or Germany) is likely to dismiss his professional qualifications and call himself 'a general student of French (or German) antiquities'. The difference expresses the peculiar situation in ancient history.

Common sense is no substitute for professionalism. When Westermann wrote, 'Serious revolts of slaves did not occur during the period 500–320 B.C., which is a significant commentary upon the generally mild treatment of slaves during that time', he implied a common-sense generalization, namely, that slaves revolt when they are treated harshly, not when they are treated mildly.[15] It happens to be, almost certainly, a false generalization, as a study of slavery in other societies reveals. I cannot, of course, recapitulate Westermann's mental processes when he wrote that sentence, but the practice is common enough. We all do it. Given fact A–in this instance the almost total absence of slave revolts for two centuries–fact B is at once linked with it as an obvious explanation. What I mean by professionalism is, among other things, the habit of mind, which comes from experience with historical study and reflection, that sends up a warning light every time one makes such a connection. Professionalism tells a historian what questions to ask, not what answers to give.

V

Obviously no historian can be asked to make explicit, let alone embark upon a systematic personal study of, every term, concept, assumption and interrelation he employs. If he were, he could never accomplish anything. The conclusions I draw from what I have said are merely: (1) historians generalize all the time at the beginning and in the course of every study they make, and the more conscious they are of this, the more control they will have over their generalizations; (2) since generalization is inherent in the work of the historian, it is absurd and even self-contradictory, for him suddenly to become 'cautious' and to refuse to generalize at the end of a study, which amounts to a refusal to explain in a proper way the very institutions and events he has devoted himself to studying.

Ultimately the question at issue is the nature of the historian's function. Is it only to recapture the individual, concrete events of a past age, as in a mirror, so that the progress of history is merely one of rediscovering lost data and of building bigger and better reflectors? If so, then the chronicle is the only correct form for his work. But if it is to understand, however one chooses to define the word, then it is to generalize, for every explanation is or implies one or more generalizations. There is a curious fallacy in many minds that the whole issue is a product of the late nineteenth century, stimulated simultaneously by modern physical science on the one hand and by Marxism on the other. Let us grant the impact of both, on history as on other disciplines. But even the most casual acquaintance with pre-nineteenth-century historians, from Herodotus to Vico or Herder, ought to leave no doubt that, each in his own way, the important historians, the ones we still read as historians (and not merely as possible sources of factual information), were deeply concerned with general truths and with the difficulties in both establishing them and communicating them, often explicitly so; in the case of Thucydides, obsessively so.

What modern science and Marxism between them have accomplished is to inject unnecessary fears into the situation. The arguments go: Human behaviour does not lend itself to quantitative analysis and to repeated re-examination under identical conditions, and therefore all generalizations are unreliable; Marxism distorts human behaviour by reducing it to a monistic theory; worse still, like all varieties of 'historicism' (in Popper's sense) it is morally noxious. The reply to such arguments is too easy. Must every discipline either be physics or be abandoned? Must all generalizations be dropped because some are demonstrably untrue or thought to be dangerous? Is a limited reliability no better than useless? Verification of historical generalizations is extremely difficult and apparently cannot be achieved, at best, beyond the establishment of a greater or lesser probability. The historian, of the nineteenth century as well as of antiquity, can only within baffling limits employ the research techniques and the quantitative analyses available to the student of the current social scene. These are aspects of the problem of historical generalizations which require careful, detailed consideration. But such an analysis need not be made, and probably can be made least effectively, in the field of ancient history. The methodological issues in one historical period are not essentially different from those in another.

4

THE HISTORICAL TRADITION: THE *CONTRIBUTI* OF ARNALDO MOMIGLIANO*

It is, I believe, a safe prediction that Professor Momigliano will never write a book entitled 'What is History?' Yet no contemporary has devoted so much energy, or contributed so much, to the study and understanding of the western historiographical tradition from its beginnings down to our own day. His *tesi di laurea* at the University of Turin in 1930 was on the composition of Thucydides' history. Early in the same year he completed his *Prime linee di storia della tradizione maccabaica.*[1] And the interest (as well as the characteristic pairing of the classical and the Hebrew) has never flagged since. With the publication of the *Quarto Contributo*, the articles and reviews explicitly concerned with historiography which have already been brought together in book form total more than one hundred. And that figure understates the case, for in Momigliano's 'substantive' studies the inquiry into historiography and the historical tradition is rarely long out of mind.

The *oeuvre* is too dense and wide-ranging to be appreciated in a

* This is a slightly abridged version of a review-essay on A. Momigliano, *Terzo Contributo alla storia degli studi classici e del mondo antico* (2 vols., Rome 1966), which appeared in *History and Theory* 7 (1968) 355–67.

The first of the *Contributi* was published in 1955, the second in 1960, the fourth in 1969, and a fifth is in the press. The third is the first to include the words 'e del mondo antico' in the title. Apart from a few previously unpublished essays, the *Contributi* consist of published articles and reviews, each reprinted, unchanged, in its original language (English or Italian, with a few book reviews in German), often with addenda, mostly bibliographical. My citation method is to use a Roman numeral for the *Contributo* number, Arabic numerals for the pages. Thirteen of the contributions have also been published as *Studies in Historiography* (London 1966), where three are translated from the Italian. In quoting from them I have used the published translation.

Copyright © 1968 by Wesleyan University, and reprinted by permission of Wesleyan University Press.

single review of reasonable length. I shall focus on a single recurrent question–why do historians write their histories in the way they do?

The question is recurrent not because Momigliano happens to be passionately interested in it but because it recurs in every generation and every age. 'Too much historical research,' he wrote in 1953, 'is being done by people who do not know why they are doing it and without regard to the limits imposed by the evidence' (I 373). For the functionalist, the question is not, what is history?–demanding epistemological or metaphysical answers–but rather, why this kind of history? on this particular subject?–inviting historical answers. The historian, in this sort of discourse, studies his contemporaries and his predecessors (and himself) as subject-matter, exactly as he examines institutions or monarchs or international relations.

I

It is a commonplace that every historian's notion (conscious or subconscious) of his function is based on both the social and political situation in his own world and the literary and moral tradition he has inherited. And there is nothing uncommon about the study of great historians of the past against their intellectual or political background. Publications pour out on Herodotus and Pericles, Thucydides and the sophists, Tacitus and the senatorial opposition to autocracy, on Gibbon, Macaulay and Burckhardt. What gives Momigliano's work its unmistakable stamp (apart from the prodigious learning, the intellectual power, the zest and the wit) is the persistent and complex counterpoint he weaves–between ideas and the social reality, between the topic under examination and its historiography, between the ancient world and the modern, including our own. This last deserves more extensive elucidation, for no other classical scholar is so conscious of the importance, and so willing to accept the responsibility, of analysing the writings of his colleagues and contemporaries with the same methods, and according to the same canons, which we all regularly employ in examining the Greek and Roman writers of history.

Not only were Beloch, De Sanctis and Rostovtzeff obviously as much the products of tradition and society as Herodotus, Thucydides or Tacitus, but we also know much about the former as individuals, almost nothing about the latter except for what little can be deduced from their own writings. This is no negligible distinction: it is pertinent to quote again Momigliano's complaint about the habit of writing history 'without regard to the limits imposed by the evidence'.[2] Nevertheless, whereas the impact of nationalism on the historiography of the First World War, or of Nazism on German historiography in general, has become a fairly respectable subject of historical investigation, there appears to be a taboo against similar inquiries outside a restricted range of men and events, a taboo not shared in other disciplines, such as philosophy, economics and sociology. At the very least, a man must be dead for a generation. When a young American classicist, Meyer Reinhold, wrote a sympathetic, perceptive but critical article on Rostovtzeff in 1946,[3] he was castigated in private for his 'bad taste' and he was ignored in public, though not by Momigliano (I 343 and III 791).[4]

To consider another kind of example, there is the remark of Ehrenberg, who was driven from his chair at the German university in Prague, in his review of Edouard Will's *Doriens et Ioniens. Essai sur la valeur du critère ethnique appliqué à l'étude de l'histoire et de la civilisation grecques*: 'The passages he quotes from some of the German writings of the 'thirties and 'forties are sad disclosures indeed of a prostitution of scholarship of which the authors must by now feel deeply ashamed. Will says: *scripta manent.* So they do – to some extent. It was a good thing to show what has been possible; but now it will be best to let all this sink into oblivion.'[5]

As a political programme, 'forgive and forget' has many supporters. For historians it is not so simple; or at least it ought not be. When an Italian translation of Berve's *Griechische Geschichte* appeared in 1959, under good scholarly auspices, Momigliano closed his mordant review (III 699–708) by posing the question of the failure of Italian classicists to interest themselves in 'studying the influence of Nazism on ancient history'. Two factors, he suggests, have interfered: 'One is the tradition of the academic encomium which wishes to keep silence about anything unpleasant, even if essential. The other is the habit of treating the history of historiography as a Sunday pastime, when one is weary from genuine historical labours and has not enough energy to read books, only to leaf through them' (III 708).

After all, what is under consideration is the central thread in western historiography from its first beginnings. No one will deny the following propositions: 'No other ancient civilization absorbed Greek historiography and made it its own as did the Roman. Through the mediation of the Romans, Greek historiography became the basis of our historiographical practice (*abitudini*)' (III 55). But the contribution of this *historiographical* tradition to the Renaissance is less well appreciated, and still less the remarkable achievement of the Germans at the beginning of the nineteenth century, when they invented a discipline called 'classical philology', which they proceeded to equate with humane education in general, and then persuaded most of Europe to accept their creation, axiomatically as it were. The gains to learning which resulted are not to be underestimated: one can read them up in histories of classical scholarship. What one will not find in these accounts is their deeper significance. One powerful current, the romantic school of historians whose spiritual ancestor was Wilhelm von Humboldt, aimed at something beyond a mere *techne*, and it is their political *weltanschauliche* concerns, gravitating around such concepts as 'spirit', 'essence', 'nation', which a functional inquiry seeks to elucidate and assess.[6] Momigliano, for one, has never relented in his dislike and distrust of such 'abstractions' (a favourite derogatory term with him).[7] In an 'epoch of political dissolution' they were ready to hand, easily converted into ideological weapons in the service of the enemies of the humanity they were supposed to foster.

'The antijuristic current, to which I would attribute long-term effects, is that which is represented in Greek history by W. Jaeger's *Paideia* and, at a lower level, by *Der hellenische Mensch* by Max Pohlenz (recently translated into Italian as *L'Uomo greco*). . . . In all these works, concrete situations, economic and juristic relationships, institutions, are left on one side. Jaeger speaks of Paideia, but the history of education in antiquity has been written by a very different historian, the Frenchman H. I. Marrou. . . .

'It would be erroneous to say that this historiography is a child of Nazism: this would not only go against chronology, but also against the fact that distinguished scholars like W. Jaeger were themselves victims of Nazism. Nor should we forget the conspicuous contribution of Jaeger, Heinze and certain of their disciples to the understanding of Greek and Roman ethics. But this historiography, with its scant grip on reality, bears the mark of an epoch of political dissolution. . . . That this historiography could degenerate into Nazism was a danger, which was confirmed by some of Jaeger's pupils who had remained in Germany' (III 300–301).

Werner Jaeger was for my generation the central, and ambiguous, figure in the latest chapter of the story. He was a great scholar, highly influential in Germany before the war not only through his writings and university teaching (especially as Wilamowitz's successor in Berlin) but also through the journal, *Die Antike*, which he edited until he left Germany in 1936 to accept an American invitation. Although he was also widely respected in the United States, where he remained until his death in 1961, his 'humanistic' ideal continued to make its greatest impact in Germany–'a truly triumphal career, unbroken by the catastrophes of the age', is how a German classical scholar summed up Jaeger's life.[8] Momigliano has discussed his significance time and again, though never at length; in his London Inaugural in 1952, for example, when he singled out Jaeger's three-volume *Paideia* as a symbol of one aspect of the 'crisis' through which Greek studies are passing, namely, the divorce of the study of Greek political ideas from the study of politics (I 230); most recently in a lecture on 'Perspective 1967 of Greek History' (IV 43–58), where he briefly noted the programmatic aim of *Paideia* as an aristocratic educational idea. This is worth pursuing further, textually, by two quotations from the introduction to Jaeger's book:

'We are accustomed to use the word culture, not to describe the ideal which only the Hellenocentric world possesses, but in a much more trivial and general sense, to denote something inherent in every nation of the world, even the most primitive. . . . Thus the word has sunk to mean a simple anthropological concept, not a concept of value, a consciously pursued *ideal*. In this vague analogical sense it is permissible to talk of Chinese, Indian, Babylonian, Jewish or Egyptian culture, although none of these nations has a word or an ideal which corresponds to real culture. . . . And ultimately the habit of speaking of a number of pre-Hellenic "cultures" was created by the positivist passion for reducing everything to the same terms: an outlook which applies hereditary European descriptions even to non-European things, and neglects the fact that historical method is falsified by an attempt to apply our conceptions to a world foreign to them.'

'We can now define the specific character of Hellenism, in contrast to the Orient. By discovering man, the Greeks did not discover the subjective self, but realized the universal laws of human nature.'[9]

This 'separation of the Greek and Oriental worlds as two opposing worlds' is for Momigliano the 'first and essential element' (out of eight) in the heritage of German Hellenism of the previous generation. (Another is the conviction that 'to understand the Greeks it is necessary to think in Greek or, alternatively, in German'.) Hence his summons, in 'Perspective 1967', to extend the process of 'decolonization' to the study of ancient history in Italy. In the end, his own many inquiries into the present-day historiography of antiquity are always programmatic, not on the strictly political level, as it has sometimes been thought to be, in opposition to 'forgive and forget',[10] but on the educational level, understood broadly. The 1967 call for 'decolonization' goes well beyond the demand for emancipation from German *auctoritas*, to include among other things an urgent plea for the modernization of the study of anthropology in Italy and for a closer interplay there between classical studies and sociology and anthropology. It is not by chance that this last interest seems to have arisen after his transfer to England, and to have grown stronger with the years here. 'After all, *we* are contemporaries of Lévi-Strauss, and so we ought to learn something from his analysis of pseudo-archaic cultures' (III 292). What we ought to learn, methodologically, he formulated briefly in his 'Interim Report on the Origins of Rome': 'Comparative anthropology is more likely to indicate alternative possibilities of interpretation for the evidence we have than to supplement the evidence we have not' (III 581).

The other part of Momigliano's programmatic concern thus bears immediately on the subject-matter of ancient history rather than on the training of its practitioners – in so far as that distinction can legitimately be drawn, at least for purposes of analysis – and a consideration of Momigliano on Rostovtzeff with this point in mind may help to draw together the strands of this section of my review. Momigliano's two elegantly written obituary-articles[11] include the usual biographical ingredients, employed in a superlative way to throw light on Rostovtzeff's two greatest works, the social and economic history of first the Roman Empire and then of the Hellenistic world.

'Born in a country where the bourgeoisie was hard to find, he came to idealize the Hellenistic and Roman bourgeoisie. . . . Slaves and peasants attracted Rostovtzeff's attention only in so far as they helped, or interfered with, the activity of the city builders. Agrarian history, to which Rostovtzeff had devoted so much important research when he was in Russia and in the first years of his exile, played only a secondary part in the two great Histories. . . . He is not the historian of Roman and Hellenistic society as a whole. He is primarily the historian of their traders, gentlemen farmers and professionals' (I 350).

However, 'the triumph of the Hellenistic and Roman bourgeoisie was comparatively short and incomplete',* and Rostovtzeff tried desperately, and unsuccessfully, to find the grounds for an explanation in his own experience. An early attempt to attribute the decline of Rome to a Red Army of peasants was demolished by other scholars and abandoned, to be replaced by a mixture of factors – excessive state intervention in the economy, the debasement of culture through its trickling down to the masses, and the barbarian invasions (playing the role Rome itself had played against the Hellenistic states). In the end, the restricted focus of Rostovtzeff's vision was responsible, even in his greatest work, for a 'hiatus' that

* In the present context it is unnecessary to discuss Rostovtzeff's use of the term 'bourgeoisie', which he never defined, as Momigliano was not alone in pointing out (I 353–54).

Momigliano had immediately spotted to be a structural feature of the Hellenistic book. That work proved to be a massive effort to deal with two separate themes Rostovtzeff could not 'weld together', 'the two stories of Roman conquest and Hellenistic achievement' (I 335–39). Momigliano then formulated the historical nexus:

'Both stories have long been needed. . . . They reflect a dualism which it would be erroneous to suppress. If one looks at Greece as a political organization, Rome is the next step: Hellenism is just a transition between Greece and Rome. If one looks to Greece for a faith, the next phase is Christianity, and Hellenism is the period in which, by its contacts with the East, the classical world prepares for Christianity. Overschematizing again, if one wants to explain the Roman Empire, one has to follow the first approach; if one wants to understand the Church, the second direction is best' (I 338).

With that we are plunged into the complex story of the concept of Hellenism that runs in different streams from Droysen to Wilamowitz and Tarn, about which Momigliano has written so much. And that is what I mean by calling his critique of contemporary historians programmatic: he always looks ahead to the next stage in the historical inquiry, setting the research problems, pointing to the possible evidence (or lack of it), calling attention to the traps, always insisting on retaining a 'grip on reality'.

II

The dangers inherent in the history of ideas are well known. One is the genealogical fallacy, that is, the notion that the discovery of a genealogical link between two thinkers or schools of thought is sufficient of itself to explain what the 'borrower' believed or felt or intended. Another, not unrelated, is a tendency not to pursue the argument beyond the establishment of connections. Even Momigliano is not immune, and one sometimes has the feeling that, in the fascination of 'locating' Timaeus or Josephus, he for the moment forgets to pose the question of credibility. Not for long, however. His 'grip on reality', his feeling for the realities of an historical situation, is too strong. Typical is the following aside:

'To us it naturally appears that there is something in common between the Jews who died in defending the old Jerusalem and the Christians who died in building up the new Jerusalem against the same Roman Empire. Modern scholars have found it easy to prove that in form and substance the Jewish martyr is the prototype of the Christian martyr. Such scholarly discoveries have little relevance to the realities of the fourth century. The pupils hated their masters, and were hated in their turn. With a cry of joy Eusebius, possibly a man of Jewish descent, retells from Josephus the story of the fall of Jerusalem: thus may perish the enemies of Christ' (III 88).

This passage appears in the introduction to the article on 'Pagan and Christian Historiography in the Fourth Century A.D.', to which I now turn as the first of three examples (drawn from the *Terzo Contributo*) illustrating how Momigliano applies historical analysis to the ancient historical writers, and with what results.

1. The development of large territorial empires–Persian, Hellenistic, Roman–brought about the incorporation and subsequent co-existence of civilized peoples or 'nations' each of which had its own considerable historical tradition. Although the responses which ensued cannot be forced into a single pattern, it seems true that, on the whole, the dominant group showed little interest in learning about its subjects and their beliefs about their past, while among the latter a curiosity about their rulers was inevitable, though it created difficult problems. If one compares Herodotus on Persia with the work of another native of Halicarnassus, Dionysius, who nearly 300 years later wrote a lengthy *Roman Antiquities*, in Greek, one begins to perceive the complexity of the situation and the variety of the responses. Or consider Josephus. The ancient Hebrews produced 'the well-known paradox . . . that within a few generations the most historically minded of the ancient nations turned into the one most indifferent to history. . . . Historical events lost their importance in comparison with the eternal Torah' (III 237–38). After Kings and Chronicles were compiled, there was no more serious Jewish historical writing about the past in antiquity, save for the *Jewish Antiquities*, an apologetic work composed after the fall of Jerusalem by Joseph ben Mathias, become Flavius Josephus, written in Greek for 'any of the Greeks . . . curious to learn our history'.

That many were curious may be doubted. 'Normally the educated pagans of the Roman Empire knew nothing about either Jewish or Christian history. If they wanted some information about the Jews, they picked up second-hand distortions such as we read in Tacitus. The consequence was that a direct acquaintance with Jewish or Christian history normally came together with conversion to Judaism or to Christianity. People learnt a new history because they acquired a new religion. Conversion meant literally the discovery of a new history from Adam and Eve to contemporary events.'

The Christians were thus presented with a problem, especially after the conversion of Constantine. On the one hand, their own history was one of persecutions from without and doctrinal conflicts within, both of which had to be correctly understood; hence Eusebius' 'emphasis on the struggle against persecutors and heretics and therefore on the purity and continuity of the doctrinal tradition' (III 100). On the other hand, the Christians were ready to take over the empire *and its history*, and, with the conversion of large numbers of more educated men from the eastern, Greek part of the empire, it was necessary to teach them at least a short outline of that history. For this purpose the pagan epitomes or *breviaria*, notably that of Eutropius, served well enough. They were 'neutral' in their religion and morality and no danger to the Christians. It was unnecessary to 'christianize ordinary political history', so long as the important history, the doctrinal one, was under full control.

The Christians, in short, made no effort to compete in the 'traditional forms of higher historiography'. They were content to leave that to the pagans, who, in the event, were unable or unwilling to accept the gift but preferred to read and imitate such pagan historians of the past as Sallust, Livy and Tacitus. What was new in Christian historiography was its universal chronology, the spadework for which was done in the second and third centuries; its contribution to biography (the hagiographies); above all, the 'new type of historical exposition' introduced by Eusebius, 'characterized by the importance attributed to the remote past, by the central position of doctrinal controversies, and by the lavish use of documents' (III 101).

Was there then a medieval 'school' providing the link to the early modern period? 'From the sixteenth to the eighteenth century ecclesiastical history (especially of the early Church) was treated with a much greater display of erudition, with much greater care for minute analysis of the evidence than any other type of history.... Perhaps we have all underestimated the impact of ecclesiastical history on the development of the historical method. A new chapter of historiography begins with Eusebius not only because he invented ecclesiastical history, but because he wrote it with a documentation which is utterly different from that of the pagan historians' (III 101).

2. The earlier Persian Empire, reaching to the eastern shores of the Mediterranean Sea, had a different impact, partly because its structure was different from the Roman, partly because the social and intellectual situation among its subjects and those in contact with it were not the same as the later Hellenistic condition. Hebrews and Greeks alike responded by a 'sharpening of the national consciousness' (III 814), expressed in very divergent ways. Hecataeus and Herodotus were led to a 'critical rediscovery of the national tradition when confronted by other traditions'. Contact with the Persian Empire 'made the Greeks more conscious of the world about them and also of their own cultural heritage: that was one of the

stimuli which created Greek historiography' (III 818). However, Herodotus had no eastern models. History was his own creation. On the other hand, although Ezra and Nehemiah had the Hebrew historiographical tradition behind them, they did not continue it. They, too, created something new, an account in autobiographical form of a politico-religious community activity. For Herodotus the central episode was the Greek victory in the Persian wars, which deserved memorializing for future generations along with an indication of those superior qualities which enabled the Greeks to triumph; but for the post-exilic Hebrew 'scribes' the issue was the formation of a new community, of a 'new pact between God and Israel'.

In Herodotus' own lifetime there came a shift of interest as the Athenian Empire grew into the dominant factor in Greek political affairs; the greatest and fullest expression of this change is of course to be found in Thucydides, with his history of the long struggle between Athens and Sparta. The defeat of Athens in 404 B.C. and the subsequent failure of Sparta to hold together an empire of its own as successor to the Athenian brought Persia back on the scene, and post-Thucydidean historiography was quick to respond. Unfortunately, for the whole period between Xenophon, writing in the first half of the fourth century B.C., and Polybius two hundred years later, nothing remains of the far from negligible Greek historical output save for fragments quoted or paraphrased (and sometimes distorted or falsely attributed) by later writers. Any attempt at a detailed or systematic account of, say, Ephorus or Theopompus is therefore hazardous. But the attempt must be made if we are to understand these decisive centuries in the formation of the western historiographical tradition. In a long article published in 1931 (III 367–92), Momigliano argued persuasively that one of Theopompus' objectives in embarking on a continuation of Thucydides' unfinished history was to correct the latter's failure to appreciate the menace of Persia. The whole of Theopompus' *Hellenica*, he concluded, 'in its political ideals' can be seen as a 'continuous implicit polemic against Thucydides' (III 375). Hence the admiration for the Spartan Lysander, as later for Philip of Macedon; they realized, each in his own way, the need 'for a strong union of Greek powers as the only effective practical deterrent to the power of Persia'.

3. If I were given the miraculous power of recovering some of the lost histories of antiquity, high on my list would be the works of two third-century B.C. writers, Timaeus of Taormina in Sicily and the Roman senator, Fabius Pictor. The former, son of a dynast who had ruled his native city, was exiled by Agathocles, tyrant of Syracuse, late in the fourth century, went to Athens, and for fifty

years devoted himself with monomania to investigating and writing the history of the western Greeks, followed by an account of the invasion of Italy and Sicily by Pyrrhus of Epirus in the years 280–275, which brought the story down to one of the great turning-points in European history, the completion of Rome's conquest of Italy and the first of the wars against Carthage. Much is necessarily obscure about Timaeus, but enough can be deduced from the fragments, supported by some explicit statements in later writers, for a plausible assessment of his qualities and his place in the tradition. To begin with, he never wavered in his hatred of tyrants, with whom he classed the new Hellenistic monarchs starting with Alexander the Great. His capacity for hatred was infinite; among the butts of his tirades were Thucydides, Isocrates, Theopompus, Ephorus, Plato, Aristotle and Theophrastus. But one should not conclude from that (incomplete) list that he had any genuine interest in philosophy, either of the past or in the present, despite the fact that the Athens in which he lived was the centre of four flourishing schools. Plato fell victim because of the strange episode in which the Academy had been associated with the tyrants of Syracuse, Aristotle and his school for their connection with Alexander and his successors. Contrariwise, the Pythagoreans had the merit of having lived and worked in the city-state world of southern Italy and Sicily.

Apart from these flashes of indignation, Timaeus turned his back on the old Greek world, now the hateful Hellenistic world. It was his obsession with the west which made him a pivotal figure. 'A pedant with imagination', he had learned some of his essential techniques from Herodotus, including a searching curiosity about the non-Greek peoples of the west, their legends, traditions and customs. So 'he did for the west what Herodotus had done for the east more than a century and a half earlier' (III 61), and in the process he 'discovered' Rome. Some interest in Rome and her origins had been shown by earlier Greek historians, but 'Timaeus was the first to get down to details. . . . Furthermore, he was the first to draw the consequences of the [current] situation and to devote a special monograph to a war in which Rome had fought and defeated a Greek army' (III 44). Two facts attest to his impact: Polybius felt it necessary to try to destroy Timaeus' reputation, and Romans in the age of Varro and Cicero were still reading him with pleasure. It is therefore 'legitimate to conjecture' that in third-century Rome he became 'obligatory reading for the growing minority of aristocrats educated to understand Greek' (III 50).

Among them – this can be demonstrated with virtual certainty – was Fabius Pictor, a member of one of the most aristocratic of

Roman *gentes*. In the critical days of the Hannibalic War he wrote the first history of Rome. Two questions arise. What inspired him to so novel an action? Why did he choose to write in Greek, not in Latin? Again Momigliano offers persuasive, though necessarily conjectural, answers. We know that the Romans, led by their priests, were making urgent calls on the supernatural powers to rescue them. These took various forms, including the burial alive of a Greek and a Gallic captive, and certain specific cult activities which brought 'a superstitious interest in Rome's past' to bear on current needs. Fabius Pictor, pious and patriotic, preferred to take another line: 'by the very fact of writing history . . . he transformed a nebulous and quasi-magical interest into an effort of intellectual comprehension' (III 58). And by choosing Greek he chose deliberately to 'insert himself directly into historiography in the Greek language'.

Fabius was totally successful. The future course was fixed. 'History in Rome, properly Hellenized, remained under the control of the ruling class' (III 67), and through their mediation (though they switched to Latin), Greek historiography became the basis of our historical practice.

5

ARCHAEOLOGY AND HISTORY*

MOMIGLIANO began his elegant obituary of Rostovtzeff by recalling the 'unforgettable impression' made on students of his (and my) generation by the publication in 1926 of the *Social and Economic History of the Roman Empire*:

'All seemed, and indeed was, extraordinary in the book. Even the external appearance was unusual. We were accustomed to books on ancient history where the archaeological evidence, if used at all, was never presented and explained to the reader. Here a lavish series of plates introduced us directly to the archaeological evidence; and the caption of each plate really made us understand what one could learn from apparently insignificant items. . . . Rostovtzeff delighted and surprised us by what seemed to us his uncanny gift of calling ancient things to life. He guided us through the streets of Rome, Pompeii, Nimes and Trèves and showed how the ancients had lived.'[1]

Half a century later the situation has altered in some respects. Although there are still too many books written about ancient history in which the archaeological evidence receives no more than lip service, not merely in the presentation but also in the historian's own study, it is also true that more classical and Near Eastern historians are conscious of, and knowledgeable about, archaeological evidence than was the case when Rostovtzeff's book appeared.† If it is hard to think of anyone since who possesses his gift of the illuminating caption, that is sad but not very significant. What is serious is that the demands made by historians of antiquity upon archaeology, and the methods of employing and presenting archaeological evidence in ancient history, have not advanced much beyond

* The original version of this essay was published in *Daedalus* 100, no. 1 (Winter 1971) 168–86, and reprinted in *Historical Studies Today*, ed. F. Gilbert and S. R. Graubard (New York, Norton 1972) pp. 281–99.

Copyright © 1972, 1971 by the American Academy of Arts and Sciences and reprinted by permission of the editors.

† Throughout this discussion I mean by 'archaeological evidence' only artifacts and I exclude documents–papyri, inscriptions, leather scrolls–that excavations produce.

what was possible for Rostovtzeff, and often lag behind. Yet in the same half-century archaeology itself, at its best, has advanced immeasurably, and historians ought to have advanced with it.

However, it is not my intention to produce a catalogue of grievances along these lines; it would soon become boring and unilluminating. Looking to the future, there are two central questions, in my judgment. The first is whether current trends in archaeology are departing so far from the kinds of questions historians have traditionally put to archaeologists that the gap between the two will soon be widened rather than narrowed. The second is limited to classical archaeology alone: What is it that the classical historian ought to be asking of archaeological evidence today, and how successfully are the archaeologists, from their side, adjusting their own older aims and techniques to these new demands? Implicit in this discussion is the assumption that contemporary historians, even of antiquity, *are* asking new kinds of questions. Anyone who is happy with kings and battles or with 'calling ancient things to life' (I deliberately resort to a caricature) will find the discussion wholly irrelevant.

I

In common with other disciplines in the humanities and social studies, archaeology gives the appearance of being in a crisis. That is attested by the spate of books and articles with such titles as *New Perspectives in Archaeology*.[2] At the simplest level, there is a strong reaction within the discipline against the familiar excursions into prehistoric religion, economics or art appreciation that are neither grounded in, nor controlled by, theory or adequate knowledge. There is a new mood of austerity, even of pessimism. It may seem 'hard doctrine to some people', writes Stuart Piggott, but 'the observational data of prehistory seem to me in almost every way to be more ambiguous, and more capable of varied interpretations, than the normal run of material available to historians. What we have at our disposal, as prehistorians, is the accidentally surviving durable remnants of material culture, which we interpret as best we may, and inevitably the peculiar quality of this evidence dictates the sort of information we can obtain from it. Furthermore, we interpret the evidence in terms of our own intellectual make-up, conditioned as it is by the period and culture within which we were brought up, our social and cultural background, our current assumptions and presuppositions, and our age and status.'[3]

One example demonstrating the urgent necessity for such 'hard doctrine' merits examination – the remarkable fable of the Great

Mother Goddess. For Jacquetta Hawkes that goddess was so omnipresent and omnipotent in Bronze Age (Minoan) Crete that the civilization itself is labelled a 'predominantly feminine force'. The case rests on a group of small Neolithic figurines, averaging less than two inches in height, which she describes as follows: 'The material evidences of the religious life of these Stone Age farmers consist very largely of formalized statuettes of women (carved or modelled) which they kept in their homes or sometimes provided with sacred houses of their own. In making these images they called attention to the reproductive function, giving them huge breasts and buttocks, and often the mountainous bellies of advanced pregnancy. Moreover they usually set them in a squatting position, which at that time may have been the accepted position for childbirth.'[4] Apart from Miss Hawkes's private fancy about feminine and masculine forces in civilizations, her interpretation of the figurines is a restatement of what had become virtually received doctrine in archaeology.[5] It has now been shattered beyond hope of rescue by the publication of Peter Ucko's book on the figurines.[6]

The total number of Neolithic Cretan anthropomorphic figurines known by 1969 was 103. Of these, only 28 are certainly female, 5 male, and 28 sexless; the remainder cannot be classified, primarily because of their fragmentary state. They sit, stand, kneel and crouch as well as squat. 'The majority of female figures have close-set breasts which are flat and small and which project very little from the body', and anyway the assessment 'is almost always largely subjective'. Only two figurines have come from houses anywhere in Crete, none from any structure which can be identified as a shrine (Miss Hawkes's imaginary 'sacred houses of their own'). Usually the find site can be described only as 'general habitation debris'. And there are also numerous animal figurines.

The received view is thus an extreme case of the type that David L. Clarke, a leading Young Turk in the field, criticized when he wrote, 'The degree of confidence that we are logically justified in placing in many archaeological generalizations is often undermined by failure to specify the proportion of observed cases, the variety of circumstances or the existence of conflicting examples.'[7] The wonder is that no one before Ucko had bothered to examine systematically all the 103 Cretan figurines.[8] Now 'archaeologists and students of prehistoric religion' are asked to 'overhaul present theories very critically'.[9] Beyond doubt they must, but it is not mere *Besserwisserei* to point out that some of us–archaeologists as well as historians and anthropologists–have been challenging the Mother Goddess for years. Even without Ucko's breakdown, other methodological objections had been raised–for instance, that the Mother Goddess devotees made no effort to explain the complete disappearance of these figurines in the Minoan period, and offered no foundation for their vast superstructure other than the vaguest subjective verbiage about the 'meaning' of big breasts and heavy buttocks. It should be recorded that Ucko had published his Cretan analysis as early as 1962 in the authoritative official organ of the Royal Anthropological Institute,[10] with little visible impact.

How, then, do we interpret such remains as the anthropomorphic figurines? The archaeological Young Turks reject Piggott's kind of pessimism. 'The argument', writes L. R. Binford, 'that archaeologists must limit their knowledge to features of material culture is open to serious question; and second, the dichotomy between material and non-material aspects of culture itself and the relevance of this dichotomy for a proposed hierarchy of reliability have also been the subject of critical discussion. . . . It is virtually impossible to imagine that any given cultural item functioned in a socio-cultural system independent of the operation of "non-material" variables. Every item has its history within a socio-cultural system–its phases of procurement of raw material, manufacture, use, and final discarding. . . . *There is every reason to expect* that the empirical properties of artifacts and their arrangement in the archaeological record will exhibit attributes which can inform on different phases of the artifact's life history' (my italics).[11]

Of course no one imagines that cultural items function independently, least of all the pessimists whom Binford is attacking. The issue lies in the final sentence I have quoted. Is there any reason to expect what Binford expects, and significantly can offer only as an expectation rather than as a proposition for which there is available evidence? On the contrary, there is sufficient evidence that identical artifacts and arrangements of artifacts can result from different socio-economic arrangements of procurement, manufacture or distribution. For example, we know from the chance preservation of accounts inscribed on stone, that the most delicate stone carving on the temple in Athens known as the Erechtheum was produced by free men and slaves working side by side at the end of the fifth century B.C. Nothing in the material remains (the carving itself) could have told us that. On the other hand, the surviving accounts of the temple of Apollo at Epidaurus, built thirty or forty years later, are of such a nature that the labour force is not specified. How does Binford imagine it will be possible to discover whether or not slaves were employed, at the highest level of skill, on that temple?[12]

The most radical, elaborate and sometimes brilliant argumentation will be found in Clarke's *Analytical Archaeology* already mentioned. For Clarke the crisis in archaeology is most obviously exposed by the attempt to produce 'imitation history books'.[13] His objective is to establish archaeology 'as a discipline in its own right, concerned with archaeological data which it clusters in archaeological entities displaying certain archaeological processes and studied in terms of archaeological aims, concepts and procedures. ... The entities, processes, aims, procedures and concepts of archaeology have a validity of their own in reference to the archaeological frame and despite their generation by–and partial correlation with–former social and historic entities.'[14] The 'fundamental' archaeological entities are 'the attribute, artifact, the artifact-type, the assemblage, the culture and the culture group'.[15] The major aims of the discipline are (1) 'the definition of the fundamental entities'; (2) 'the search for repeated similarities or regularities in form, function, association, or developmental sequence amongst the particular entities from every area, period and environment'; (3) 'the development of higher category knowledge or principles that synthesize and correlate the material at hand whilst possessing a high predictive value. The development of increasingly comprehensive and informative general models and hypotheses.'[16]

We know where we are now; the familiar polemic of the social scientist against history has been carried back into prehistory, though I am unable to discover in his more than six hundred pages what he means by 'a general archaeological theory'. In so far as Clarke rests on a tautology–'an archaeological culture is not a racial group, nor a historic tribe, nor a linguistic unit, it is simply an archaeological culture'[17]–his sophisticated statistical procedures, requiring extensive use of computers, will no doubt enhance and refine archaeological inquiry considerably. However, it is apparent that he does not wish to be taken too literally. That is revealed by the way the word 'function' creeps into the second of the 'aims', and by the conventional admission of social anthropology into the exclusive club.[18] When he speaks of 'religious data' and 'religious artifacts', and writes a short paragraph about Minoan Crete that includes such phrases as 'embalmed within the conservative memory of the religious subsystem', 'the later Minoan idealized bull cult', 'a religious "memory" or a cultural "dream" of such a former trajectory',[19] one is entitled to protest not only that he has abandoned 'archaeological procedures' but that he has descended to the excesses of the Mother Goddess fable.*

* The Minoan bull cult desperately needs the same sort of scrutiny Ucko gave to the Mother Goddess.

Furthermore, when Clarke leaves prehistory for periods for which there is some documentation, other than archaeological, he is surprisingly happy if his archaeological analysis seems occasionally to coincide with written documentary evidence. I say 'seems to' because it does not always do so as he claims, and because when it does, the coincidence is illusory. Of the former failing, I merely cite the inaccuracy and the misunderstanding of the nature of such Greek sources as Homer, Herodotus and Eratosthenes, which pervade the paragraph that is supposed to provide literary substantiation of his account of Hallstatt assemblages from the ninth to the fifth centuries B.C.[20] For the second, there is a more significant example. Clarke reports a computerized analysis of more than one thousand 'burial assemblages of weaponry and harness artifacts' of Turkic-speaking nomads between about A.D. 900 and 1300. The analysis produced a diachronic classification into four main groups, the transition to the fourth being marked by the replacement of horse gear in the women's graves by 'distinctive new Mongolian types . . . earrings, mirrors, birch-bark head-dresses'. 'Historically', Clarke adds, 'and by coin evidence it was possible to associate this change with the period of the Golden Horde invasions.'[21] Though the observations are no doubt accurate, the obvious comment is that, granting the Mongolian character of the objects can be established from the objects themselves, no 'archaeological procedures' would have revealed the 'Golden Horde invasions', as Clarke's own wording concedes. Why, then, does he resort to what he has earlier labelled, pejoratively, a 'nostalgic retreat into historiography'? Why does he not leave the final transition as 'unhistoriographical' as the other three, for which there appear to be no distracting coins or documents?

These questions raise the fundamental one of the purpose of the exercise. Why expend effort and financial resources to sort out in a time-series some four hundred years of burial assemblages – or to sort out, in any fashion, any group of past phenomena, prehistoric or historic? Is it only in order to achieve a more or less abstract classification of objects? To ask the question is to answer it. No one can make a claim for such a bloodless procedure, beyond the aesthetic one that can equally be made of a game of chess, the claim that elegant precision has value for its own sake. Unless one is prepared, in the study of the past, to abandon all interest in change, growth, evolution, in institutions, events, or the interrelationships among the different aspects of human society, I see no virtue in the insistence that any one type of evidence, or one type of analytical procedure, must be isolated from all other types – no virtue, in short, in David

Clarke's 'validity of their own despite their correlation with social and historical entities'.* No more do I see any virtue, as I have already said, in the practice of historians who similarly neglect archaeological materials. And perhaps I should repeat that, on all available evidence, it is impossible to infer social arrangements or institutions, attitudes or beliefs from material objects alone.

None of this is an argument against more and better quantification of evidence. But it is an argument against the view, sometimes expressed explicitly, that what cannot be quantified cannot be dealt with at all, that only quantification produces 'scientific' (as distinct from 'subjective' or 'ideological') analysis and results. The objection is simply that large areas of human behaviour thereby disappear from the 'scientist's' view altogether, including all historical events or series of events. This is the point at which I believe the Young Turks in archaeology and in history meet. Historical demographers are now able to provide complicated graphs of the trends over long periods of time in life expectancy, size of family, illegitimacy. These are important data for the history of the family, but they are not equal to the history of the family, and never will be. Likewise, it is interesting to know that central Asian women took horse gear to the grave with them in one period, and in another preferred ear-rings and mirrors, but no table of correlations will reveal the thinking and the value judgments behind the habits.[22] Admittedly the latter kind of interest requires speculation, with a low coefficient of reliability, and explanations cannot be verified in the same way as frequency tables can be, but that seems insufficient ground for dismissing serious, disciplined efforts as mere 'counterfeit history'.

II

It is self-evident that the potential contribution of archaeology to history is, in a rough way, inversely proportional to the quantity and quality of the available written sources. It is also self-evident that the line between prehistory and history is not a sharp one, that for centuries after the introduction of writing, the historian's evidence remains almost exclusively archaeological, at least for some civilizations, notably the Greek and the Roman. Perhaps the most frustrating example is that of the Etruscans: despite some

* 'Although most prehistorians have come over the last twenty years or so to admit that prehistory is about men and the way they lived and developed in time, too many European archaeologists have contented themselves with animating their pet artifacts by equating them with human groups and putting on something like a museological puppet-show . . . the proper study of archaeology is not things but men . . .': Grahame Clark, in a review in *Helinium* 10 (1970) 170–77, at p. 171.

10,000 more or less deciphered texts and a considerable, though late and distorted, Roman tradition behind them, assemblages of artifacts remain not only the base of all accounts but nearly the whole of the evidence. An Etruscan tomb is nothing more than an assemblage of artifacts, despite the sophistication of the technology or of the wall-paintings, so long as there is no adequate literary key to the conventions and values represented by the artifacts. Nowhere is Piggott's hard doctrine more necessary, and nowhere is it more systematically ignored in a continuous outpouring of counterfeit history, in the literal sense of that phrase.

For the earliest historical periods, an extraordinary complication is introduced by oral tradition and historical legends. The problem is then not simply one of correlating archaeological and literary evidence but of using archaeology to assess whether, and how far, the literature has any worth at all. How difficult that is, and how little agreement has been reached so far, in large part because of unclarity about the canons of discrimination, are clear from the current debates about the Minoan and Mycenaean civilizations and the Trojan War.[23] Apart from the anomalous Linear B tablets, there is no contemporary written evidence for this long period, and it remains the province of the prehistorian rather than of the historian; in the final analysis the work is one of reconstruction from archaeology, even if one is prepared to take more from the legends than I am.

The earliest Roman history presents a different situation, because it began late enough to fall within the period of literacy and because the Roman traditions about their origins, unlike the Greek, have the external appearance of a very detailed history, full of narrative and of constitutional and institutional information ordered in a coherent time sequence. Roman history cannot be said to begin before the period of Etruscan rule, the sixth century B.C., and the contemporary documentation for the following century, the first period of independence, though scrappy, includes annalistic fragments and the Twelve Tables.[24] The 'histories' are of course very late – the early books of Livy, who died in A.D. 17, and of his contemporary, Dionysius of Halicarnassus, and several lives by Plutarch, still later by about a century – and largely fictitious. However, Theodor Mommsen and others had already demonstrated, long before there was any relevant archaeology of value, that there are techniques by which some data could be pulled out, chiefly in the constitutional, legal and religious spheres, to which one could with some confidence attach the name of genuine history. Today we have available a full synthesis of the archaeology of early Rome and its environs, unrivalled in Graeco-Roman archaeology in its completeness, and it is important to assess its impact on the received view of early Roman history.[25] In the first place, by itself it reveals perhaps less than some had hoped, in broad terms that sixth- and fifth-century Rome was a fairly primitive village, with strong Etruscan traits, far removed from the great Livian Rome of the kings and early Republic, but one that was rising in its material level and its size by the end of the fifth century. In the second place, archaeology has confirmed the chronological outlines of the tradition – that is to say, historians are satisfied that it has, whereas the individual archaeologists most directly involved in the discussion insist, for some reason I am unable to fathom, that the literary chronology must be downdated by about half a century.[26] And in the third place, we are in all other respects left with no tools of analysis other than those inherited from the nineteenth century, refined, occasionally supplemented by new epigraphic fragments, checked by modern comparative studies, but unchanged in their fundamental nature.

From this particular, pessimistic report it is tempting to draw the rather paradoxical conclusion that the contribution of archaeology to history becomes greater as the volume and reliability of non-archaeological evidence increase (until the latter reaches the volume and nature of modern, even early modern, documentation). There is truth in that proposition, but not the whole truth, as I shall illustrate in a moment. It would be pointless to catalogue the many important contributions archaeology has in fact made to our knowledge of ancient history. Instead, I have selected three further examples that raise major problems about future possibilities and needs, examples that fall within the field of economic history.

The first example is at the same time a demonstration of the limits of my paradoxical proposition – the history of what is conventionally called Greek 'colonization', in reality the history of Greek expansion between about 1000 and 550 B.C., to Asia Minor and the coastal areas surrounding the Black Sea in the east, to southern Italy, Sicily, and along the Mediterranean in the west. The Greek tradition, scattered in a multitude of writers from Herodotus to Eusebius, consists of a chronological framework (and, by the end, in very precise dates), anachronistic propaganda on behalf of the Delphic oracle, and anecdotes. No history of colonization was possible on that basis. Archaeology has confirmed the chronological frame, though of course not the precise dates (as with early Rome), but it has also achieved very much more. In combination with the literary materials, it has made possible a kind of history, not a narrative political account but a picture of settlement, growth and movement, or urban organization, of trade and manufacture, of relations with the native populations, of cults and temples. The picture exists only in broad outlines, it is very incomplete, much is uncertain and controversial, but hardly any of it could be derived from the ancient traditions alone–or from the archaeology alone.[27] The lines of further archaeological exploration are now clear–and so are the difficulties and weaknesses in our methods of interpretation.[28]

The second example is the history of money and coinage in antiquity. Systematic study began in the eighteenth century, but it was dominated, almost monopolized, by the interests of collectors until the last few decades, and that interest still retains a strong hold. However, the function of coins, as distinct from their rarity or their aesthetics, has become an increasingly prominent subject of research, and the results have been considerable. Discussions of money and coinage are uncommon in ancient Greek and Roman literature; only from the coin finds can significant conclusions be drawn about the volume of minting, for example, or the circulation of coin. As a preliminary step, it was necessary to devise better techniques for dating Greek coins than the aesthetic canons that once prevailed (since the coins lack dates and, before the Hellenistic period, portraits), and this has been achieved by intensive studies of the dies. It was also necessary to appreciate that coin hoards, not excavation coins, are the fundamental source material; that hoards must therefore be published promptly and completely; that they must be subjected to proper, and not partial, statistical analysis. Other recent advances need not be enumerated. Nor need it be argued that what we now know, or think we know, about monetary history, as about the history of colonization, rests on archaeological evidence but not on 'archaeological analysis'. And the interpretation of the archaeological evidence is the point at which the dialogue between historians, numismatists and archaeologists is still unsatisfactory.[29]

My third example is a curiosity–the perverse refusal by some distinguished experts in the history of technology to permit either the historian or his documentation to make a contribution. They prefer to write the history of technology largely, if not solely, from the artifacts, carrying Clarke's psychology to a *reductio ad absurdum*, without the saving grace of his rigorous techniques. The consequences can be exemplified by comparing the first two volumes of the much praised *A History of Technology*, edited by Charles Singer and others,[30] with the painstaking, often unrewarding, but always more fruitful and more accurate studies during the past decade or so, by scholars who combine the archaeological and documentary evidence in an investigation of agricultural technology in Gaul and other parts of the western Roman Empire.[31]

It will be apparent that much of what I have been calling an advance has been the consequence of a new focus, of new historical interests, and of new questions that the historian had not earlier put to himself, and therefore not to the archaeologists either. What do we now wish from the archaeologist, and, more narrowly, what have the new ways to offer to the ancient historian?

Immediately I must express my belief that the rapid development and application of sophisticated scientific techniques provide only a small part of the answer. Of course they have proved valuable, especially in locating the most promising places to explore. A more interesting example, providing stimulating implications, is the spectroscopic analysis which revealed that the obsidian (volcanic glass) used for tools, by 6000 B.C. at the latest, in a region extending from southern Macedonia to Crete, all came from the island of Melos, where on present evidence there was no settlement for several thousand years after the obsidian mining began.[32] Or, as an example from the historical era, it is not yet possible to determine the source of the marble used in any specific Greek statue or building. The usual, and casual, statements about marble sources in archaeological reports turn out often to have been mere guesses of no value. However, new techniques open up the possibility in the future of answering a complex of questions of the highest interest for social and economic history–questions such as: How much weight was given to costs, especially transport costs, in the decision to select one marble rather than another for any given temple, as against other considerations, political, technological (the preference of the architect and the masons) or aesthetic? Until now the information has been so lacking that it has been pointless to tackle such a question (and indeed no adequate study of quarries in antiquity has ever been undertaken). Now the possibility exists, but its realization will require laborious examination on a large scale of widely scattered artifacts and of marble outcroppings.[33]

A note of caution about carbon-14 dating is also necessary here. It is a familiar complaint of prehistorians that classical archaeologists do not make proper use of this most widely known of all the new scientific techniques–an unjustified complaint. In the first place, the accumulated experience with carbon-14 dating has revealed more eccentricities and complexities in the method than had originally been suspected, particularly for the centuries and millennia before about 2500 B.C. 'The archaeologist', David Clarke warns us, 'can rarely, if ever, date excavated strata and their assemblages to precise points in time–all archaeological dates are relative, even the so-called absolute isotope decay datings.'[34] More to the point, relative dates, or dates $\pm$ 50 or 100 years, are not precise enough, and often virtually useless, for the sequences and interrelationships we seek to establish in the late Bronze Age, let alone the historical age. They cannot help resolve such current controversies as the date of the destruction of Cnossus, the connection between the volcanic explosion at Santorini and the destruction of sites in eastern Crete, the dates of the earliest Greek colonies in southern Italy and Sicily.

In the end, what ancient historians now require of archaeologists is something much simpler, much more primitive–a willingness to devote themselves to precisely formulated historical questions and a far greater consciousness of the value of statistics, for which pencil and paper and elementary numeracy are on the whole sufficient, though a simple computer would do no harm. Rostovtzeff made the point directly a generation ago. In discussing the extraordinary position of Hellenistic Rhodes as the greatest entrepot and financial centre, and perhaps the wealthiest city, of the Mediterranean world, he wrote:

'We have only slight knowledge regarding the volume and the character of the Rhodian transit trade. I have discussed the evidence which refers to it above and I have mentioned the stamped jar-handles of Rhodes and Cnidus, and the problems connected with them. One of the most important of these problems is that of their respective dates. *A full catalogue of Rhodian stamps will certainly help us to establish their chronology*. Some progress has been made in this direction. We are able to date a considerable group of stamps found at Pergamon (220 to 180). Another group of stamps found at Carthage is certainly earlier than the year of the destruction of the city. Thus we have some indications with regard to those stamps which belong to the period between 220 and 146 B.C. . . . *We require comparative statistics* of the various stamps for each place where Rhodian stamps have been found in order to determine whether modern scholars are right in assuming that the Rhodian stamps of the period 220 to 146 are the most common stamps in all the centres of Rhodian commercial activity. *As things stand, we must confine ourselves to some very general statements*' (my italics).[35]

That was published in 1941. We still await the full catalogue and the comparative statistics, and we are still confined to very general statements.[36] The reluctance of archaeologists to embark on such projects (comparable to the analysis of marbles I have already mentioned) deserves sympathetic understanding. Archaeology is an expensive activity; patrons are chiefly attracted by the prospect of museum pieces, or of a public sensation. Presumably that is the psychological explanation of the fact that complete catalogues and comparative statistics are becoming increasingly common for coins, geometric pottery, archaic Greek sculpture and the like, whereas Gjerstad's catalogue of the archaeology of early Rome remains an exception, the catalogue of Rhodian jar-stamps still a desideratum. Yet it is an explanation the historian cannot accept–and he is not by profession competent to do the work himself.[37] Nor is it the whole explanation. A few years ago Snodgrass collected all the identifiable remains of cutting tools and weapons found in mainland Greece (excluding Macedonia) that could be dated in the period *c.* 1050–900 B.C. His tabulation of these finds follows:[38]

	Bronze	Iron
Swords	1	20+
Spearheads	8	30+
Daggers	2	8
Knives	0	15+
Axe-heads	0	4

No sensation there, yet this simple table answers a question that had not been posed in quite that way before, while vague statements were based on the Homeric poems and guesswork: How rapid was the shift from bronze to iron, not 'in general', but in the decisive weapons and implements? Once the chronological question was formulated that way (the only correct way), no alternative remained, if one wished an answer, to the *total* collection and tabulation of the evidence.

That illustration–and I hasten to add that there are others–explains why I rank an interest in precise historical questions on a par with numeracy and closer attention to statistics in stating what I consider to be the urgent requirement in the immediate future. My own experience suggests that Snodgrass's task was exacerbated by the poor state of the archaeology and the archaeological reporting with respect to graves and grave-goods. I have twice in recent years tried to use such evidence, first for the complicated and ill-understood linguistic situation in Roman Sicily, then for the history of military grave-goods in Greece during the late Bronze Age and the subsequent 'Dark Age'. Both times I was reduced to impressionistic remarks and to complaints, much like those of Rostovtzeff about the Rhodian jar-stamps. In too few cemeteries have both the excavation and the subsequent publication been systematic and complete.[39] Worse still, it would require a large research project on its own merely to collect the bibliography. Whereas the historian of Anglo-Saxon England has Audrey Meaney's *Gazetteer of Early Anglo-Saxon Burial Sites*,[40] I know of no comparable guide to any district of Greece or any province of the Roman Empire.[41]

We have thus come full circle to Ucko and the Mother Goddess. To multiply examples further would be pointless.[42] But it is necessary to look at the other side, at the historian's needs from the viewpoint of the archaeologist. One common objection can be dismissed out of hand: classification and chronology are still uncertain, it is argued, and until they are fixed more firmly, historical questions must wait. That is nothing but Cornford's Principle of Unripe Time.[43] More serious is the plea that archaeologists are already overworked, that there is so much excavation still to be done, that publication would be even further delayed. There is no answer to that, only a choice of values. Of what use, I should reply, is the vast outpouring of annual reports on the year's work from which little emerges, more often that not, other than isolated facts, soon to be cancelled or corrected in the next year's work or the third or the fourth year's? Of what use are more and more excavations when so many older ones have not been fully reported, and no small number have not been published at all? And, finally, of what use is archaeology anyway, apart from the museum pieces that sometimes come out of the debris, if it leads to nothing more than reports?

One solution that is being mooted to the genuine difficulty created by overwork, insufficient manpower and insufficient funds is the employment of good sampling techniques. I must demur. No sampling technique is 'good' except in terms of a predetermined range of questions. It would be a bold archaeologist who believed he could anticipate the questions another archaeologist or a historian might ask a decade or a generation later, as the result of new interests or new results from older researches. Computer experience has produced examples enough of the unfortunate consequences, in just this respect, of insufficient anticipation of the possibilities at the coding stage. A similar failure in archaeology is more harmful, because it is in the nature of archaeological excavation literally to destroy–to destroy for ever–whatever is dug up and neither fully recorded nor preserved.[44]

There is of course the crushing retort: *tu quoque*. That I accept, as I have already indicated. Ancient historians are also too often satisfied with impressions, too often non-numerate and non-quantitative, too often imprecise in the questions they put to themselves, about documentary as about archaeological evidence.

III

The Greek city of Akragas (modern Agrigento) in Sicily was famed for its wealth and its conspicuous consumption in the fifth century B.C. The visible symbol that still survives is the number and quality of its stone temples, perhaps ten of which were constructed in that one century. Ten is an extraordinary number and there are interesting social problems to be studied. But what is a fair standard for temple construction in this period? To answer that question today would involve one in a massive research operation, for the reasons I have already given–the absence of gazetteers, and, as I discovered when I looked at the question, of easily available summary statistics even for such major cities as Corinth or Miletus. In the absence of literary or epigraphical documentation, only archaeology can provide the figures (with an admitted margin of error), and the archaeologists have not done so. Temples are not paltry grave-goods; they are central to Greek art history and the volume of publications on the subject grows annually, but always by example alone.

I have introduced this illustration in closing not just to introduce one more complaint, but to pile a second paradox on to my earlier paradoxical half-truth. If it is often the case that the usefulness of archaeology to history increases with an increase in documentation, it is also the case that certain kinds of documentation render archaeology more or less unnecessary. If one posed the Akragas question for the Middle Ages, one would find the answer in papal and diocesan records. And one final example. By an ingenious calculation, based wholly on the results of stylistic analysis of remains, R. M. Cook arrived at a reasonable estimate of the number of men engaged in the Athenian fine pottery industry in the fifth century B.C.[45] That was an important contribution to economic history. The same question about the English potteries in 1800 would be answered with far greater precision, and with a breakdown by skills and functions which remains out of reach for Athens, simply by going to the pottery archives. It is hardly surprising, therefore, that the relatively new field of industrial archaeology remains a backwater. I should be much more surprised if it ever turns out to be more than that.

6

ANTHROPOLOGY AND THE CLASSICS*

'AND last I would thank my critics. They have kindly warned me that, in the study of Alpha there is danger lest I lose sight of Omega. Intent on *origines*, on the roots of things, I fail to gather in, they tell me, the tree's fair, final fruit and blossom. I thank them for the warning, but I think they have not read my *Prolegomena*, or at least its preface. I there confess, and still confess, that I have little natural love for what an Elizabethan calls "ye Beastly Devices of ye Heathen". Savages, save for their reverent, totemistic attitude towards animals, weary and disgust me, though perforce I spend long hours in reading of their tedious doings. My good moments are when, through the study of things primitive, I come to the better understanding of some song of a Greek poet or some saying of a Greek philosopher.'

That was the penultimate paragraph of Jane Harrison's introduction, written on New Year's Eve 1911, to her *Themis*. It didn't help. 'I think', said Gilbert Murray in his Memorial Address (1928), 'there was, in conservative or orthodox circles, rather more dislike of *Themis* as a "dangerous book" than there had been of the *Prolegomena*.'[1] 'Dislike' is too weak a word, though not many Hellenists were as frank as the American authority on Plato, Paul Shorey, who wrote, with reference to Murray's *Four* (later *Five*) *Stages of Greek Religion*:

'Professor Murray has done much harm by helping to substitute in the minds of an entire generation for Arnold's and Jebb's conception of the serene rationality of the classics the corybantic Hellenism of Miss Harrison and Isadora Duncan and Susan Glaspell and Mr. Stark Young's "Good Friday and Classical Professors", the higher vaudeville Hellenism of Mr. Vachel Lindsay, the anthro-

* The Jane Harrison Memorial Lecture, delivered at Newnham College, Cambridge, on 13 May 1972, previously unpublished and now slightly revised, with the help of comments by J. R. Goody.

pological Hellenism of Sir James Frazer, the irrational, semi-sentimental, Polynesian, free-verse and sex-freedom Hellenism of all the gushful geysers of "rapturous rubbish" about the Greek spirit.'[2]

Gilbert Murray has since been rescued from the onslaught, but by a divorce from Jane Harrison that he himself would not have agreed to, despite his addiction to the word 'beauty'. Thus, Isobel Henderson wrote about the same *Five Stages*, in a testimonial volume published after Murray's death: 'He re-asserted the humanizing value of the Olympian "reformation" against the brute theogony. If Murray seems to insist too much on the better parts of Hellenism, it was done to redress a balance which had tipped over to the slimy side.'[3] The reference to Jane Harrison is explicit in the context.

The value judgments and the extraordinary language in which they are expressed do not interest me in themselves, but certain consequences do. The *Prolegomena to the Study of Greek Religion* was published in 1903, *Themis* in 1912, the brief *Epilegomena* in 1921, all by the Cambridge University Press. The first two were reprinted in 1922 and 1927, respectively, the *Epilegomena* not again; they remained out of print until the 1960s, when American reprint houses re-issued them, *Themis* and the *Epilegomena* by a firm that specializes in books on the occult and spiritualism. The Cambridge School (a term to which I shall return) had become a pejorative by-word, shorthand for 'the dreadful consequences of the straying by Hellenists into the slime of anthropological Hellenism, not only of the Frazer variety but equally of all other schools of anthropology'. By-words are by nature self-evident; it was sufficient to say 'the Cambridge School' and one grasped the implications at once, without bothering to read their works seriously or trying to place them within the history of modern classical study–with a few honourable exceptions.

The outstanding exception is of course E. R. Dodds, successor to Murray as Regius Professor of Greek in the University of Oxford, whose preface, written in August 1950, to his *The Greeks and the Irrational*, both echoes Jane Harrison and sums up the position I have just sketched: 'To my fellow-professionals I perhaps owe some defence of the use which I have made in several places of recent anthropological and psychological observations and theories. In a world of specialists, such borrowings from unfamiliar disciplines are, I know, generally received by the learned with apprehension and often with active distaste. I expect to be reminded, in the first place, that "the Greeks were not savages", and secondly, that in these relatively new studies the accepted truths of today are apt to become the discarded errors of tomorrow.' Yet Dodds himself cites Jane Harrison only once, as far as I can discover, in an unnecessary reference to her *Epilegomena*, along with Rivers, Lévy-Bruhl and Kluckhohn, for the more or less Freudian metaphor that myth 'is the dream-thinking of the people, as the dream is the myth of the individual'.[4]

More recently, Geoffrey Kirk, whose radical account of Greek myth shares one fundamental premise with Jane Harrison, expressed by the latter on the first page of the introduction to the *Prolegomena*, that the 'habit of viewing Greek religion exclusively through the medium of Greek literature has brought with it an initial and fundamental error in method'; who himself commented that the two currently standard manuals on Greek religion and mythology, by Martin Nilsson and H. J. Rose, respectively, 'have done much to perpetuate an essentially Victorian view about the clear air of Greece and its tonic effect on the Greek mind that Gilbert Murray and Jane Harrison laboured in vain to overthrow',[5] could nevertheless not resist joining the chorus: Jane Harrison's books, he writes on page 3, 'are lively, learned, yet unpedantic–and utterly uncontrolled by anything resembling careful logic'.

A classical scholar of course has the right to prefer 'serene rationality' to maenadism, and to expend his energies on what he prefers. It may be doubted that knowledge is much advanced by the addiction to aesthetic-botanical metaphors–trees, fruit, blossoms, slime. It may also be doubted that blinkered concentration on the serenely rational can produce a proper understanding even of that which it pretends to examine. But I do not discuss that. Nor am I about to embark on a detailed examination of Jane Harrison's work.

My point is both methodological and historical. When Jane Harrison was wrong, as she certainly was in her insistence on the ritual foundations of all myths, that was because she mishandled the Greek evidence, not because she had spent long hours in reading of the tedious doings of savages. The latter is more relevant to the psychobiography of Jane Harrison, not a classical subject. That is the methodological point. The historical one is that the hostility engendered by the legendary Cambridge School, hostility that stemmed from bad reasoning and strong emotion, was a powerful contributory factor, if not the cause, of an almost total cessation in the dialogue between anthropology and the classics, a cessation, at least in the mainstream of classical studies, not only in this country but everywhere else.[6] The long years of indifference and resistance to Milman Parry's fundamental discovery about the nature of oral poetry, which he made among the illiterate bards of Yugoslavia, a resistance now weak but not wholly beaten back, exemplifies the situation.

In recent years, however, there has been a revival of the dialogue, on one side, and there is need for further reflection on the methods, the implications and the limits. But first I must lay the Cambridge ghost, for whose re-emergence into daylight I seem to be unwittingly responsible by having written *The World of Odysseus*. The distinguished anthropologist who wrote the unsigned front-page review of Kirk's *Myth* in the *Times Literary Supplement* (14 August 1970) began with Frazer and Jane Harrison, and went on to say that, despite the embarrassment she caused among the 'more orthodox members of the Cambridge classical faculty, . . . there has been a persisting Cambridge tradition, currently reflected in the work of M. I. Finley' and of G. S. Kirk, though the latter is only a 'half-convinced convert'. The facts are that I both wrote and published *The World of Odysseus* before I ever set foot in Cambridge; that Geoffrey Kirk began to work on myth after he left his Cambridge post for Yale; that Gilbert Murray, an unregenerate Oxford Australian, was a full member with Francis Cornford of the original unholy trio; that, for all Jane Harrison's admiration for the *Golden Bough*, her intellectual mentors, as she said explicitly more than once, were Durkheim, Nietzsche, Bergson, later Freud and Jung.[7] The dank Cambridge air is as irrelevant as the clear Greek air to the problems of classics and anthropology, Greeks and savages.

Next I must define the terms in my title. The second half, 'the classics', is not difficult: it is conventional, if not very happy, shorthand for the Graeco-Roman world; not only Graeco-Roman myth and religion, on which a preponderant share of the discussion concentrates, but all aspects of the life of the Greeks and Romans, material or symbolic. 'Anthropology' is less easy to define. The laymen among us customarily think of anthropology as the study of primitive peoples, with some uncertainty as to whether the subject embraces both contemporary groups and prehistoric societies or only the former, a combination that is still reflected in the term 'physical anthropology' and in the existence of university departments of 'archaeology and anthropology'. Professional anthropologists tend to shy from that definition for two unrelated reasons. The first is the semantic difficulty with the word 'primitive'. The second is an internal disagreement over the scope of the discipline. At one extreme is the global claim, recently expressed by Sol Tax, for example, when he wrote that the 'subject matter of anthropology is the origin and development of the whole of *Homo sapiens*, and its varieties',[8] a claim that would embrace within anthropology most of human knowledge with such few exceptions as theoretical astrophysics and geology, making nonsense of the very idea of a discipline with its own theoretical and methodological rules and its own subject matter. The more modest definition is the one I shall adopt, in Leach's phrasing, 'the study of the behaviour of small groups operating within a defined structural-cultural matrix',[9] with the addition of the term 'non-literate'–small non-literate groups. I believe this definition is adequate for the bulk of anthropological study, despite the fact that anthropologists, including Leach himself, sometimes study aspects of larger and more advanced groups, when, it seems to me, either they migrate to the kindred discipline of sociology or they select small units, such as Indian villages, in order to be able to retain their specific methods of investigation.

Earlier I used the word 'dialogue'. Today the word is scarcely applicable, because, as Clyde Kluckhohn noticed in his lectures, also called *Anthropology and the Classics*, delivered in 1960 and published posthumously in 1961, 'the flow of ideas and materials between the two fields of classics and anthropology has become over the years increasingly one-sided'.[10] Maine's *Ancient Law* and Fustel de Coulanges' *La cité antique* find their place in anthropologists' lists of 'early classics' in their field,[11] but they appeared more than a century ago, and they have no successors. Much of the explanation lies in the central role of fieldwork in the post-Boas, post-Malinowski era of anthropology, with some assistance, I suspect, from the notoriety of the Cambridge School. Whether or not anthropology has suffered by its withdrawal from the dialogue is not for me to say,[12] though I may perhaps note that some recent exceptions have not been encouraging, including, regrettably, Kluckhohn's own third chapter, entitled 'A Brief Grammar of Greek Culture'.

Consider Kathleen Gough's procedure in examining the notion of 'widespread literacy'.[13] She first takes figures for the population of fifth-century B.C. Athens from William McNeill's *The Rise of the West*, a derivative source with no standing in the matter, adds in a note an 'estimate' by Talcott Parsons which is simply preposterous, then asserts explicitly that a majority of the women were illiterate and implies the same for slaves and for those she inaccurately terms 'disfranchised foreigners', none of which is correct, and on that foundation, which I cannot even call sand, concludes that 'it is possible that Gupta India . . . or even the central region of the Maurya empire . . . had almost as high a percentage of literate people'. She then goes on to place the Greeks (not just the Athenians any more) 'in Parsons' category of "advanced intermediate" societies . . . those having full literacy for adult males of an upper class', a definition that is too restrictive for Athens. A remarkable qualifying remark closes the discussion: 'More precise research may, however, reveal quantitative differences in literacy which are in fact crucial . . .'; remarkable because Miss Gough, 'side-stepping tedious historical chores',[14] has made no effort to consult *any* of the available research. It would not be difficult to imagine her reaction were a classical historian to treat her subject matter in so cavalier, I might say contemptuous, a manner.

Again I acknowledge the existence of important exceptions. There are always exceptions, but I must try to look to the mainstream, not on a statistical computation but by the *auctoritas* of the experts to whose work I turn as exemplars (wherever possible, to recent works). In 1950, Evans-Pritchard made his celebrated plea in defence of Maitland's dictum, 'by and by anthropology will have the choice between being history and being nothing'. He returned to the subject eleven years later in another lecture, entitled 'Anthropology and History', which he began with the following comment on his earlier lecture, 'I will not say that there was a storm of protest, but I had certainly, as the criticisms levelled at me showed, run into a bad patch of anti-historical prejudice'.[15] In 1968 I. M. Lewis replied, rather sourly, that 'appearances . . . are . . . somewhat deceptive'; anthropologists have in fact 'long been trying to write some history'.[16] He seems to me, however, to have missed an essential part of Evans-Pritchard's argument, which was a plea for the resumption of a dialogue. The anthropologists' history to which Lewis refers, historical accounts of the societies anthropologists normally study – and that is of course proper – seem as indifferent to inter-disciplinary study as we historians are accused of being.

It is often impossible for me to recognize my profession in the descriptions given of it. For example, Lewis writes that, 'with the exception of Namier and others with a similar approach, it is I think generally true to say that they [historians] tend to emphasize the uniqueness and particularity of their subject-matter, and in their interpretation of events place greater stress on such cultural artifacts as "the spirit of the age" than on institutional imperatives.'[17] Which historians later than Voltaire, one is tempted to ask, has Professor Lewis been reading besides Namier? I find it difficult to think of a single important historian about whom this statement is even partially true.

One can compile a considerable anthology of quotations from distinguished contemporary anthropologists denigrating the study of the past: 'History is never history, but history-for', 'all history is conjectural', 'the past may be treated to a considerable extent as myth'. Several important issues lie beneath these gnomic statements, aside from the essentially irrelevant historical point that, beginning with Malinowski, anthropologists over-reacted to the historical conjecturing and the unilinear evolutionism of their predecessors by rejecting not only their bad methods but the subject of their inquiry as well, a procedure which, though understandable, is not justifiable.

One important issue has been formulated brutally by a current school among prehistoric archaeologists: archaeologists and anthropologists together must abandon the 'notion of historical explanation as a valid category of intellectual activity and, with even more force, of scientific activity'.[18] The search for certainty, for being 'scientific', this lusting for the non-scientist's notion of what is a natural science, with physics as the model, with its proliferation of laws and predictions, is widespread among the various disciplines dealing with human behaviour, including history. If we narrow the consideration to anthropology and ask what kinds of wide, non-conjectural generalization has the discipline produced, let alone laws, the only ones known to me are either 'for the most part speculative, and . . . in any case too general to be of value' (Evans-Pritchard[19]) – I cannot resist one example that has just reached my desk: 'People have to adapt and expend energy to do work'[20] – or trivial or commonplace (Boas[21]) or tautological (Leach[22]). I find no warrant there for the dismissal of history as, in contrast, conjectural or as myth. Philip Abrams has recently noted that when historians 'wish to move to a *slightly* more generalized type of explanation' than the conventional analysis of individual events, 'they can do so without difficulty and without ceasing to be historians in any meaningful sense. What is not recognized . . . is that it is only at this *slightly* more generalized level that sociology explains anything either'[23] (the italics are his). When Einstein discovered the law, $E = mc^2$, he initiated a chain of actions that destroyed Hiroshima and Nagasaki and landed men on the moon. What anthropological 'law' leads to the Parthenon or the *Corpus Iuris*?[24]

The pursuit of the will-o'-the-wisp of scientific certainty and scientific laws has led to some remarkable conclusions, not least in the work of Lévi-Strauss. His ideas about history are extraordinarily difficult to pin down; I dare not say that Lévi-Strauss is self-contradictory, so I shall content myself with Barnes's recent phrase, that his ideas of history are 'invincibly antisystematic'.[25] At one extreme there are the opening pages of *Structural Anthropology*, in which he appears to identify himself with Franz Boas's dictum, 'To understand a phenomenon we have to know not only what it is, but also how it came into being.'[26] At the other extreme, and I am not the only reader who comes to this conclusion, he is not far from regarding 'history as "just one damn thing after another" '.[27]

However, there are two formulations that reappear so persistently as to constitute a safe ground for reflection. One is that history 'is not a continuous flow of events but a discontinuous choice by men of those incidents and processes which are fitted into a logical order by a human mind. Chronology is, therefore, important not as a statement of actual continuity or development, but as an indication of how the mind groups, codes, and imposes meaning upon a set of constituent units drawn from the uninterrupted sequence of events.'[28] Hence it is not possible to write a history of the French Revolution. This is of course consistent with his fundamental conception of anthropological science as the discovery of the unconscious patterns, structures, the codes and symbols that underly observable social phenomena. 'History,' he writes in *La pensée sauvage*, 'is a method with no distinct object corresponding to it . . . history is tied neither to man nor to any particular object. It consists wholly in its method. . . . As we say of certain careers, history may lead to anything, provided you get out of it.'[29]

It is not to deny the existence of unconscious structures or the existence of codes and symbols to argue, in reply, that human behaviour cannot be reduced *only* to structures and symbols. The Bastille no longer stands at the Place de la Bastille, the excessively centralized French educational system was created by Napoleon more than a century and a half ago, goods are shipped up and down the great French rivers without paying tolls at various points to this count and that prince. It is neither arbitrary nor wholly subjective to link such data with a history of the French Revolution. Nor, to change the example, is the bureaucracy we encounter at every turn in our lives *only* a Weberian ideal type, let alone only a symbol.

Overt behaviour is as legitimate a subject of systematic inquiry as the unconscious structures underneath. Social institutions are as much a form of overt behaviour as codes or symbols. The denial of that proposition implicit in so much of the 'history is like myth' (and, presumably, 'anthropology is like physics') talk current among anthropologists produces the despair recently reflected by Gerschenkron when he closed a review of a book on the concept of continuity in German anthropology with these words: 'And what culture is this reviewer once had understood much more clearly before he was induced to read the book by A. L. Kroeber and Clyde Kluckhohn (*Culture. A Critical Review of Concepts and Definitions*, New York, 1963) which offers 160 definitions produced by 111 authors.'[30]

But then, Gerschenkron is an economist and historian. May I therefore quote a proper anthropologist, John Barnes: 'to escape from an amusing but ultimately sterile ballet of symbols in which history and anthropology, synchrony and diachrony, consciousness and unconsciousness, reversible and irreversible time dance endlessly round each other until the audience decides to go home, we have to break down the dichotomies, establish continua and feed in more facts.'[31]

'Synchrony and diachrony' refer to Lévi-Strauss's well-known and widely repeated Janus metaphor. Borrowing terms from structural linguistics, Lévi-Strauss has said that anthropology discovers synchronic structures or models, history diachronic structures or models. There is, it seems to me, a fallacy, or at least a trap, in this seductive formulation, namely, that the two faces of Janus are conceived as no more than two alternative systems of coordinates on a plane surface, that anthropology compares institutions or modes of behaviour among contemporaneous groups, history within a single group at two or more points of time. An essential distinction is overlooked. A structural comparison between groups A and B cannot be the same as a comparison between A and A′ because in the latter the factor of change has been introduced, not in the former. Change is an important part of social behaviour.[32] That is a commonplace, which unfortunately bears repeating, as is the point that synchronic analysis can never reveal change, or the point that the notorious difficulty in getting at the past of non-literate societies is no excuse for pretending they had no past or that their past is irrelevant. Change, furthermore, requires explanation. 'Were it not for the idea of transformation,' Piaget has said, 'structures would lose all explanatory import, since they would collapse into static forms.'[33]

I could document at length Evans-Pritchard's charge that the functional school of anthropology, in particular, at best pays 'lip-service . . . to the possibility of a scientific study of social change'.[34] However, I shall restrict myself to two examples, large generalizations which appear to make even lip-service barely necessary. 'Although the past may be one source of the imperatives which control the shape and content of men's actions in society,' writes Lewis, 'its role in determining how men behave now is secondary to the interconnections between their *current* beliefs, actions, and institutional arrangements. Current custom replaces the past as the repository of the springs of social behaviour.'[35] The either-or formulation is meaningless. How did the present come into existence except by reproducing the past? The past and 'current custom' therefore are not *alternative* 'repositories of the springs of human behaviour' but complementary. I do something because it is the acceptable thing to do, according to the prevailing customs of my society; it is acceptable because it was handed on to my generation from previous generations. That is a statement of an ideal, to be sure, since there are also changes over and within the generations, but the reality is always near enough to the ideal to render the Lewis formulation meaningless. Beyond that, Lewis asserts an explanatory hierarchy–the past is secondary as a source of imperatives–and at once slides into the implication that anything secondary calls for little analysis. The equilibrium fallacy of functionalism has strange progeny.[36]

Lucy Mair is more cautious: 'We must ask, not, *Is* history relevant [to an anthropologist]? but *What* history is relevant? The answer will not be so far from Malinowski's dictum that the past is significant in so far as it lives in the present. Those recorded events of the past which can be shown to have bearing on the phenomena under investigation are significant.'[37] Apart from the erroneous narrowing of the field to 'recorded events', the dictum is meaningless. How on earth is the investigator to determine which events of the past have bearing on present phenomena under investigation, even if only a secondary bearing, without a systematic study of the past? And so lip-service brings us back to Boas's 'To understand a phenomenon we have to know not only what it is, but also how it came into being'. I find it remarkable that this truism has now to be restated polemically.

The passion for the present, for contemporaneity, is at least in part a by-product of a fallacy that pervades the more recent history of anthropology. Having abandoned the crude evolutionism of their forerunners, anthropologists slide into abandonment of evolution, of progress itself. Thus, Leach quotes with approval the following remarks of Godfrey Lienhardt: 'If I report without further comment that some primitive men speak of pelicans as their half brothers, I do little more than offer the reader a form of words which, as it stands in English, suggests the atmosphere of fairy tales and nonsense. . . . In order to make this understood in English it would be necessary to give a full account of views about the relations of the human and non-human quite different from those we entertain, but not, therefore, necessarily less reasonable.'[38] There is a sense of the word 'reasonable' that can comprehend pelicans as half-brothers to men, but there is another, far more important, sense, understood by every one of us, which renders that form of words simply unreasonable. The shift from Lévy-Bruhl's *mentalité prélogique* to Lévi-

Strauss's *pensée sauvage* has not removed one particle of progress from human history.

Not all anthropologists drift into this fallacy, of course: Evans-Pritchard protested in 1950,[39] Goody in 1968,[40] but the very fact that they were moved to protest justifies my contention. The latest edition (1951) of the authoritative *Notes and Queries on Anthropology*, prepared by a committee of the Royal Anthropological Institution, exemplifies the slide (p. 28): 'Striking as is the diversity of human cultures it can no longer be maintained that this indicates fundamental differences in human mentality. Recent advances in psychology have established the basic identity of human mental structure in all branches of the human race. Sociologists have discovered similar principles at work in all types of society. . . .' In what sense can it be said that a 'basic identity of human mental structure', an ambiguous phrase at best, implies 'similar principles at work in all types of society'? I need not repeat my view that such an equation requires a narrowing of focus to meaningless or banal 'principles', but there have been practical consequences for the disrupted dialogue between anthropology and history that merit concrete examination, and I propose to look at two areas of human behaviour, literacy and politics.

On literacy I can be brief, because Goody has said what needs to be said.[41] One is often given the impression that the most significant difference between non-literate and literate societies is in the eye of the beholder, the consequence of the different sources of information available to the investigator. Basically that difference is the essentially unimportant one of technique,[42] whereas what really matters is that literacy profoundly affects the whole of social activity. I will not waste time on the question whether literacy is a sufficient or only a necessary condition for this or that social development, an argument that is largely a diversionary tactic.[43] The proposition holds beyond dispute that there is not a single aspect of human behaviour that has not been given new possibilities for development, change, progress, with the introduction of literacy into any given society, and especially literacy that diffuses beyond a small, closed priestly or ruling class. That proposition can and has been demonstrated in the fields of politics, religion, economics, law, education, historiography and the sense of the past, and others, not to mention 'culture' in its narrow sense. It is sufficient to cite Goody's observation that 'the religions of conversion, the excluding religions, are all religions of the book'.[44] The specific consequences of literacy may be neither automatic nor universal nor inevitable, but consequences invariably flow, and that fact implies severe limitations on any proposition or generalization derived solely from the study of non-literate societies.

The situation with respect to politics is more complicated. It may be oversimplified to say that a particular society either is or is not literate, but statements of that order are not meaningless, whereas there are too few societies wholly lacking in government and politics, at least in the sense of the expression of power relations, to permit any either-or formulation in this area of behaviour. Suitable definition for analytical purposes of such terms as 'government', 'politics', 'state' exercises anthropologists, sociologists and political scientists, but I need not enter that thorny field. My present interest is in the prevailing tendency in political anthropology, and for that purpose the common-sensical meanings are sufficient.

In his preface to that pioneering work, *African Political Systems*, edited by Fortes and Evans-Pritchard, Radcliffe-Brown defines the 'task of social anthropology, as a natural science of human society' to be 'by a careful examination of diversities to discover underlying uniformities'. The editors themselves are even sharper: '*We speak for all* social anthropologists when we say that a scientific study of political institutions must . . . aim *solely* at establishing and explaining the uniformities among them . . .' (my italics). I said earlier that this (to me) false conception of science must lead to a level of generalization of little or no use to anyone; in this instance, the disinterest in differences removes from the field of study the most important problems about government and politics.* When M. G. Smith begins by eliminating 'process and content' as posing 'insuperable obstacles' and goes on to reject function, too, because 'it remains to be shown that Bushmen, Pygmies, or Eskimos have governments which are functionally homologous with those of the United States and the Soviet Union'[45]–not said in irony, I must stress–there is an obvious retort. It was made recently by John Dunn in another context: 'If the development of a sociology of revolution means the loss of the capacity to tell the difference between a Sierra Leonean military coup and the Chinese revolution, any funds devoted to supporting its development will be money excessively ill-spent.'[46] I must confess a total inability to appreciate the value of removing all the differences between Bushmen, Pygmies or Eskimos and the United States or the Soviet Union in the search for some notional homologous residue.

How in fact does one establish a governmental homology between Pygmies and the United States? The indispensable first step is reductionism again, in this case elimination of the state. 'Amongst

* Anthropologists are not alone in their obsession with 'underlying uniformities': see chapter 8 below.

some writers on comparative politics,' said Radcliffe-Brown, 'there is a tendency to concentrate too much on what is called the "sovereign state".'[47] More recently, Georges Balandier, a member of what I earlier called the global school of anthropology, has demanded 'breaking the spell' cast by the state, dissociating 'political theory from the theory of the state',[48] a programme for which he claims Aristotle as a spiritual ancestor on the basis of mistranslation and misunderstanding of two famous passages in Aristotle's *Politics*.[49] 'The traditional state cannot be defined by a sociological type (or model) that would oppose it *radically* to the modern state'[50] (if not Pygmies and the United States, therefore, at least Zulus and the United States). One further recent example: in order to 'discover some of the general principles in political manœuvre which transcend cultures', begin by thinking of 'politics as a competitive game'; then 'just the same patterns of political competition can be perceived alike in the behaviour of Vallacchi's associates [in the American criminal organization known as Cosa Nostra], Indian villagers, university committee-men, General de Gaulle, and that most civilized of men Herbert Henry Lord Oxford and Asquith'.[51] But politics are not *just* a competitive game: the different consequences of Vallacchi's behaviour, victory in the 10,000 metres at Munich and the German elections late in 1932 sufficiently expose the fallacy of such reductionism.

We must agree with the author of the chapter on political anthropology in the 1969 *Biennial Survey* when he writes, without intended irony, 'It is not hard to see why anthropologists should eschew a definition of politics phrased in terms of the society as a unit' as well as 'a definition of politics that requires an irreducible minimum of centralized authority'.[52] He is himself consistent to begin his section on 'political systems' with two pages on primates on the one hand, and on the other hand to demand removal of the 'bias' inherent in Easton's 'assuming that political systems always coincide with governments and societies'.[53]

Two specific consequences of the method merit consideration. First a search through five of the best known and most highly regarded books on political anthropology and two survey-articles uncovered exactly one use of the word 'citizen' and one of the word 'naturalize',[54] both times in inverted commas as a warning that the word is not to be understood literally, a warning that was hardly necessary when it emerged that 'citizen' among the Hottentots was a rough English equivalent for a specific social class, distinguished not from 'foreigner' or 'alien' but from 'servant'. I cannot guarantee that I did not overlook another instance or two, but that does not matter: neither word appears in any index and their use is precluded by the 'politics' under examination.

Second, in those primitive societies that can be said to have achieved statehood, the form of government is invariably chieftainship, so much so that Lucy Mair, for example, slides into the following generalization: 'If we were to try to put in a single sentence the essence of the state system, we might say that it consists in the delegation of power by *the ruler* who holds final authority, in such a way that *he* can expect *his* orders or decisions to be carried out throughout the land which *he* claims to rule' (my italics).[55] That this is meant to cover more than primitive states is revealed by the qualifying parenthesis, 'or its [the state's] name in some modern states'. Furthermore, that chieftainship is the sole form of government not only existing in primitive states but also conceivable to their people is demonstrated by the acknowledged fact that in these normally unstable states, rebellion is common, revolution unknown: 'In the event of rebellion,' write Fortes and Evans-Pritchard, 'the aim, and result, is only to change the personnel of office and never to abolish it or to substitute for it some new form of government.'[56]

Now I submit that such politics, without citizens, without revolution, without any dynamics, without either a concept or an institution of the state other than chieftainship, provide little substance for a dialogue with the classical student, beyond a whispering conversation for the most archaic eras in Graeco-Roman history, those characterized by Louis Gernet by the phrase, *prédroit*, awkward when rendered into English, pre-law.[57] Nor is the difficulty with politics alone. Citizenship was an important, sometimes a decisive, factor during the classical periods in such diverse institutions as marriage, land tenure and taxation. The erosion of citizenship in the Roman Empire was one of the main symptoms of the changing structure of imperial government and of the slow transformation from the ancient world to the medieval. Debates about government and the state abound in ancient cultural expressions, in epic, tragedy and historiography as well as in ethics or political theory in the narrower sense.

By now it may seem puzzling that I continue to refer to a 'dialogue' when 'feud' appears to be more precise. But that is not the case. As a firm believer in–I think I may fairly claim to say practitioner of–the dialogue, I am trying to formulate some rules and establish the limits. Years of indifference and misunderstanding have not made that easy, and, if I have been polemical, that is because I find it essential to strip away false claims, and to specify possible meanings in the vague rhetoric of 'cross-fertilization' and 'interdisciplinary study', if the dialogue is to become genuinely fruitful in my field. For, I must repeat, it is my side of the dialogue that I am ultimately concerned with, and my aims and aspirations are modest ones, the same, though for a wider range, as Jane Harrison expressed when she said simply, 'better understanding of some song of a Greek poet or some saying of a Greek philosopher'. The dialogue between anthropology and the classics is a branch or subdivision of what is now called 'comparative history' or 'historical sociology', and 'understanding' is the key word, by which, it will be obvious from what I have already said, I do not mean universal laws or symbolic structures but, and again I use the word 'modest', understanding and explanation at a 'slightly more generalized level' than the conventional analysis of individual events found, for example, in the traditional narrative.[58]

A sympathetic reviewer of my book, *Early Greece: The Bronze and Archaic Ages*, expressed regret that in the archaic section I abandoned the 'anthropological methods' I had employed in *The World of Odysseus* for a 'class-conflict model'.[59] I should not myself employ those particular terms, but her meaning is clear, and my answer is simple. For the world of Odysseus, I found Marcel Mauss's concept of gift-exchange a cogent model; modern anthropological work on kinship equally useful, but in the negative sense of revealing how wrong the traditional stress on kinship has been in the accounts of the society I was analysing; an occasional anthropological parallel for one Homeric practice or another heuristically valuable. But I do not find the work of anthropologists of much use, in a concrete way, for archaic Greece (the period roughly between 750 and 500 B.C.), which saw the emergence of the city-state, conflicts over tyranny, the first appearance of democracy, the *Theogony* of Hesiod, Ionian philosophy and science, the Pythagoreans and the poetry of Sappho. (For archaic Rome, it is enough to mention the replacement of kingship by a republican system of government and the early law code known as the Twelve Tables.)

What I am saying can easily descend to a tautology: a dialogue is useful in so far, and only in so far, as it is useful. Because anthropology illuminates one period (or one aspect) of the classical world, it does not automatically follow that it also illuminates all other periods (or aspects). Societies and their cultures are complex, and the mere presence of some similarities is of itself not sufficient ground for rushing to conclusions without full inquiry into the location of those similarities within the totality, the structure of the societies under examination. Sparta offers a model example. For more than a century scholars have drawn upon anthropological parallels for an explanation of Sparta: comparative materials on primitive age-classes, polyandry, blood-letting as an initiation rite, marriage by capture, even the Zulu barracks appear and re-appear in modern books about Sparta. What has been largely overlooked is that all the anthropological models are inadequate for classical Sparta, the Sparta which, with Athens, gave the Greeks effective leadership in defeating the Persian invaders, and which, half a century later, entered into a twenty-seven-year war that destroyed the Athenian Empire; inadequate because those 'peculiar' features in Spartan life that appear to be illuminated by anthropology were, by the classical period, fossilized rites which had lost their original function (and which the Spartans themselves no longer understood) and had acquired new functions within a complex society of a kind that eludes meaningful comparison with non-literate, primitive groups. What anthropology illuminates about Sparta, paradoxically, are certain aspects of her lost early history rather than the Sparta from which the fossilized evidence comes.*

A different kind of example is provided by the work of Karl Polanyi. One of the intellectual roots of his insistence that the market model of trade is not universal was the work of the German anthropologist, Richard Thurnwald, who formulated a scheme of types of exchange which he called 'reciprocity', 'redistribution' and 'market (or commercial) exchange'. These Polanyi tried to convert into systems of 'integration', and, though that effort must be deemed a failure, his insights remain indispensable in the study of classical trade, indeed of trade in all pre-industrial societies.[60] The implication was irresistible that the student of classical trade should steep himself in the available studies of primitive trade, as did Polanyi himself. At least I could not resist, until I discovered that these studies, thorough, sophisticated and increasingly numerous though they are, were more misleading than illuminating for my purposes. Peasants and peasant markets, administered trade (a technical phrase in Polanyi's usage), ports of trade (another Polanyi phrase), conventional 'prices', barter are to be found in both worlds. But the intrusion of genuine market (commercial) trade, on a considerable scale and over very great distances, into the Graeco-Roman world had a feedback effect on peasant markets and the rest to such a degree as to render the primitive models all but useless.[61]

One consequence of my judgment that the dialogue should become most intensive for Gernet's *prédroit* periods of the ancient world, is that the classicist has most to learn from anthropology in the fields of kinship and of myth and ritual. Much can be (and has been) said in

* See in detail chapter 10 below.

detail about that, as about 'survivals' in the more advanced periods or about individual social practices which have been illuminated, sometimes unexpectedly, by anthropological comparisons. However, this is not the occasion for such detailed study, and, besides, there is a general point that transcends all detailed considerations. That is, simply, that the greatest value to the classicist in the dialogue is in the end the cultivation of an approach, a habit of thought–I might say a methodology, but I will not go so far as theory, a word used frequently and, I believe, much too loosely and imprecisely, by anthropologists, as in the opening paragraphs of *Notes and Queries*.[62]

There are several factors in this approach: the careful formulation of concepts and models, from which flows a precision in selecting the significant questions to be studied and, if possible, answered, which are often not the questions directly posed by the sources (in our subject, Greek and Roman writers);[63] an explicitness and consciousness about the generalizations we constantly and unavoidably employ even in the most matter-of-fact narrative or literary analysis, not always with either sufficient realization or sufficient foundation;* the habit of stating propositions in such a way that they permit either validation or falsification, and the deployment of arguments suitable for that purpose, of which the familiar argument by example is normally not one; a grasp of the distinctions and the interrelations between social institutions and systems on the one hand and 'culture' on the other, what Leach has called the 'form, the "dress", of the social situation',[64] which includes the unconscious codes and symbols as well as the overt cultural statements of a society–function and structure, in other words, but without functionalism or structuralism. There is no intrinsic reason why this approach should not have been achieved as well in history or literary criticism as in anthropology, but the historical fact is that modern anthropology has developed sophisticated and satisfying habits, whereas the classics have not (apart from such ancillary techniques as textual criticism and epigraphy).†

I deliberately select anthropology, not sociology, as the mentor. Granted that the distinction between those two disciplines is largely, perhaps wholly, one in the organization of teaching and research, stemming from the two different concentrations, on small non-literate societies for the former, on industrial societies for the latter, the resulting literature is sufficiently divergent to permit the choice I have made.[65] It is not only that, for comparative study, modern

* See chapter 3 above.

† The weakness must, of course, be conceded that no past society can be observed in actual operation.

industrial society is very limited in its usefulness to the classicist, but also that sociology has, so far at least, been most illuminating when it deals with very narrow, precise, temporally bound questions, quickly flying off into over-generalized and commonplace propositions when it becomes macro-sociology, as the jargon has it. Ideally, we should create a third discipline, the comparative study of literate, post-primitive (if I may), pre-industrial, historical societies. (I include the attribute 'historical' because the larger and more complex societies, non-literate or literate, which anthropologists do study are severely contaminated by their contact with the modern European world.) For most of the concerns of the classicist (and for most of the periods on which he concentrates), pre-Maoist China, pre-colonial India, medieval Europe, pre-revolutionary Russia, medieval Islam offer a more appropriate field for the systematic investigation of uniformities and differences, and therefore for an increased understanding of the society and culture of his own discipline. And that, as I have been trying to stress throughout, is the object of the exercise. As Gilbert Murray said, in rather extravagant language, in his Memorial Address, 'It was said of a certain great Scotch savant that to him all facts were born free and equal. To her [Jane Harrison] it was much the reverse. If the fact had a living message she embraced it and loved it; if it had not, it was entirely unimportant to her.'

7

THE ANCIENT GREEKS AND THEIR NATION*

NEAR the end of the Persian wars a rumour spread that Athens had been solicited, and was tempted, to betray the Greeks. Sparta rushed a delegation to Athens, where they were quickly and emphatically reassured. 'And then there is our Hellenism,' Herodotus has the Athenians say (8.144), 'our being of the same stock and the same speech, our common shrines of the gods and rituals, our similar customs. Should the Athenians become traitors to all this, it would indeed not be well.' And indeed it was often not well with the Greeks: many communities, supported by advice from the Delphic oracle, refused from the very first to resist Persia. But Herodotus' sentiments, if not an accurate statement of a universal and unequivocal Hellenic faith, cannot be brushed aside as propaganda of the moment. They recur too often in Greek literature.

What, precisely, was Herodotus saying? A modern political scientist or sociologist might explain that he was enumerating the elements in Greek life and thought that justified the inclusion of the Greeks within that class of social organisms we call nation or nationality: common descent, common language, common religion, common customs and a consciousness of belonging together. However, what Herodotus failed to include is equally noteworthy. Their common Hellenism may have made it unthinkable that Athenians should join Persians against Greeks; it never prevented Greeks (including Athenians) from fighting or enslaving Greeks and from employing foreign mercenaries in the attempt. Nor was there the faintest intimation that a single governmental structure was either necessary or desirable. In other words, being a Greek meant a great

* This chapter is so completely rewritten a version of an article originally published in the *British Journal of Sociology* 5 (1954) 253–64, as to be in effect a new essay. For the standard modern literature, see F. W. Walbank, 'The Problem of Greek Nationality', *Phoenix* 5 (1951) 41–60; 'Nationality as a Factor in Roman History', *Harvard Studies in Classical Philology* 76 (1972) 145–68. I am grateful to James Roy and C. R. Whittaker for helpful comments.

ideal in Herodotus, intellectually, spiritually, morally, but it had no political content apart from the one point of not assisting non-Greeks to defeat and subjugate Greeks.

'In respect to political sovereignty,' wrote George Grote, 'complete disunion was among their most cherished principles. . . . Such co-existence of entire political severance with so much fellowship in other ways, is perplexing in modern ideas; and modern language is not well furnished with expressions to describe Greek political phenomena. We may say that an Athenian citizen was an *alien* when he arrived as a visitor in Corinth, but we can hardly say that he was a *foreigner*; and though the relations between Athens and Corinth were in principle *international*, yet that word would be obviously unsuitable to the numerous petty autonomies of Hellas, besides that we require it for describing the relations of Hellenes generally with Persians or Carthaginians. We are compelled to use a word such as *interpolitical*, to describe the transactions between separate Greek cities, so numerous in the course of history.'[1]

For Grote, a representative of the mid-nineteenth-century English liberal establishment, the Greek pattern was merely perplexing–he made no attempt to explain it, so far as I can discover–but on the continent, and particularly in Germany, it had by then become an exemplary fault. No ancient Greek had proclaimed the same principle as the *Confession of Faith*, presented to a great meeting of the *Burschenschaften* in 1817, the ideological fundament of the movement for German unification: 'Germany is, and shall remain, ONE. We cannot accept the belief that Germany is composed of thirty-eight islands.' So the sad fate of the Greek city-states, subject to fratricidal strife and then to foreign conquest, became a favourite lesson in the ideological battle for unification.[2]

The *failure* of the Greeks to unite politically has been an almost unchallenged concept among historians of antiquity ever since.[3] Implicit is the modern identification of nation with nation-state, with its corollary that any 'nation' which neither united nor even strove to unite politically suffered from inherent defects, failed, whether in the nineteenth century or in the fifth and fourth centuries B.C. 'The important and *perhaps somewhat disheartening* fact. . . . The failure of the Greeks *to realize their potentiality as a nation* . . .' (my italics).[4] As living ideology such a simple doctrine is understandable enough, often effective and not rarely catastrophic. As an analytical tool, it crumbles quickly. 'The tendency has always been strong to believe that whatever receives a name must be an entity or being, having an independent existence of its own.'[5] In what sense may one legitimately say that the Greeks failed to do something that, demonstrably, they never conceived of, as either a possible or a desirable end? In what sense, indeed, were the Greeks a nation at all if we insist on equating nation with nation-state?[6]

When Herodotus was writing, Greek communities, most of them tiny, severely restricted in population and in space, were scattered from Phasis at the eastern end of the Black Sea all the way to Marseilles.* The Greek peninsula itself was solidly Greek, as were the islands in the seas around it. The western coast of Asia Minor (modern Turkey), most of Sicily, the southern tip of Italy from Naples down were heavily Greek, but they also contained substantial non-Greek populations. Elsewhere in the extensive territory in which there were Greek communities they tended to be more or less non-contiguous little dots in an alien world of Scythians, Thracians, Libyans, Gauls and dozens of others. Unless prevented by another power, each community had its own government, its own coinage, calendar and laws, its own temples and cults. The variations were infinite, yet Herodotus could speak, without descending to nonsense, of their common language, religion and customs. These were the grounds on which every one of the innumerable scattered communities was accepted to be as Greek as every other, in its own opinion and in the judgment of the rest (discounting the inevitable local claims to a superior brand of Hellenism). They also had a common label for all other peoples–*barbaroi*. Its deployment was a clear signal of a qualitative differentiation, commonly but not always with a pejorative implication.

Paradoxically, it can be argued that both the dispersion of the Greeks among barbarian nations and the absence of a central Greek political or ecclesiastical authority served as centripetal forces holding their common culture together. The former compelled them to cling to their Hellenism, their identification with other Greeks, as a means of retaining self-identity. The latter prevented the emergence of regional loyalty, rebellion, heresy and similar centrifugal forces familiar from later epochs in European history. The several Greek dialects remained recognizably and intelligibly Greek for many hundreds of years, in contrast to the transformation of late Latin into Romance languages. So did art and architecture; religion, too, though in this sphere the variations, changes and accretions were bewildering in their number and range.

I am of course suggesting not that any Greek offered these arguments against unification, but that *we* must propound such proposi-

* In the centuries after Alexander the Great, there was a considerable growth of Greek cities further east, into Asia Minor, in Syria and Babylonia, but that did not significantly alter the situation under examination.

tions if we wish to explain, not evade, the history of the Greek 'nation'. Instead we are commonly served up with a mixture of tautology, rhetoric and mysticism resting on the notions of immanence and failure. In an influential work on the history of nationalism in Germany, written at the beginning of this century, Friedrich Meinecke gave currency to the categories of *Kulturnation* and *Staatsnation*. 'We may distinguish between an earlier period, in which nations on the whole had a more plantlike and impersonal existence and growth, and a later period, in which the conscious will of the nation wakens in that it feels itself to be a great personality (even if only through the instrumentality of its leaders) and claims the hallmark and right of the developed personality, namely, self-determination.'[7] Individual Greek city-states never emerged from the vegetable state.[8] Why not? Even if one accepts Meinecke's metaphorical formulation as meaningful, the key question has still to be answered. In 1800 one could have said of the Prussians that they were Germans culturally but Prussians politically, as the ancient Athenians were Greeks culturally but Athenians politically. Why did the situation undergo a radical change in the former instance, not in the latter?

'The failure of the Greeks to realize their potentiality as a nation'– so runs a widely accepted view–'was due to several causes of which the particularism of the *polis* was only one (though an important one)'.[9] This is a tautology disguised by the (misused) word 'cause'. City-state particularism was no fixed entity, neither was it a mere prejudice, pure emotionalism. The *polis*, wrote Aristotle, exists by nature and is prior to the individual (*Politics* 1253a19–20). 'A *polis* has its proper scale like all things, animals, plants, inanimate instruments. Each will lose its power [to function properly] if it is excessively small or excessively large; it will either be robbed of its own nature entirely or it will be defective. . . . A state composed of too many . . . will not be a true *polis* because it can hardly have a true constitution. Who can be the general of a mass so excessively large? And who can be herald, except Stentor? . . . The optimum size of a *polis* occurs when the numbers are the greatest possible for self-sufficiency, while living within sight of each other' (*Politics* 1326a35–b24).

These sentences are the culmination of a complex, coherent argument, in which the components are Aristotle's concept of nature, his doctrine of the mean, and his ethics, with its systematically developed notions of justice, community (*koinonia*), virtue and the good life.* City-state 'particularism', for Aristotle at least, was the

* Aristotle's 'the *polis* is prior to the individual' is therefore a far more embracing

outcome of all these elements, and if they constituted a powerful block to what we call 'nationhood', they point in directions wholly unrelated to any modern theory or ideology on the subject. To charge Aristotle with being blind to the potentiality of the Greek nation, to its right to self-determination as a developed personality, is therefore a sterile, meaningless way of looking at the distant past.

Aristotle died a year after Alexander the Great, whose exploits initiated important changes in the realities of the city-state, but, as we shall see, no equally fundamental shifts in attitudes to nationhood. All Greek thinkers, philosophers, poets, historians, were equally 'blind' to the idea of a *Staatsnation*. And when they began to probe into the components of Herodotus' 'definition' of Hellenism, into the Greek *Kulturnation*, they found themselves troubled and confused, unable to formulate an agreed, or even fully consistent, conception. Common language seemed obvious enough as a starting point. Common descent was a stereotype, and it is doubtful that many Greeks took it very seriously.[10] Common religion, symbolized by such Panhellenic institutions as the oracle at Delphi and the quadrennial games in honour of Zeus at Olympia, had its ambiguous side. 'Homer and Hesiod', wrote the sixth-century B.C. philosopher Xenophanes, 'have attributed to the gods everything that is disgraceful and blameworthy among men: theft, adultery and deceit. . . . If cattle and horses and lions had hands or could draw with their hands and produce works of art as men do, the horses would draw their gods horselike, the cattle cowlike, and give them bodies, as every species has its own.'[11] Xenophanes' target was not merely Homer and Hesiod but the traditional conception of the Olympic gods and, so to speak, the Olympic morality, which the two poets had fixed in as scriptural a way as is possible in a culture without a sacred book.

'Much learning does not teach reason, understanding. Otherwise Hesiod would have learned it. . . . But Hesiod is the teacher of most. They are convinced that he knows the most, he who does not even know day and night. There's one for you.'[12] That bitter comment by Heraclitus was an expression of the great rationalist movement in Greek philosophy, in open conflict with the majority. Aristophanes' *Clouds* is an effective, though caricatured, presentation of the popular response; the 'Republic of wise men' of the founder of Stoicism, Zeno, is the extreme counter-statement. But the battle was

notion than the superficially similar one to be found in the literature of the 'interactionist' school of social psychology, e.g., 'the temporal and logical pre-existence of the social process to the self-conscious individual that arises in it': G. H. Mead, *Mind, Self & Society*, ed. C. W. Morris (Chicago 1934) p. 186.

not always restricted to intellectual debate; the last third of the fifth century B.C. witnessed a series of impiety trials in Athens that began with the exile of Anaxagoras and closed with the death of Socrates.[13] The same Heraclitus, it is to be noted, found the faculty of rational thinking to be a peculiarly Hellenic trait: 'Eyes and ears are poor witnesses for man if he has the soul of a barbarian.'[14] Plato rejected that but was equally opposed to the traditional morality and theology: he banned from his Republic all poetry, Homer in particular, 'with the sole exception of hymns to the gods and encomia of the good' (*Republic* 607A).

Obviously a determination of what the Greeks or any segment of the Greeks meant by common religion and common customs, Hellas and Hellenism, cannot be made by the prevailing method of selecting apt quotations, overt programmatic statements. What is required is a systematic, quantitative where appropriate, multivariate analysis of everything in the available documentation that pertains to national consciousness; of the casual as of the programmatic references, of the unintended as of the intended meanings, of the silences, too, and always in correlation with the precise context in which something is said or is not said.[15]

What I mean by the silences is quickly illustrated from the *Works and Days* of Hesiod, an 800-line poem which is a brilliant compound of apparent autobiography, myth, moral indignation with a prophetic undercurrent of doom, farmer's almanac, and instruction in ritual.

It was Hesiod, apparently, who first gave literary expression to the belief that all Greeks had a common progenitor, Hellen, grandson of Prometheus and great-great-grandson of Heaven and of Ocean. Hence the collective name, Hellenes. Yet in the *Works and Days* there is no role for the Hellenes. Kinsmen, neighbours and the community make up the whole of his set of identifications. 'A man grows eager to work when he considers his neighbour, a rich man who hastens to plough and plant and put his house in good order; and neighbour vies with his neighbour as he hurries after wealth. . . . A bad neighbour is as great a plague as a good one is a great blessing; he who enjoys a good neighbour has a precious possession' (lines 21–24, 346–48).[16] For those 'who practise violence and cruel deeds far-seeing Zeus, the son of Cronos, ordains a punishment. Often even a whole community (*polis*) suffers for a bad man who sins and devises presumptuous deeds, and the son of Cronos lays great trouble upon the people, famine and plague together' (lines 238–43).

A note of doom hangs over the *Works and Days*, at its blackest in the account of the five ages of man. 'Would that I were not among the men of the fifth generation. . . . For now truly is a race of iron, and men never rest from labour and sorrow by day and from perishing by night; and the gods shall lay sore trouble upon them. . . . And then Aidos and Nemesis, with their sweet forms wrapped in white robes, will go from the wide-pathed earth and forsake mankind to join the company of the deathless gods: and bitter sorrow will be left for mortal men, and there will be no help against evil' (lines 174–201). All mankind is threatened, unlike 'O ye children of Benjamin, gather yourselves to flee out of the midst of Jerusalem, and blow the trumpet in Tekoa, and set up a signal of fire on Beth-haccerem; for evil appeareth out of the north, and a great destruction. . . . Be thou instructed, O Jerusalem, lest my soul depart from thee; lest I make thee desolate, a land not inhabited' (Jeremiah vi, 1, 8). The Hebrew prophet had one and only one point of reference, his people, his nation, while the Greek poet had several, of which his nation was not one. The moment he left the daily concerns of his farmers to consider more universal matters, he leaped from the community to the human race.

Hesiod and his farmers had little contact with non-Greek states. When war disturbed the closed circle of their existence, as happened often enough, the enemies who raided his fields and destroyed his crops, and against whom he retaliated in kind while serving in his community's militia, were as Greek as themselves. Finally, there came a time when old Greece (as we may call it) was invaded by a foreign power, Persia. In assemblies and councils everywhere decisions were urgently debated. Should the great Persian armies be resisted at the probable cost of rout and perhaps extinction, or should discretion prevail and the best possible bargain be made with the invaders? No doubt orators made frequent use of the increasingly pejorative word 'barbarians' in the debate, but nothing in the actual behaviour suggests that the basis for decision was any different from what it was when the threat came from another Greek state or coalition (except in so far as the Persian threat was unprecedented in its scale). In the *Persians*, a tragedy produced in Athens eight years after the decisive Greek naval victory at Salamis, Aeschylus gave the call to battle: 'Advance, O sons of the Hellenes, liberate your country' (lines 402–3). However, one should not draw implications too quickly. The appeal is identical, even to the key word, liberate (from slavery), with Thucydides' version (1.124) of the Corinthian plea to Sparta in 432 B.C. to take the initiative against Athens: 'Believing that the city that has been establishing itself as a tyrant in Hellas has been established against all alike . . . let us attack it and reduce it, so that we ourselves may live safely in the future and the Hellenes now enslaved be liberated.'*

After all, the trouble with the Persians started in Asia Minor, and there the Greeks had lived in their cities for more than half a century in quiet acceptance of Persian suzerainty. Why they finally revolted is unclear, but it was certainly not because they had come to the conclusion that their Greek nationhood was incompatible with barbarian rule. Mutual animosities among the Asia Minor Greeks had a long history behind them. Herodotus himself was not immune. If these animosities had not led to outright war for some decades, that was only because the Persians would not permit it. Everywhere else that Greek communities were established among other nationalities they warred with each other as freely as on the Greek peninsula itself.

None of this is to suggest that Hellas had no meaning whatever. But it is essential to catch the right contextual note. Every ancient Greek, living in a complex society, belonged to a multiplicity of groups.[17] By the time of Herodotus and Thucydides the list of possibilities, apart from purely informal groups which should not be underestimated, included the family and household; the neighbourhood or village; the occupational group or military unit; the community and its political subdivisions (whether in a highly structured city-state like Athens or in the looser, more primitive societies of Thessaly or Aetolia); the *ethnos*, a category (for which there is no English equivalent) of regional subdivisions of the Hellenes, normally larger than a *polis*, such as the Boeotians or Arcadians; a social stratum; the age-group and the table-fellowship. It is self-evident that the interests and demands of these varied groups were not always consonant, and often enough conflicting. It is also self-evident that the nature and intensity of an individual's ties, institutional and psychological, to each group with which he had an affiliation varied substantially–according to the context or activity; according to his status within the group (few were egalitarian) and within the social hierarchy itself; according to his own self-image, aspirations and ambitions, lack of ambition or feeling of deprivation.

Hesiod's peasants could not have had the same identification with the community as did his 'bribe-devouring princes'; nor the same as the peasants two centuries later, after they had attained more or less full membership in the political community. In the second half of the fifth century B.C., when Athens had a tribute-paying empire,

* Cf. Aristotle, *Rhetoric* 1396a18: the Athenians 'enslaved the Hellenes, they reduced to slavery those who were bravest in fighting with them against the barbarians, the Aeginetans, the Potidaeans and all such others'.

which, among other things, gave many poor citizens the opportunity of a livelihood in the fleet, peasants were entitled to sit in the popular assembly and vote directly on the issues and proposals surrounding the empire and imperial policy. Then they were entitled to vote for war with Sparta, in which many of them were required to fight as infantrymen and which caused considerable devastation of their farms, orchards and pastures. There was grumbling at times, yet the evidence is indisputable that at every critical moment, popular morale held fast, until the Athenians were at last defeated militarily, after twenty-seven years, thanks in considerable measure to the support the Spartan enemy received from the barbarian, the Persian king.

There were Athenians who turned traitor, Alcibiades the most famous of them. But treachery was not an important element in the war except for a brief period, in 411 B.C., when a hard core of oligarchs saw an opportunity to destroy the democratic system in Athens and seized it even though that meant surrender to Sparta. They failed. The identification of the vast majority of Athenians with their state, in its existing form, was overpowering. That was not always the case in Greece by any means. An exemplary text is provided by a little collection of stratagems written as a handbook for military commanders by a fourth-century B.C. mercenary captain from Arcadia in the Peloponnese, named Aeneas. The stratagems are restricted to the needs of siegecraft, particularly in defence, and an astonishingly large proportion are directed to the single end of security against betrayal from within. The tone is set at the very beginning of the book (1.4–7):

'In the first place the most skilful and experienced soldiers must be set apart to form the magistrates' bodyguard; it then remains to make a roll of the men who will be most capable of exertion and to divide them into companies. . . . These must be men who are well disposed to, and satisfied with, the established government; for a united body like this is a protection as strong as any citadel against the plots of others, and will intimidate malcontents within the city. Their commander and supervisor should be a stout and able soldier, and also a man who has everything to fear from a change of government.'[18]

The incidents Aeneas cites, the majority from the period 400–360 B.C. and nearly all from wars entirely within the Greek world, combined with the other available evidence, fully warrant his preoccupation with betrayal. Furthermore–and that is what matters most in the present context–the problem of loyalty is directly and repeatedly linked by Aeneas not so much with individual psychology or corruption as with considerations of economic condition and social status.[19] In a crisis, he writes at one point (14.1.2), debtors are 'very dangerous to have sitting by, watching for their opportunity. Those in want of the necessaries of life should be amply provided for. How this may be done fairly . . . I have described in detail in my *Ways and Means*' (a work unfortunately lost).

What the Greeks called *stasis* was endemic in their world so long as the autonomous city-state remained the characteristic political unit: 'city-state particularism' evidently included a considerable incapacity to live peacefully with one another within the individual, autonomous communities. *Stasis* is a very broad term, impossible to translate directly; its connotations range from faction to outright sedition, open civil war, bloodshed and mass exile. 'Intra-state violence with political, economic or social motivation', though cumbersome and rather imprecise, will perhaps do, and that definition brings me back to the main theme.[20] When *stasis* reached the stage of civil war, all other group loyalties were sacrificed if necessary. Thus, in 197 B.C., early in the long history of Roman military and political intervention in the Greek peninsula, the lower-class 'faction' of little Opus in Locris, near the Straits of Euboea, requested the Aetolian army to assist them, 'but the richer faction shut out the Aetolians, and sending a messenger to the Roman commander, held the city until he came' (Livy 32.32.2–3). This unimportant little incident was typical of Greek behaviour from early times, including the intervention, by invitation, of a foreign army, the barbarian, when circumstances permitted.[21] 'National' Hellenic patriotism had a feeble appeal when in conflict with other overriding demands.*

Other demands were always overriding. That is precisely the point at issue, and a satisfactory explanation cannot be found by the prevailing preoccupation of historians with ideas and ideology in the abstract.† I have stressed how little we actually know about Hellenic attitudes to Hellas, and that we can know far more, but now I must add that no matter how much we extend that knowledge, it will never tell us why the ancient Greeks did not transcend their 'city-state particularism'. The relationship between ideology

* Analogous is the enslavement of Greeks by Greeks, a practice untouched by the protests of some moralists, Plato among them. It is a fundamental rule that only outsiders may be enslaved, and in the Greek world, citizens of the next city-state down the valley were outsiders.

† Other manifestations of this preoccupation have been noted in the first part of chapter 4. For an important critique of a similar flaw in contemporary social psychology and sociology, see John Urry, *Reference Groups and the Theory of Revolution* (London 1973).

and social behaviour is a dialectical one. Neither can be held steady by the analyst as if it were merely a passive receiver of impulses from the other, as in Meinecke's study of nineteenth-century German nationalism, in which the Industrial Revolution is never mentioned while we are led systematically through the ideas of Wilhelm von Humboldt, Novalis and Schlegel down to Ranke and Moser.[22] What philosopher, poet or other representative of high culture brought about the English nation centuries before the Germans achieved that goal? William the Conqueror, a Norman, was driven by the ambition of royal power, not by national consciousness. Aristotle was no less intelligent than Schlegel or Ranke, but he came to the opposite conclusion. And the rich men of Opus were 'intelligent' enough to distinguish Greeks from Romans.

Stasis was a terrible malady: ancient commentators and modern historians are agreed on that. But the Greeks never succeeded in finding a remedy, and for reasons. The most profound *staseis* were between the few and the many, as the Greeks commonly referred to them, between the rich and the poor: the references in Aristotle's *Politics* alone are too numerous to be cited.* They disputed and warred for control of the state, for the power to make public policy, not only for its own sake–and I do not underestimate the attractions of power as power–but also for the substance of the measures to be adopted over a range of issues. Once the Greeks took the astonishing and unprecedented step of incorporating within the community all the free men of the community, peasants, craftsmen and sailors as well as landholding aristocrats and noble warriors, they opened the door permanently to *stasis*. The political rights of the poorer members varied greatly, between Periclean Athens and oligarchic Corinth, for example, but the gulf was far greater between a Corinthian peasant and an Egyptian or Persian peasant. If the latter wished to alter his condition fundamentally–and he scarcely ever tried to–he was driven to flight or rebellion, precisely like a slave, not to *stasis*, a prerogative of free men.

The freedom of all members of the community, citizens of the *polis*, was not easy to maintain; citizenship entailed rights as well as duties, and the poorer members, the 'many', naturally included the right to life, to a livelihood, among them. For that the material and technological base was much too weak. Not even the most perfect system of distribution could have fulfilled their expectations, except

* There were other kinds of *stasis*, for example, within an oligarchy or in the attempts of tyrants to establish sole control of a *polis*. These can be shown to rest on the same foundation as the type I have selected and do not require separate consideration here.

at the expense of someone else, either of the more prosperous citizens—hence the perennial revolutionary cry, Cancel debts and redistribute the land—or of outsiders, by pillage and conquest, through war, tribute-paying empire or outright subjugation. Any other form of expansion, specifically a combination of city-states into a larger nation-state would, under ancient conditions, merely have extended the scale of the difficulties without substantially altering the fundamental condition of Greek life, including the malady of *stasis*.[23] Modern critics of Greek particularism should first decry their failure to have an industrial revolution.

There was one practical alternative, to replace the city-states by larger territorial units, at the cost not only of the subjected peoples but also of the traditional social structure and values of the Greeks themselves. Within a generation after the death of Alexander the Great in 323 B.C., two extensive monarchies were firmly established, by the Ptolemies in Egypt and the Seleucids in Syria and (for a time) Mesopotamia. They were absolutist, bureaucratic regimes, backed by a relatively closed élite of Macedonian conquerors and Greek immigrants exploiting a subject non-Greek population, Egyptians, Syrians, Hebrews, Chaldaeans, Persians and so on. In the Greek peninsula itself, another of Alexander's generals, Antigonus, and his successors tried to emulate Ptolemy and Seleucus, but they failed. They lacked the essential ingredient, a conquered barbarian population; for them to establish an absolute monarchy required that the Greeks be the subjects, not the élite, and they resisted. It remained for the Romans to achieve in Greece what the Antigonids could never manage.

Greek political affairs were henceforth a matter of '*ethnē, poleis* and dynasts'[24]—dynasts, not nations. If one asks, Of what nation, territory or country was Ptolemy king?, the answer is that he was not king 'of' anywhere, neither in his titulary nor on his coins nor in any official documents, whether edicts, letters or treaties. He was just 'King Ptolemy', of wherever his writ ran at any moment. And the same was true of the other Hellenistic rulers, major or minor.[25] That is what *dynasteia* signified. Nor were Roman emperors essentially different. The titulary of Trajan, for example, the last of the conquering emperors, ran as follows (in a late version): 'Imperator Nerva Caesar Traianus Augustus Germanicus Dacicus Parthicus, tribunicia potestas 21 [times], [acclaimed] imperator 13 [times], consul 6 [times], proconsul, pater patriae.'* What is missing is

* 'Germanicus', 'Dacicus' and 'Parthicus' commemorate military victories or conquests (even when they were not much to boast of), as was customary in Roman imperial titulary.

anything comparable to 'of the United Kingdom of Great Britain and Northern Ireland and of Her other Realms and Territories Queen'.

The disappearance of the city-state occurred in an age when cities were burgeoning. Hellenistic rulers founded some and encouraged others in the eastern territories that had previously been outside the Greek orbit. The Romans followed suit in the relatively undeveloped west. That was much the best way for them to govern large areas: urban élites not only provided the personnel required to collect taxes, finance and supervise public works, build roads and provide essential postal and similar services, and so on; they could also be given administrative responsibility for the surrounding rural districts in return for various privileges, material and honorific. A Greek still remained a citizen of his local community, even when, as became increasingly common among the élite in the course of the Roman Empire, he also acquired Roman citizenship. However, important aspects of local citizenship could be regulated by the emperor, and that one fact symbolizes the fundamental transformation that had occurred. A city-state which no longer controls its own membership is a contradiction in terms. At a low level, politics went on, but all the main prerogatives of autonomy were lost to the higher power. Aristotle would have dismissed all these cities *en bloc* as a negation of the genuine *polis*. The philosophical schools which came after him, Cynic, Stoic, Epicurean and the rest, took the inverse position: they dismissed the classical Greek *polis* as meaningful; they depoliticalized ethics and sought virtue within the individual independent of the social relationships in which he lived and worked. 'I am a *cosmospolites*', Diogenes the Cynic is supposed to have said,[26] a citizen of the cosmos, the universe. That of course meant, 'I reject citizenship as a valid notion'.

However, the small minority symbolized by Diogenes apart, identification of a Greek with his city continued with apparently undiminished intensity. Those with sufficient means contributed substantially to its adornment and welfare, and they assumed the various municipal offices and priesthoods at a considerable financial outlay. When formal identification was required, that was provided by the name of the city.[27] No Greek in Ptolemaic times ever called himself an Egyptian; no Greek under Roman rule ever identified himself by reference to the province of Achaea. When the specific context warranted it, of course, he might refer to himself as a Greek. The *Kulturnation* survived all the political changes and even expanded through the Hellenization of barbarians. It was in the Hellenistic age that for the first time a common literary dialect emerged, called the *koinē* (the adjective for 'common' employed in the feminine gender as a noun).

A Roman, of course, would often have referred to a Greek as a Greek, not as an Athenian or Ephesian (as they would call a man a Gaul or a German), just as the Greeks had always identified non-Greeks by 'national' labels. Differences between self-identification and the identification by others are common in all societies, including our own, on many levels of which the ethnic is only one. There are interesting implications in that pattern, but they are essentially irrelevant to the subject of Greek 'nationhood'.[28]

The end of the city-state also meant, at last, the end of *stasis*. There was still violence enough, including hunger riots, but not the political *stasis* of the autonomous city-state, incompatible with *dynasteia* and effectively suppressed by the dynasts. The 'few' had triumphed, and nothing in their world either suggested or permitted the nation-state.

8

THE PROBLEM OF THE UNITY OF GREEK LAW*

So long as the Greek city-states retained their political autonomy, they legislated for themselves, and only for themselves. Other communities could, and sometimes did, then adopt a new law or practice, but that is not a denial of the self-evident proposition that autonomy extended to all branches of the law. Nor is the fact that many legal practices had their origins in an earlier, pre-city-state age, from which they passed to the classical cities more or less changed and adapted.

It is then a legitimate historical question to ask whether, and how far, the undisputed 'cultural nationhood' of the Greeks embraced the law even before the transformations following Alexander's conquests. The starting point for all modern discussion of the subject has been Ludwig Mitteis's *Reichsrecht und Volksrecht*. 'The innumerable individual statutory laws of the Greek cities rested in essence on identical juristic conceptions (*Anschauungen*) and the same institutions developed with only slight nuances.'[1] The Greeks themselves, he continued, were conscious of this, hence the 'frequent' reference to common *nomoi* and to the contrast between Greeks and barbarians in this respect.

Often as this passage has since been quoted, one flaw in the formulation seems generally to have escaped notice. The Greek word *nomos* may mean 'law' or even more narrowly 'statute', to be sure, but it just as commonly means 'custom' or 'institution' in the broadest and vaguest possible sense. In his own text here, Mitteis also slides from law (*Recht*) to custom (*Sitte*). However one under-

* A paper read at the 1st Congresso Internazionale della Società Italiana di Storia del Diritto, in Rome in December 1963, and published in the *Atti* of the Congress (Florence: Olschki, 1966) pp. 129–42; now considerably revised with the help of comments by Jean Bingen, Emily Grace, D. M. Lewis, J. Modrzejewski, P. Vidal-Naquet and H. J. Wolff.

Reprinted by permission of the Società Italiana di Storia del Diritto.

stands the relationship between law on the one hand and custom or morality on the other, a distinction must be drawn if there is to be a fruitful discussion of Greek law and the extent to which it was or was not commonly shared. At the very least, there is the difference that 'moral rules or principles cannot be brought into being or changed or eliminated' by 'deliberate enactment', whereas legal rules can.[2] Unfortunately, the texts Mitteis adduced as evidence of what the Greeks themselves thought turn out, with one exception, to be either empty rhetoric or so broadly directed to a small number of moral questions as to be of little use for our purposes. How empty the rhetoric could be is well exemplified by one of the forensic texts (Isaeus 2.24), where the speaker, talking about adoptions, says that all men, Greeks and barbarians alike (not, as Mitteis implies, Greeks as distinct from barbarians), recognize the value of the institution, except, of course, his opponent. Otherwise the passages contrast Greek monogamy with barbarian polygamy, or refer to the un-Greek practice among the Lydians of prostituting their female children, or say that it was an ancient Greek custom to marry by capture (which is untrue) or that the Lusitanians of Spain marry according to Greek customs, whatever that may mean.[3]

All these things can be said with equal truth about the Romans, which demonstrates that they do not get us anywhere. But there is one text which is in a different class from his others. Mitteis cites Xenophon as saying in the *Memorabilia* (4.4.15) that the Spartans differ from the rest of the Greeks only in their greater obedience to the laws. That misplaces the emphasis. Xenophon actually has Socrates say that it is precisely the quality of obedience which enabled Lycurgus to make the Spartans different from their fellow-Greeks. This suggests that, remaining on the same vague level for the moment, it was as much a commonplace among the Greeks to contrast the Athenians and Spartans or the Dorians and Ionians as to contrast Greek and barbarians. There are, for example, the passages in which Thucydides (6.4.3–5.1) tries to sort out some of the Sicilian Greek cities as to whether their *nomima* were Dorian or Ionian. There is the contrast implicit (and often enough made explicit) in the procedure Plato adopted in the *Laws* of developing his legislative programme through a 'conversation' among an Athenian, a Cretan and a Spartan. And there are the concrete examples scattered through Aristotle's *Politics* (not tied to the Dorian-Ionian stereotype).

Then there is the work of Aristotle's successor, Theophrastus, also called *Laws*, a more or less systematic collection of existing legal rules from many communities (not like Plato's 'personal' codification). Unfortunately, little can be said about it, since only one continuous, not very long, extract survives in a Byzantine florilegium.[4] Perhaps, as has been claimed, it was no more than a 'comparative description of statutes and institutions, but not an analytical commentary'.[5] But Aristotle's *Politics*, the model for Theophrastus' *Laws*, leaves no doubt that this philosophical school, profoundly concerned with analysis, with principles, found the endless variety of laws in the Greek world deserving of a large-scale, systematic research effort. Merely to record 'slight nuances' of 'identical juristic conceptions' (to repeat Mitteis's language)? No student of Aristotle is likely to believe that.

Few of the examples given in the *Politics* (or in Thucydides) pertain to private law, as distinct from political and constitutional arrangements. That was presumably the gap filled by Theophrastus' lost work. Private law is often compatible with a variety of constitutional systems and may survive a political revolution fundamentally unchanged, as we are told explicitly, for example (Diodorus 16.82.6), about Timoleon's legislative programme in Syracuse. Plato in his *Laws* combined much Athenian private law with a social and political structure that more closely approached Sparta, in so far as it resembled any existing Greek system.[6] In the process Plato also revealed the limits beyond which such a combination becomes impossible. In two fields, at least, real property and commercial law (including credit transactions), he broke altogether from the law of Athens. And in those two fields Athens and Sparta were as far apart, in practice, as were Greeks and barbarians with respect to marriage. Even if Sparta were unique in these matters, which she was not, that would not excuse the way she has been ruled out of the Greek world, by implication, in virtually all modern literature about Greek law. Whether one likes it or not, Sparta was also a Greek state.

No one wishes to deny that there were certain institutions common to the Greek communities everywhere: monogamous marriage, some form of servitude and so on. But I do not believe anyone can legitimately deny that the property regime and the institutions of commerce were equally not uniform, and that raises the fundamental question: What is really the point at issue? With respect to property, Mitteis wrote (pp. 69–70): 'Greek law reveals the same firmly held basic ideas despite breaches which the principle suffered by arbitrarily experimental legislation in one region or another. The time when all real property had a community (*genossenschaftliche*) character may not have lain so far in the past for the Greek states as for Rome, but in the classical period private ownership was recognized everywhere, and though the sale of land, like the manumission of slaves, may have required the agreement of heirs by blood, it was never restricted by claims of next-of-kin.' He then went on summarily to contrast Greek ownership with Roman *dominium*.

That is all. It is not an accurate statement of the situation, but I do not want to raise that point now, nor do I want to consider the overworked distinction supposed to be implicit between the Greek protection of ownership by *diadikasia* and Roman *dominium*. I want instead to ask the following: Is it illuminating or useful to reduce the basic principles of the law of property to three assertions–that private ownership exists, that the next-of-kin other than blood-heirs have no claim, and that the metaphysics of ownership are not Roman–and then to dismiss all else as minor detail, mere nuance? If that is all that is meant by the unity of Greek law, there can be no argument, but there is equally nothing worth discussing. What does such a generalization tell us about the Greeks or their law? Of what use is it conceptually or as an analytical tool?

At the other end of the scale, there were legal rules of a technical nature–for example, how long the waiting-period must be before a transfer of real property becomes valid–which can properly be dismissed as negligible nuances, the inevitable but not significant consequences of the fact that there was no single legislative authority for all the Greeks. Between the two extremes, however, there is a vast area. How does one decide which rules are basic, which insignificant? Which adjective does one apply, for example, to a rule prohibiting alienation of inherited property? Such a rule does not invalidate the generalization that private ownership exists, but I submit that, both in those Greek communities where the rule was enforced and for us who are trying to understand the Greeks, the rule reflects a very fundamental conception. Or, if I may just this once tread on the treacherous ground of the Greekness of the law of Hellenistic Egypt, I suggest that the whole of the law of real property there, starting from the very notion of royal land (*basilikē gē*), was much more not Greek than Greek, and that the distinction cannot be magically dismissed by pointing to the existence of some more or less private property.*

* Behind my suggestion lies a protest against the frequent citation of a vastly disproportionate number of papyri from Ptolemaic (and even Roman) Egypt, as we shall see, in the discussion of pre-Hellenistic Greek law. The practice is no doubt convenient: the papyri include tens of thousands of private documents, of a nature almost completely unavailable from the city-states. Convenience, however, is not sufficient warrant for a question-begging procedure. That the Hellenistic monarchies, administered by Greek élites, saw the emergence of a common law,

The Greeks had a history. So did their law. Any discussion of the unity of Greek law, whether unity is deemed to be total or partial, must eventually come down from the stratosphere of juristic mode of thought (*Rechtsdenken*) and juristic sensibility (*Rechtsgefühl*) to mundane operational–and that means historical–questions. We know exactly how Roman or English law developed as a more or less integrated, coherent body of rules. But by what process did the Greeks achieve the same results, as is claimed, when they were scattered over vast distances east and west, in many separate, often unrelated moves over several centuries; when they were politically fragmented; and when their institutional history shows such very different rates, and even directions, of development?

Mitteis at least noticed that there is a problem and he had an answer of sorts, namely, racial kinship (*Stammesverwandtschaft*). Properly, he added (pp. 62–63), we ought to differentiate according to the individual stocks–Dorians and Ionians, in particular–but the evidence does not permit that. Is that really an operational answer? Let us look at one concrete situation. In the Homeric poems marriage may be called monogamous, but juridically it was established without any required formalities and the status of children was a matter for the head of the household, the *oikos*, to decide.[7] In classical Athens and elsewhere only a marriage between a man and a woman who had the right to marry each other, established by formal 'handing-over' procedures, known as *ekdosis* and *engyesis*, was a legitimate one, in the sense that their children alone were eligible for the full rights of succession and often of citizenship.[8] The law of Gortyn in Crete, however, was in this matter, according to Wolff, a 'compromise' between 'legal principles not only quite different in kind but essentially incompatible'.[9] Wolff understates the difference between Gortyn and Athens, but even his doctrine is sufficient for my present argument, for that puts an end to race as a serious factor of explanation. In simple logic a single constant factor cannot explain two such divergent developments as the Athenian and the Gortynian, not to mention Sparta again.

In the field of marriage and the family there is an altogether different approach available, and that is to link the Greek developments (in the plural) with the varied history of the growth of the *polis*. What then emerges is precisely what one could have guessed if one had no information, namely, that different kinds of *poleis*

---

under new political, social and economic conditions, and that declining autonomy had a similar effect, much later, in old Greece, constitute another matter, not the one under examination here.

formulated different rules about marriage, legitimacy, the rights of women, and inheritance. A few examples, all taken from Wolff's fundamental article, will suffice.

1. Periclean Athens went as far as it was possible to go in one line of development: restriction of legitimate marriage to members of the citizen body on both sides; the formal requirement of *ekdosis* and *engyesis*; the classification of all children not the offspring of such marriages as 'bastards' (*nothoi*), with their consequent exclusion from intestate succession when there were legitimate children, and, at least in the case of children of a 'mixed' marriage, from citizenship;[10] denial to women of all rights to an inheritance, of the right to administer or control property, of freedom from tutelage.

2. In the Gortyn code there is no trace of *engyesis* (though that does not necessarily mean that there were 'free' marriages); daughters had mandatory claims to a share in the succession; women owned and controlled property, and an orphaned daughter without brothers had certain freedoms and privileges denied her Athenian counterpart, the *epikleros*.

3. Elsewhere we are dependent on single bits of evidence which suggest that the total Greek picture was variegated, but which do not permit any systematic formulation. It is certain, however, that neither the Athenian exclusion of women from property rights nor the extreme Athenian rejection of *nothoi* was universally shared. (Perhaps I should add that the differences constantly cross the Dorian-Ionian line.)

4. The Greeks in Egypt, as far back as the relevant documentation goes (which is to 311 B.C., a very early date some years before Ptolemy assumed the title of King), recognized the property and testamentary rights of women, showed no trace of *engyesis* or the *epikleros*, and reduced the giving of the bride by her father to an empty formality. 'Marriage', writes Wolff, 'is no longer a transaction between the *oikoi* on both sides but only a personal agreement of the two partners with the blessing of the bride's parents.'[11]

Within the limits of our information this makes an intelligible story. We now have a classic account by Wolff, which remains valid even if some elements are challenged or modified. But the account is disfigured by illogical pronouncements on the side, seeking to preserve the unity of Greek law at any price. I quote two examples. (1) From the Homeric picture 'to the legal situation of the early *polis* was only a step. The basic conceptions of Greek family law were already worked out in the Homeric age, and all that was necessary was their adaptation to the new conditions. . . .' (2) 'It is beyond doubt that the marriage law of Gortyn corresponded in all essentials to the principles which prevailed everywhere in the Greek sphere.'[12] If we take as nodal points the Homeric poems, Gortyn, Athens and the earliest Greek papyri from Ptolemaic Egypt, I am unable to discover a single common 'basic conception' or 'principle' except for the notion, familiar from societies of the most diverse kinds all over the world, that marriage is an arrangement involving families past, present and future, and the transmission of property. Nor has Wolff stated any. It is not even easy to think of a significant principle common to any three of these four systems which one cannot also find in many other civilizations. And when one gets down to the actual rules laid down for marriage and the family, one is struck by the differences, the meaningful historical changes, not the identities.

Nor is it only in marginal pronouncements that the *idée fixe* of unity misleads; explanations of concrete data suffer also. When Wolff says that in the earliest preserved Graeco-Egyptian marriage agreement, an Elephantine papyrus of 311 B.C.,[13] the parties had already *abandoned* certain Greek principles, he *assumes* the existence of the principles. In the edition of the text regularly cited, the bridegroom's origin is not indicated, but the bride is identified as legitimate and a Coan.[14] What do we know about the law in Cos? The answer is that we know absolutely nothing. Earlier in the same article Wolff asserts, on the basis of a single inscription, that Cos had a 'system essentially similar to the Athenian'. The inscription, a century later than the Elephantine papyrus, gives a list of some 300 men and women and of their contributions to a fund, possibly for the maintenance of soldiers in wartime.[15] The contributors are distinguished as to whether they are citizens (male or female), *nothoi*, resident non-citizens or non-resident aliens (*xenoi*). That is the whole of the 'evidence' from which Wolff deduces the principles of Coan family law, and it is not unfair to label it worthless.[16] We cannot assume that the law of Cos at the end of the third century B.C. had not changed in the previous century. We know, as Wolff himself pointed out, that *nothoi* did not have the same status in all *poleis* or at all times in the same *polis*. We do not know, nor have we any good reason to take it for granted, that in Cos itself in 311 B.C. marriage was not already essentially 'a personal agreement of the two partners with the blessing of the bride's parents', the words Wolff used to describe the Elephantine papyrus.

In that agreement, incidentally, the husband promises not to have children by any other woman (lines 8–9). I see no reason why an agreement could not have been drawn up in Cos at that time in exactly the same language. Had the husband then violated this particular clause, the children would have been *nothoi*, subsequently identified, as in the later Coan inscription, by their father's name. I hold no strong brief for that last bit of speculation of my own. My point is that we can do nothing but guess in our present state of ignorance once we step outside three or four communities. Where we have solid evidence, it seems to me, the alleged unity of Greek law in the field of marriage and the family turns out to be more of a dangerous illusion than a valid generalization.

As a second test case, I turn to property. I have already indicated one important distinction to be found among the Greeks, as to whether women could or could not own and control property. Much more can be said on that subject, but I prefer to go on to some aspects of the alienability and inheritance of real property. I am not concerned with the controversy that has been revived in recent years about how long inalienability may have survived in Athens, but with the situation in the Greek world at the time when Athens had achieved, on any account, a maximum degree of freedom to alienate.* No society has ever allowed absolutely unrestricted alienation, so that the general question must always be reduced to one of alienation by whom, to whom, of what and under what conditions. Aristotle believed that there was a fundamental political issue here. Equality of property, he explained (*Politics* 1266b14–24), has been recognized as an important influence on the political community, a brake on *stasis*, class war. He enumerated three proposals, all tried in actual practice: (1) to set a limit on the size of holdings, for which he gave no current example; (2) to prohibit the sale of estates, as in Locris where such sale was allowed only on evidence of misfortune; and (3) to prohibit the alienation of the 'original allotments', for which his sole example was Leucas, where the prohibition had been removed at an unspecified date with bad political consequences. It would be a mistake to infer from Aristotle's almost non-existent documentation that these were merely utopian or archaizing proposals. Although our knowledge of the laws of property is fragmentary, it is not difficult to demonstrate that Aristotle could have exemplified the proposals adequately had he so chosen.

The surviving evidence is fragmentary: Aristotle surely knew much more. We are dependent on accidental finds, epigraphical texts that were inscribed on bronze or stone in the first place because of weighty special circumstances, and then discovered in modern times by chance. 'Normal' legal developments and changes rarely received such treatment. Primarily it seems to have been a coloniza-

* See chapter 9.

tion or resettlement which fostered more permanent publicity, about restrictions on 'original allotments' or on land grants to new settlers.* But that does not invalidate or weaken the evidence: a very large part of the classical Greek world arose from just such conditions of colonization; resettlement was a continuing factor; and there can be no disputing the conclusion that in scattered communities the idea of prohibiting or severely restricting the alienation of land and houses was still operative, under some conditions, at the end of the third century B.C. In Athens and many other cities, in contrast, there had been considerable freedom to alienate. No single 'conception' of the law of property can meaningfully underly all these sets of rules.

Other complications and variations of a different sort arose out of the claims of children to their paternal (or maternal) estates in the present or in the future. Sometimes a patrimony was more hemmed in, with respect to alienation, than property otherwise acquired. Where women had property rights, it was necessary to distinguish further between a paternal and a maternal inheritance. And all these elements entered into the question of whether other members of the family, and which among them, had to agree to the alienation of various forms of property, including the manumission of slaves.

How common the variations were, or how they were distributed in place and time, is unanswerable today. In a significant sense, however, such questions are irrelevant to our present concern. It is enough to have suggested that there were variations and that they were not simply different points along a single, continuous evolutionary line. In other respects Greek institutional history was surely far from uniform, and it would have been miraculous had the law in all its aspects somehow managed to go its own way, all of one piece save for trivial nuances. There were no miracles. Rather than pretend that there were, it would be more profitable to study Greek legal history as history, analysing the similarities and the differences, and trying to explain both.

'Nobody', wrote Hermann Kantorowicz in a general jurisprudential context, 'has been able to give a clear idea of what is meant by the metaphysical term "Wesen", or "essence", nor has anyone been able to indicate a method of teaching the intuition necessary for grasping it.'[17] I suggest that this comment applies directly to modern study of Greek law, and that the less said about 'essences' the better. Law is a system of rules. Even in a highly codified system

* The evidence and further bibliography for the statements in this paragraph and the next will be found in chapter 9. I had given them in the original publication but have deleted them here to avoid repetition.

or in one in which jurists have been working actively to find or impose general principles, there must always remain a large area of what Kantorowicz called 'free law', situations in which a judge, for example, is compelled to create a rule. With the Greeks, we are in a world of amateurs, as remote from jurists and legal theorists, from codification in its contemporary sense, as it is possible to get in a relatively advanced state of political organization. That does not preclude our trying to provide their jurisprudence for them, so to speak, to seek such regularities or patterns as may be observable in their rules. In doing that, however, we ought not impose our ideas on the Greeks retrospectively by assuming that in practice the rules were systematically worked out from explicit and recognized general conceptions, or that the juridical implications of an innovation were analysed by Greek rulers, legislators or priests (as would have been the case with the Roman jurists).

In Delphi, for example, an ingenious device for the manumission of slaves was employed for much of the Hellenistic period, and at least a century thereafter under Roman rule. The core of the device was the sale of a slave to the god Apollo 'on account of freedom'. Some formal procedure for the freeing of a slave was essential for his own protection, should his free status subsequently be challenged, and some form of publicity was also common, for the same reason. Over the centuries a number of different procedures were invented in one part of the Greek world or another, but the variations on the whole come under the heading of legal rules of a technical nature which I earlier dismissed as insignificant for our purposes. Not the Delphic technique, however, because for a jurist it creates extraordinarily difficult questions. Greek temples (and therefore gods) owned slaves as they owned farms, buildings, treasure, and they bought and sold slaves in the usual fashion. The Delphic manumissions were accomplished by sales transactions in the strict sense and in strict form, save for the phrase 'on account of freedom', which meant that the slave whom the god bought at once ceased to be a slave and became a free man, no longer property, whether of the god or of anyone else.

Did the priests or magistrates of Delphi think through the juridical principles by which a sale led to the immediate extinction of the property 'sold'? I know no reason to believe that they did. Legal fictions were familiar in Greece, as in every other civilized society.[18] Here was a brilliant one; it produced the desired effects in a novel and powerful way, and that was good enough. Not a trace of any ancient discussion of the procedure survives (if it ever existed); only the accident of archaeological exploration at Delphi has uncovered more than one thousand inscriptions recording these manumissions.[19] But modern legal historians cannot tolerate such untidiness: there must be an underlying 'juristic conception', even though no attempt to discover one has so far resulted in anything but a tangle of confusions and Procrustean manœuvres. When it becomes necessary to fall back on the notion of 'beneficial ownership' borrowed from the English law of equity–a notion that cannot be rendered in Greek and for which the Greeks lacked the indispensable institutional base–it is time to abandon the pursuit of will-o'-the-wisps.*

Were this excessive concern with essences and juristic modes of thought merely a waste of time, I should not be very much interested to raise objections. However, I believe the consequences are more serious, that they lead to distortions in the analysis of individual rules and institutions, and I hope I may be permitted one illustration from what is perhaps the most important book on a single branch of Greek law for many years, Fritz Pringsheim's *Greek Law of Sale*. When the book appeared, I wrote a long review in which I tried to raise some fundamental questions of method.† My criticisms have not been taken very seriously by jurists, I must confess, but I must add that I have never seen them answered either.

In his chapter on 'contracts for cash payment with deferred delivery', Pringsheim begins by enunciating the proposition that since 'liabilities for future performance are not compatible with the Greek conception of sale', the Greeks first tried to solve the problem of enabling a farmer to sell a future crop by 'recourse . . . to the law of loan' (pp. 268–69). The detailed analysis which follows does not mention a single instance from Greece but rests solely on Egyptian papyri and on one short passage in Plautus's *Asinaria* (a Latin comedy based on an early Hellenistic Greek prototype), although Pringsheim says (without giving any citation) that there are 'a few references to contracts with deferred delivery' from Greece proper. The conclusion of his intricate analysis is that there finally emerged 'a new type of contract which is neither sale nor loan. . . . The intelligence of the Greek and Hellenistic notaries found new ways for the satisfaction of economic requirements which were evidently irresistible. The new contract brought into existence a duty to deliver goods which could be enforced by an execution clause and guaranteed by a surety' (pp. 285–86).

One pertinent text is an inscription from the Aegean island of Thasos, to be dated probably in the last quarter of the fifth century B.C., containing several market regulations. The relevant one reads

* See the latter part of sect. III in the appendix to this chapter.

† I reproduce excerpts of my review in an appendix to this chapter.

as follows: 'It is forbidden to buy the crop on the vine before the first of the month Plyntherion [which falls somewhere between April and June].'[20] For some reason Pringsheim reserves this text for brief notice in the chapter on 'contracts giving the purchaser a right of seizure'. He writes as follows (pp. 296–97): '. . . it has already been observed that the Greeks had difficulty in conceiving and an aversion to acknowledging the sale of future fruits. Such scruples find expression in certain restrictions. A fifth-century inscription from Thasos prohibits the sale of . . . wine still on the vines before May–June. . . . Hence it was first impossible to sell future goods, like fruits. Restrictions, however, were later caused not by such dogmatic difficulties, but rather by economic considerations, especially by an aversion to speculative transactions. This is one of the many examples of the general principle that dogmatic causes are in the course of time replaced by economic and social causes. . . . All such restrictions suggested to the Greek notaries the idea of avoiding the sphere of sale and of making use of the rules governing leases.' After which there is a long section on leases, based as usual on the papyri.

The text, I repeat, says only that it is not permitted to *buy* the crop on the vine *before* a date which, at the latest, falls in the month of June. Whoever drafted that text wrote 'buy' and 'sell', not 'deliver' or 'lease'. Moreover, the new law did not prohibit the sale of future goods; it merely fixed the earliest time in the year when such a sale was allowed. September was the vintage month, so that any sales made in the month of Plyntherion would still be of a future crop. Hence the law has nothing whatever to do with any assumed 'scruples' or 'dogmatic difficulties' stemming from an assumed 'Greek conception of sale'. Obviously the practice of sales of future grape crops was already in existence, at least on Thasos, well before the end of the fifth century B.C. Then, perhaps in order to curb speculation, as most commentators including Pringsheim believe, the state decided to modify the practice, but not to stop it, by limiting the period of time within which it was permissible. There is no reason for saying that this decision had anything to do with the enforceability of contracts or 'dogmatic causes' or the purchaser's 'right of seizure'. The 'economic requirements' supposedly 'irresistible' to Hellenistic notaries were already being 'satisfied' in fifth-century Thasos. Pringsheim's reconstruction of the Thasian situation is a fiction to which he is driven by 'dogmatic difficulties' of his own creation.

Who, finally, is imagined to have been wrestling with these dogmatic problems in fifth-century Thasos? The inevitable answer, as we have seen, is 'notaries'. Until someone finds actual notaries in pre-Hellenistic Greek texts and until a reasonable explanation is given for the total absence of notaries from fourth-century Athens, about which we really know something, notaries ought never again be dragged back from Ptolemaic Egypt into the classical *polis*. Hellenistic notaries were the direct descendants of the ubiquitous scribes of the ancient Near East. One of their accomplishments was to help create a common private law. That was an inescapable objective in the Hellenistic monarchies, with their authoritarian hierarchical structure and their élite composed of Greeks and Macedonians who had migrated from hundreds of separate Greek communities.[21]

Neither scribes nor notaries were part of the civilization of archaic and classical Greece (or, for that matter, of the old Greek sector of the Hellenistic world). They have been invented – that is the precise word – by modern scholars as a desperate measure, for one cannot escape the need to answer the operational question I posed earlier. The correct answer is complicated, and not always evident. It is not difficult to grasp both the mechanism and the reasons for the emergence of a common law of maritime salvage, the so-called 'Rhodian sea law'. Every *polis* with cargo vessels on the high seas faced the same problems, exacerbated by the frequency of shipwreck, and the seamen and shippers required neither notaries nor jurists in order to come to an agreement with each other across the political boundaries of small autonomous states. The same was true of commercial law more generally.[22] And there matters ended: no amount of inter-city intercourse required or stimulated alteration or coalescence of deeply rooted laws of the family and property. Nor can any mechanism of transmission explain why so important an innovation in the matter of juristic personality as the 'family foundation', originating about the time of Alexander in the Doric Hexapolis on the coast of Asia Minor, was adopted in a number of communities on the Greek mainland, but not in Athens.[23]

I close with a commonplace. Legal rules constitute one of the ways of defining and regulating human behaviour. There is no perfect correlation between legal institutions and other institutions, but to grant that is not to concede its opposite, that there is no correlation at all. The widely accepted unitarian dogma comes near to implying just that.

APPENDIX*

I

The theory part of the book opens with a two-page chapter called 'Thesis', subdivided into seven points. In essence, this is the sound theory of Josef Partsch (to whose memory the volume is dedicated), 'amplified and reshaped'.

1. 'Greek law never abandoned the principle of cash sale.'

2. 'Since consensual contracts do not exist in Greece the mere informal agreement to sell and to buy is not a contract which binds both parties.'

3. 'Therefore there are no actions arising out of sale.'

4. 'Greek law separated the delivery from the cash sale, so that only the payment was left. . . . No "traditio" is necessary', but for real property 'and probably slaves and ships . . . certain forms . . ., varying in different cities, are required to give publicity to the transaction.'

5. To validate credit or deferred-delivery sales, various legal devices were made available: combining the sale with a fictitious contract of loan, *arrha* (earnest money), or a special agreement giving the right of seizure of the goods (by self-help) to the purchaser.

6. 'Although no binding contract of sale exists some agreement must obviously precede each cash sale. . . . But no liability (*Haftung*) arose; it was merely a duty (*Schuld*).'

7. If eviction is threatened, 'the vendor has to take over the purchaser's defence in the ensuing procedure. Otherwise he is liable and must pay a penalty. But this liability does not arise out of the contract.'

If one does not insist on too narrow a connotation of 'thesis', three more may be added. Though they do not pertain to sale specifically and they are not elaborated in the same way, they are as essential a part of the book as the seven principles of sale.

8. The law of the Greeks has a 'special character', based on 'their unique method of thinking and research, their flexibility of mind and their critical reasoning' (p. 5).

9. 'The simple Greek concept of sale was able to survive in a

* I reprint three sections numbered II, III and V in the original, unchanged except for the elimination of much of the annotation, of my review of F. Pringsheim, *The Greek Law of Sale* (Weimar 1950), in *Seminar* (an annual extraordinary number of *The Jurist*), vol. 9 (1951) 72–91.

Reprinted by permission of the then editor of *Seminar*, Stephan Kuttner.

highly developed cultural and commercial civilization' thanks to 'the adroit versatility with which Greek and Hellenistic practitioners managed to satisfy the requirements of a highly civilized world' (p. 501).

10. 'In spite of many variations among the laws of more than a hundred independent cities the similarity of Doric and Ionian institutions allows us to speak of "Greek law" as a unity' (p. 5). ('More than a hundred' is a curious understatement.)

II

'Sale is a contract.' With that sentence Pringsheim opens his second chapter. But what is a contract? If, for example, one accepts the definition of the American Restatement, that a contract is a legally enforceable promise, then the whole of Pringsheim's book is devoted to proving that in Greek law sale is *not* a contract.

Pringsheim continues, in the next sentence but one: 'But sale is not only and not mainly a contract. Its result is the transfer of ownership.' There is either a logical or a semantic fallacy here. The fact that the result of a sale is transfer of ownership has nothing to do with the question, Is sale only, mainly or not at all a contract? Nor does Pringsheim suggest what else sale is beyond contract.

The proper juridical classification of sale is a most complex problem. In Anglo-American law, for example, it is a commonplace to say that, 'The law of Sales . . . is in one phase part of the law of contract, in another phase part of the law of property.'* The complexity is multiplied many times over when, as Pringsheim points out, 'The whole Greek law of contract must be rewritten, or rather must be written for the first time' (p. 14). Pringsheim is also right in saying that 'this cannot be done here and now'. Where he is not right, in my judgment, is in avoiding the issue by resorting to axiomatic formulations. More is involved than the proper classification of sale. Behind that lies the most basic question of all: On what principles and along what lines should Greek law be categorized and analysed?

If Pringsheim ignores the problem in an explicit sense, he actually answers it implicitly. His unqualified and unquestioning, 'Sale is a contract', is apparently the automatic response of an experienced Romanist and civilian, the moment he discovers that conveyance was not a necessary component of the legal transaction. Roman-law

* K. N. Llewellyn, *Through Title to Contract and a Bit Beyond* (New York Univ. School of Law, Contemporary Law Pamphlets, series 1, no. 5, 1938) p. 1. Despite a superficial similarity, this formulation is qualitatively different from the three sentences by Pringsheim quoted in the text.

classification appears throughout the book. The chapter on contract starts with the question, 'Greek consensual contracts?' and ends with the answer, No, for 'real' and 'formal' elements were both essential. All three adjectives, consensual, real and formal, are of course Roman. They are often convenient and helpful notions in the analysis of contracts; they are not indispensable, but Pringsheim's formulation precludes alternative analysis. Again, he explains the familiar distinction made by Plato and Aristotle between 'voluntary and involuntary agreements' in terms of contract and delict, not only in direct violation of their language but on the unquestioned assumption that the Roman antinomy, contract-delict, is equally appropriate to Greek law (p. 36). Anglo-American law lacks it: contract-tort is not the same. Perhaps our legal analysis would be improved by its introduction. Perhaps, too, it suits Greek law perfectly. But these propositions require demonstration, and none is offered.

At other times, English law serves as a guide, particularly the concepts of legal and equitable ownership. Of several available examples, perhaps the best is Pringsheim's interpretation of the Delphic manumissions, which were accomplished through the legal fiction of selling the slave to Apollo. In such manumissions, says Pringsheim, 'the slave supplies the god with the money with which he purchases him from his master. The sale results in formal ownership by the god, which means freedom for the slave. The situation can be illustrated by a comparison with the English trust . . . legal ownership belongs to the god but in equity the slave is free. . . . The ownership he gives to the god in trust so that the god becomes the legal, the slave the beneficial owner' (pp. 185–86).

Nothing in the whole of Anglo-American law is more subtle, more complicated, and more peculiarly rooted in the particular history of that one legal configuration than the trust and its concomitant notions of legal and equitable (beneficial) interests and estates. Some five hundred years of activity by Chancellors and Masters of the Rolls went into the formulation. When they had ended their work, they built a structure that caused Gierke to say to Maitland: 'I can't understand your "trust".'* Yet Pringsheim would have us believe that Athenian and Delphic magistrates and jurors anticipated the English by 1,500-odd years. He is not even satisfied with an analogy. The slave is not *like* a beneficial owner, he *is* the beneficial owner. (Cf. p. 108: '. . . the god who is only a trustee is made to speak like a genuine purchaser.') 'In equity John Doe has a right of redemption' means that a Court of Equity will uphold that right.

* F. W. Maitland, *Equity*, rev. edn. by J. Brunyate (Cambridge 1947) p. 23.

What can it possibly mean, with reference to Delphi, that 'in equity the slave is free'? The word *pisteuo* appears throughout this group of documents, to be sure. And 'trust' is a fair translation of *pistis*–but 'trust' as 'faith' or 'credit', not the 'trust' which Gierke could not understand. . . .

III

What is Greek?

In analysing contracts, Pringsheim criticizes 'modern writers' who 'neglect the essential connection between the proof of a contract and its enforceability', i.e. 'in court' (pp. 17–18). What, then, is a 'Greek' court? Were the popular dicasteries of Athens, the royal judges of the Ptolemies, the courts of Doura-Europas and Avroman, the tribunals of Byzantine Egypt all 'Greek' courts? Was Justinian a 'Greek' and the courts of his empire 'Greek' courts? And what kind of law did these courts enforce? When we say that the Twelve Tablets and Julian's *edictum perpetuum* (not to mention the Digest) were codifications of Roman law, we mean that they summarized the law to be enforced by the courts of the Roman state–and nothing else. Similarly, the law under Henry II and the law under George VI of England are both 'English law' in that political sense alone.* No one will pretend that the law of property, for example, was alike or even comparable in Rome five centuries before Christ and five centuries after, or in England in 1150 and 1950. Nor is 'spirit' a safe refuge. It is time, therefore, that we recall that never in antiquity was there a Greece in the sense in which there was a Rome. A few elementary facts may be reviewed briefly.

1. In Aristotle's time, the land-tenure systems of the Greek world ranged from prohibition of alienation to free alienability. A century later the range was extended because 'Greek' rule of Egypt and parts of Asia added 'royal land' and 'royal peasants' to the possibilities. Is it conceivable that the law regarding the sale of real property could follow similar principles for (a) inalienable land, (b) freely alienable land, and (c) Seleucid royal land?

2. From roughly 600 B.C. (Solon's time) to the end of Greek civilization some communities absolutely prohibited execution against the person for private debt whereas others permitted it. Is it not a necessary consequence that the law of debt, of pledge, of execution–even the notion of the person in law–must have been radically different in the two spheres?

* Complications arising from such problems as law for foreigners, colonial law, or the reception of a developed legal system into another country are not germane to the present discussion.

3. Plato's *Laws*, however one interprets the work, is in the form of a dialogue among three persons, a Cretan, a Spartan and an Athenian. It is implicit in the very conception and structure of the book, and it is made explicit by Plato over and over again, that the legal conceptions of the three communities were worlds apart, in spirit as well as in concrete application. Whether Plato stated the spirit and provisions of the respective legal systems accurately or not –or even intended to–is of no moment. His fundamental premise, that basic differences existed, cannot be dismissed without powerful evidence.

Whatever one's theory of the origin of the Greeks, it cannot determine the history of Greek law. 'The similarity of Doric and Ionian institutions allows us to speak of "Greek law" as a unity' (p. 5). Emphatically, I must say no.* At best, this supposed similarity indicates common *beginning* of the law in the days of Greek prehistory. It neither allows nor disallows us to say anything about fourth-century Athens, third-century Delphi, or the second-century Egyptian *chora*. Similarly, 'the law of Gortyn . . . represents an early stage of Greek law' (p. 15) is equivocal and misleading. Did the law of *all* the Greek communities go through this stage? If so, why was fifth-century Athens no longer in that stage, when fifth-century Gortyn was? What evidence is there that Gortyn ever transcended that stage; if not, why not?

To be sure, there is difficulty with the sources. 'We should like to trace the variations due to race, constitution, development. But in view of the scarcity of our material such an aim is not yet attainable' (p. 6). Unattainable–not unessayable. That the effort is both necessary and feasible is quickly demonstrated. (1) For nearly a century scholars have dealt with the so-called Hellenistic family foundations, always in universals about the Greeks. Now Werner Kamps has discovered that in fact this institution began in a small group of communities in the sphere of the Doric Hexapolis, and that there a major legal innovation was made in the direction of juristic personality which spread to some, but by no means all, of the Greek cities, notably not to Athens. (2) It has already been indicated that Pringsheim rests heavily on the Delphic manumissions. But this form of manumission, by fictitious sale to a god, is known only from central Greece and Epirus.† Whether these geographical limits

* Note Pringsheim's own statement regarding strong Rhodian influence on the law of Alexandria (p. 8): 'So the addition of Ptolemaic law enables us to balance Athenian with Greek law of a very different sort.'

† When I wrote this, I overlooked the discovery of a similar procedure in the Hellenistic East, in Susa. That does not invalidate my argument.

entail substantive distinctions or merely formal, the problem cannot simply be ignored. Further, these are scarcely the regions to which one would turn for evidences of ingenious manipulation of the law to meet the needs of a 'highly developed commercial civilization'.

Egypt presents the most difficult problem of all. With commendable caution, Pringsheim makes the following programmatic statement (pp. 6–7): 'Ptolemaic law depends to a high degree on Greek law from the motherland. . . . Of course the influence of Egyptian law has always to be considered. But as long as such a small part only of the existing Demotic papyri has been published conclusions will always remain provisional and risky.' Again (p. 8, n. 1): 'Before the influence of Greek law in Egypt is investigated in detail, every formulation is risky.'

Nevertheless, much of the material in the book is Egyptian, even Roman and Byzantine Egyptian. How does Pringsheim know that a particular legal institution attested in the papyri is 'Greek'? Actually, that question is not meaningful until the prior question–what does one mean by 'Greek' in such a context?–is answered. Since the latter is not raised, the argument often becomes either circular or ungrounded. One extreme instance may be noted. Pringsheim refers to 'contractual clauses usual in Ptolemaic Egypt and probably found also in Greece which reserve the ownership of the crop to the lessor until the rent is paid' (pp. 295–96). In a footnote, he adds: 'The Ptolemaic clause appears so early (228–1 B.C.) and is in such striking contrast with the Egyptian form (Wilcken, P. Freib. III, p. 84) that it seems to be imported from Greece. From Greece itself we know only a clause . . . which gives to the lessor not ownership of the crop, but a title to seizure.'

Thus, the only citation for the statement that contractual clauses were 'probably found also in Greece which reserve the ownership of the crop to the lessor' is a text proving precisely the opposite, *ownership by the lessee*. On the present evidence, a reversal occurred in Ptolemaic Egypt on a specific legal provision. Was the new law also 'Greek'?

9

THE ALIENABILITY OF LAND IN ANCIENT GREECE*

THE background of this paper is provided by the considerable discussion in recent years of the history of the right to alienate real property in Greece.[1] My aim is to define the historical problem, not to survey the subject systematically. I make no claim to completeness in any respect. The texts cited are offered by way of example. For purposes of definition such a selection is both legitimate and sufficient.

I

'The definition of secure possession is possession of things in such a place and manner, that the use of them depends on one's self:– the test of things being one's own, in one's having the power of alienating them; by alienation I mean giving and selling.' So Aristotle in the *Rhetoric* (1361a19, in Jebb's translation). By 'giving' (*dosis*) he meant any form of alienation without a monetary quid pro quo. Aeschines (3.21) lists some of the possibilities when he says that a retiring Athenian magistrate awaiting his audit (*euthyna*) may 'not consecrate his property or make a votive offering or accept adoption or dispose of his possessions by will and much else'.

Two elementary generalizations follow, which must be put down at the start, commonplace though they are.

1. In the fourth century B.C. alienability was, juridically, the accepted condition of ownership. Aristotle's 'definition' in the *Rhetoric* may be unsatisfactory to strict modern (or Roman) jurists, and it is possible to argue that one ought not to speak of 'ownership'

* This 'point of view' is based on a communication to a 'Colloque sur l'*oikos*', held in Paris in April 1967 under the joint sponsorship of the ancient history centres of the Sorbonne and the École Pratique des Hautes Études. I am grateful to the participants for their comments and criticisms, and also to A. Andrewes, M. K. Hopkins and J. Pečírka, who kindly read my manuscript before it was published in *Eirene* 7 (1968) 25–32, then in French in *Annales: Économies, Sociétés, Civilisations* 25 (1970) 1271–77.

Copyright © 1968 Academia, Nakladatelstrí Československé Akademie Věd.

in strict modern or Roman terms. But such familiar arguments are red herrings. The questions of possession and ownership among the Greeks and of the changes with respect to alienability or inalienability are not answered by juristic quibbles. When Eumaeus enumerates the herds of Odysseus, we may properly paraphrase his words and say that these were the cattle, pigs, sheep and goats which Odysseus 'owned' (*Odyssey* 14.96–104). The basic question, as with land, is about the nature and limits of his right of disposal, about real life-situations, not about formal arguments over labels or abstractions.

2. The conditions and rules of alienability varied widely by the fourth century, and earlier too, from a variety of causes. Three bronze tablets from Greek settlements in southern Italy, recently dated on epigraphical grounds to about 475 B.C., record the *dosis* from husband to wife of all the former's possessions, one saying more specifically 'the house and everything else'. It may be uncertain how these donations are to be classified juristically,[2] but what matters is that there was at least this much right to alienate real property in some Greek communities early in the fifth century. And that this particular right did not exist in contemporary Athens because there no *woman* could be 'given' a house.

II

The question of alienability cannot be so phrased as to permit a simple or meaningful yes-or-no answer. One must ask, rather, alienation by whom? to whom? of what? when? under what conditions? in what forms? These are the questions I now propose to look at, schematically, for the classical period before proceeding to speculations about earlier times and about historical developments. I shall concentrate on the juristic side, that is to say, on what was permitted or prohibited under the law, rather than on practice. There have been many societies in which the 'law' was frequently broken on the one hand, or in which, on the other hand, the alienation of land (other than transmission to descendants) was a rare and disapproved practice even when it was legally permissible. The two aspects may be interlocked; they are not identical. Nor shall I be concerned with what has been called the increasing 'commercialization' of real property. Even in fourth-century Athens citizens did not lightly give up their holdings in land, and a property market did not develop. That is an interesting and important extension of the questions under review, but I shall not carry the discussion that far. I shall therefore not be primarily concerned with sale as distinct from other forms of alienation.

In the age, then, when alienability was accepted in principle, certain broad distinctions are apparent, some of which were newly created in an attempt to prevent alienation (and perhaps I should say once more that I make no claim to completeness):

1. Restrictions on alienability could stem from a general rule or from rules laid down in particular cases or situations, and the latter subdivide into public rules and private agreements. Examples of general rules will soon emerge in the discussion. Here I give three examples of rules set out in particular cases: (a) In the foundation of a small new Greek community in the northern Adriatic island of Kerkyra Melaina, in the Hellenistic period, it was laid down that a portion of the original allotments to the first settlers should belong permanently to them and their descendants, which presumably means that they were declared inalienable. (b) When Miletus took in a number of Cretan refugees in 228/7 B.C. and gave them citizenship and land, it was specified that none of this land could be alienated 'by any means whatsoever'. (c) The decree of the Arcadian League admitting Orchomenus to membership, probably about 233 B.C., included the clause, 'None of those receiving an allotment or house in Orchomenus . . . may alienate them for twenty years.'[3]

For restrictions created by purely private actions, it is sufficient to note the family cult foundations, first introduced in the Doric Hexapolis of Asia Minor before 300 B.C. and then rapidly adopted in much, though not all, of the Greek world. The pertinent clause of one of the earliest, the foundation established by Diomedon of Cos, reads: 'No one may appropriate, sell or hypothecate either the buildings adjoining the *temenos* or the *temenos* itself.'[4]

2. There were differences in rules as between alienations while the parties were alive and those which were to take effect after death (whether by *donatio mortis causa* or by testament). In the Gortyn Code, for example, the distribution of an inheritance was strictly regulated, permitting the testator no freedom in this respect, but at the same time the code is shot through with special permissions and prohibitions of what the same man (or woman) may do in his lifetime with precisely the same property.[5] This double approach seems to trouble commentators, yet it is basically no different from the approach of the Roman emperor Augustus when he restricted the number of manumissions by testament while allowing unlimited lifetime manumissions; or, in a way, of modern law, which in cases of intestacy accepts the claims of remote kinsmen who otherwise have none whatever.

3. The rules may vary as between property acquired by inheritance and property acquired in other ways. The distinction is

explicit in the Gortyn Code (VI 2–12). There are other texts, from quite different kinds of communities (e.g. Athens and Thera[6]), where the full implication is less clear. I shall not discuss them beyond noting that the deliberate introduction of such a word as *autoktetos* ('self-acquired') must, at the very least, reflect social attitudes if not always juristic prescriptions. A further distinction could then be drawn, in communities which permitted women to hold property, between paternal and maternal inheritances.[7]

4. My final distinction refers in the first instance not to the alienator but to the recipient. The variations with respect to women have already been mentioned. It is enough to add those linked with political status. And, of course, if the law does not permit a woman or a non-citizen to hold real property, it imposes a restriction on any potential alienator at the same time.

III

If we now turn to the historical development leading to the classical and Hellenistic conditions, we must first repeat the obvious, namely, that all the texts I have noted presuppose alienability. The various restrictive clauses would not have been necessary if land were in principle and in fact inalienable. It should also be pointed out that we have no evidence that in the new foundations, such as Kerkyra Melaina, the attempts at restriction were actually successful over any longer period of time. Perhaps the Arcadian League was being more realistic when it modestly tried to hold the newcomers for a mere twenty years. That the question is serious is shown by another clause in the Kerkyra Melaina document: 'The magistrates shall swear that they will not, under any circumstances, make a redistribution of either the city or the countryside.' As Asheri says, 'the regime of inalienability was not sufficient to crystallize and perpetuate the primary partition'.[8] So they added the familiar prohibition of a redistribution, extended to the alienable as well as the inalienable allotments – a point which tends to be overlooked – and I find it hard to accept Asheri's further comment, that this proviso was aimed at future dissension between the beneficiaries of 'primary partition' and later arrivals, who would receive inferior land. The more natural explanation, in a document actually signed by all the original settlers, is that they realistically accepted the impossibility of holding firm to inalienability or equality for any length of time.

Be that as it may, the question is in no way answered whether or not it is legitimate to argue back from these late and unimportant foundations to the early foundations, in the west, for example, in the eighth and seventh centuries B.C. To my knowledge there are only two early texts which may be thought to provide any information at all. One is *Odyssey* 6.7–10, on the establishment of the Phaeacians in Scheria, which is silent on the critical questions, quite apart from the point that a 'colony' with a king (Alcinous) does not sound like a very good model for Syracuse or Croton. The second is the story, which may go back to Archilochus, that a certain Aithiops of Corinth bartered his land allotment for a honey-cake on the voyage to Syracuse.[9] I hold no brief for this story, but to treat it as an 'exception', as scholars do, seems to me methodologically remarkable. If there are exceptions (and this particular story neither offers a reason nor permits one to be deduced), then the 'principle' of inalienability has simply disappeared. Besides, it is odd to dismiss this explicit text as an exception when we have not a single text stating the supposed rule.*

We do better to admit that we do not know the original land regime of the western foundations. But we do know that in Syracuse there arose a hereditary oligarchy called Gamoroi and that class war, *stasis*, broke out in the western colonies in the late archaic period very much like the class war in old Greece of the time. Logically there are the following possibilities. Land was either alienable or equal or both or neither at the time of the foundation. If it was neither, or if it was equal but alienable, then we have nothing further to discuss in this context. If it was inalienable but not equal, the subsequent *stasis* could have developed, again purely as a matter of logic, without a breach of the principle of inalienability. If, however, it was equal and inalienable, *stasis* shows either that alienability had somehow crept in or that, as Asheri projected for Kerkyra Melaina, conflict arose between, and was restricted to, the newcomers and the original settlers or their descendants.

In the absence of evidence, there can be no conclusive answer from the 'colonial' world. We must return to old Greece from which the settlers had emigrated, and ask about the land tenure there. Before we do that, however, there are two final points to be made. The first is that in one vital respect, the later texts cannot be the model they are claimed to be. The later texts all assume alienability and seek to restrict it. If it really was the case that land was in principle inalienable in the eighth or seventh century B.C., then no one would have bothered, or even thought, to write in the provisions we find in the Kerkyra Melaina document. The second point is that I do not see that it is axiomatic that in the new foundations they automatically repeated the rules of the world they had left behind,

* I remain unconvinced by those who cite proposals made by Plato in the *Laws* as evidence for archaic practice.

or that the rules were identical in all the new settlements. If the Kyllyrioi of Syracuse were indeed the helot-like subjects they seem to have been, it is at least possible that Syracuse developed a different land regime from that of Rhegium or Leontini, where the social structure was different.

IV

To begin by posing the crudest possible question, What are we asked to believe, about Athens of all Greek states, with its tradition of autochthony which archaeology has confirmed to a degree that is sufficient for the present discussion? That land was handed down rigidly within each 'family' until the time of Solon, or even down to the latter years of the Peloponnesian War as some now argue?[10] To simplify the discussion, let us concede that the 'principle of inalienability' is not breached if property went to the wider kinship in the absence of direct male heirs. Are we then to believe that from some original date (the settlement of Greek speakers in Attica before 2000 B.C.? the break-up of the Mycenaean system by 1200 or 1100 B.C.?) no migrant ever acquired land in Attica and no 'Athenian' family ever lost some or all of its holding? This is not a frivolous question. The fact that no one openly makes such assertions is beside the point, for they are an inescapable consequence of the belief in absolute inalienability. I need hardly add that I find them unbelievable, without parallel from any known society as advanced as that of Bronze Age or early archaic Greece. That is not to say that alienation took the same forms or was in other respects, such as frequency, the same in earlier as in classical times. The differences were structural and deep. The historical development, it seems to me, can be studied only when we abandon the either-or approach, which compels its proponents to find specific acts bringing about changes at fixed dates (which they are in fact unable to find), and replace it by a structural and developmental analysis.

In a pre-urban, pre-*polis*, pre-monetary society, alienation of land would have been extremely rare no matter how free the holder may have been 'by law' to dispose of it. Why should anyone in such a society dispose of land to someone other than his male descendants? The Homeric poems provide enough examples from which to construct an answer: (1) Diomedes' father migrated to Argos, where he acquired land, flocks and other wealth, presumably as a dowry (*Iliad* 14.119–24). (2) Alcinous offered Odysseus a household and land if he would remain in Phaeacia (*Odyssey* 7.311–15). (3) There are two references to a promise by Odysseus to give Eumaeus a house and land, and Melanthius the goatherd is bracketed with Eumaeus the second time (*Odyssey* 14.61–64; 21.213–15). It is evident that such alienations were instruments of the power-and-status structure of this world, by which the network of personal relations was strengthened and elaborated, services were secured or rewarded, amends were made, and so on. That this was a far cry from the sales of land reported by fourth-century Attic orators is indisputable. But they were the kinds and forms of alienation which were appropriate to their society, and we should expect nothing more – or less.

With the interlocked development of urbanism and the *polis*, profound structural changes followed, in the land regime as in other respects. Urbanization created new uses for land and wealth, introduced chattel slavery, made possible the existence of classes (and even of considerable wealth) not tied to land, and eventually fostered a considerable monetization of the economy. There were now new motives for acquiring and even for disposing of land. It is no coincidence that the various examples given by Aristotle in the *Politics* of communities which were still struggling (or had only recently abandoned the effort) to preserve more archaic property regimes were without exception drawn from the more backward, non-urban Greek regions.

At the same time there were new political conditions and requirements. The growth of the *polis* meant the shift from the pre-law stage (in Gernet's phrase) to the law stage,[11] with its more specific and more formal rules and a formal machinery for their administration. It meant *political* control over the rights of land ownership, in particular the exclusion of non-citizens. Diomedes' father could not have done in fifth-century Athens what he is said to have done in Argos once upon a time: the *polis* would not have allowed him to acquire wide fields, not even as a dowry. Nor could the disguised Odysseus have told the tale of his having received a small share of his father's inheritance, though a bastard. Even membership in the family was now a matter for the state to define. In sum, the *polis*-world saw the emergence not only of new kinds and new aims of alienation and of increasing frequency, but also of new restrictions.

It follows that there can be no question of dating the change-over in narrow terms. Alienability of land was one facet of a long, uneven and complicated process of change, little of it, in so far as alienability was concerned, in the form of legislative enactment. On the contrary, most formal rules for which we have textual evidence, whether introduced by public action or by private, look like attempts to stop change rather than to bring it about. If one believes, as I do, that the western migrations, starting early in the eighth century B.C., presuppose a sufficient political organization in Greece to have launched them, then it is at least arguable that in the new settlements more rigorous restrictions were imposed than were in existence in the homeland. New settlements in sometimes hostile environments may well have introduced formal inalienability as a measure of self-preservation. That is what such texts as the Kerkyra Melaina suggest, and from that point of view the Aithiops story serves as a nice cautionary tale rather than as a meaningless and improbable 'exception'. None of this is to suggest that the full classical situation was already visible in the eighth or seventh century. My argument, on the contrary, calls for continual development, and therefore repeated change of various kinds.

10

SPARTA*

I

THE Sparta I shall consider falls within a rather restricted period, from about the middle of the sixth century to the battle of Leuctra in 371 B.C. I exclude the earlier history, apart from a few certain events and general trends, because I believe that our information is almost wholly fictitious (especially anything referring to Lycurgus); that all attempts to reconstruct that early history in detail, with names and exact dates, rest on totally unsound methodological principles; and that the excessive concentration on assumed distant origins in a legendary migration period is equally unsound in method.[1] I stop at Leuctra because I accept the virtually unanimous Greek tradition of a qualitative change fairly early in the fourth century. Thereafter, despite certain continuities, Sparta was being transformed into a different kind of society again.

What this means is that I accept that the decisive turning-point in Spartan history came in or about the reign of Leon and Agasicles (Herodotus 1.65–66), soon after 600 B.C., as the culmination of a crisis perhaps a century old, a crisis in which the so-called Second Messenian War was the main catalytic occurrence, and which produced persistently revolutionary potentialities and threats. Much about that war is obscure, not to say legendary, but the poetry of Tyrtaeus is contemporary and illuminating. It demonstrates that the Spartan army was in a disorder and turmoil unlike anything known from the later, classical period, the community in a state of *stasis*; and that the Lycurgus myth was not yet current. Once the war was finally won, a number of profound changes were

* This essay was originally presented at the Sorbonne on 5 April 1965 in one of the series of seminars which eventually produced *Problèmes de la guerre en Grèce ancienne*, ed. J.-P. Vernant (Paris and The Hague 1968). My contribution appears on pp. 143–60. I am grateful for suggestions and criticisms offered by those who participated in the seminar, subsequently to P. A. Brunt, R. M. Cook, G. T. Griffith, M. K. Hopkins and A. H. M. Jones, and especially A. Andrewes.

Copyright © 1968 by Mouton & Co., and École Pratique des Hautes Études, who have given me permission to reprint.

introduced: political, economic and ideological. I do not know how rapidly they were brought about (a question to which I shall return), or by whom, but in the end we have the Sparta which was a unique structure in the Greek world, which the Sparta of the poet Alcman was not. I stress the word *structure* in order to divert attention from the customary over-concentration on certain elements in the system, and on what regularly goes with them in the modern literature, namely, a mystique about Dorians and Dorianism in general and a few largely irrelevant Cretan parallels in particular, the latter, in my judgment, essentially misleading constructs of fourth-century theories or propaganda (in which Carthage also figured, at least for Aristotle, let it be noted).

If the excavations of the shrine of Artemis Orthia were as revealing of the transformation in Sparta as it is sometimes said, we could date the break rather near the year 600 (or several decades later in Boardman's newer chronology).[2] However, apart from the rather problematical disappearance of ivory from the deposits, I do not see that Artemis Orthia provides evidence from which to prove anything. The 'evidence', which it had been rather more fashionable to stress ten or twenty years ago than it is now, turns out to consist of little more than highly subjective judgments about the quality of Laconian pottery in various periods, on which the experts do not agree. Besides, we do not know whether the Spartans ever made this pottery themselves or whether much (or even all) of it was already in the hands of the *perioeci** well before 600, in which case the decline is irrelevant anyway, even if it really could be placed in the middle of the sixth century. On the other hand, if those who believe the ephor Chilon to have been the great reforming 'lawgiver' could be shown to be right, then we should have a firm date about 550, although I cannot imagine how we should then fill out the very long interval between the end of the Second Messenian War and 550. Since all this is largely irrelevant to my subject, I propose to by-pass the chronological puzzles and speak, as a kind of shorthand, of the 'sixth-century revolution'.[3]

Let me elaborate a bit on this 'revolution'. Schematically (and rather inexactly) one may divide the classical Spartan structure into three broad strands:

1. the infrastructure of land allotments, helots and *perioeci*, with everything that includes with respect to labour, production and circulation;

2. the governmental system (including the military);

* Citizens of neighbouring communities who, though free men probably enjoying local self-government, were subject to Sparta in military and foreign affairs.

3. the ritual system: *rites de passage*, the *agoge*, the age-classes, *syssitia*, etc.*

These strands had different origins and a different history; they did not develop and shift *en bloc*; and they did not have the same unchanged functions at all times. The 'sixth-century revolution' was therefore a complex process of some innovation and much modification and re-institutionalization of the elements which appear to have survived 'unchanged'. I use the word 'revolution' even more loosely than is perhaps customary, but I do not use it capriciously. It is loose because I do not for a moment suggest, or believe, that the classical Spartan system was created at one stroke, or even in one reign. After all, the introduction of the hoplite army was one of its necessary conditions, and that must go back early in the seventh century, at least before the Second Messenian War. Helotage in some form was even older. And we must not rule out the possibility that other elements were effectively introduced, or raised to new prominence, as late as the fifth century (as we know certain changes in the army organization to have been). On the other hand, it was not a system that somehow just evolved. Some innovations and modifications had to be introduced at a single stroke (whether one at a time or in combination). The Great Rhetra, for example, reflects something very fundamental of this kind.[4] In a negative way, the prohibition of the use of silver coinage by Spartiates was another obviously sharp decision made by somebody at some moment (and one, incidentally, which more than most can be almost exactly dated to the time of Leon and Agasicles).

By speaking of the 'sixth-century revolution', in sum, I am trying to underscore the necessity for looking at the structure, and not at isolated elements and their antiquity or persistence. I include the whole of the ritual system in this argument, particularly in what I have called rather awkwardly 're-institutionalization', because even if it were the case that the ritual externals were all very old and unaltered (a most unlikely possibility), their function within the new structure was necessarily a new one in significant respects, in effect if not always by deliberate intent. No one will pretend that the whipping ceremony at Artemis Orthia in Roman times, when a great theatre was built for the convenience of the spectators, bore any meaningful connection with the superficially similar rite of

* *Agoge* is a conventional label for the system by which all Spartan boys were brought up by the state. There is good Greek authority for the term; 'education' in the normal modern sense is too narrow a translation.

Syssitia were the dining-groups or mess-companies to which every Spartan male belonged as a necessary condition of full citizenship.

Xenophon's day.[5] *A priori* we must assume the same discontinuity in function between the fifth century and, say, the eighth, and sometimes we have evidence to confirm the assumption, for example, in the case of the *krypteia*, as we shall see shortly.

Classical Sparta may have had an archaic, and even a pre-archaic look about it, but the function of the 'survivals' is what chiefly matters, not the mere fact of survival. Before the reign of Leon and Agasicles, writes Herodotus, the Spartans were the worst governed (*kakonomotatoi*) of all the Greeks; then they switched to good order (*eunomia*). Translation destroys the full sense of the judgment: both *eunomia* and *kakonomos* characterize a whole way of life, not only (or perhaps not at all) a form of constitution.[6] That transformation was the 'sixth-century revolution'.

II

At this stage I want to consider the structure as an ideal type. In what follows, furthermore, I am not much concerned with the accuracy of any individual text. Unless one believes that the picture the Greeks have left us is altogether a fiction, few of the details are of themselves crucial for an apprehension of the ideal type.

I go immediately to the adult male citizens, the *homoioi* as they were frequently called, who are our subject. We must, at the start, take the word in its full connotation–Equals.[7] At birth, if they were permitted to remain alive, all Spartan males were strictly 'equal' with two exceptions: (1) two of them were potential heirs to the kingship; (2) some were richer than others; the rich men (*anthropoi olbioi*) of Herodotus (6.61; 7.134); the wealthy (*plousioi*) of Xenophon (5.3),* who provided wheaten bread for the *syssitia*; or the winners of Olympic chariot-races, of whom there are eleven within my time-limits in Moretti's catalogue, one a king and another the daughter of a king.[8] Being equal meant sharing a common, well defined life-cycle, including:

1. a common, formalized, compulsory upbringing designed to inculcate obedience, valour, discipline and professional military skill;

2. a single vocation or profession, that of a hoplite soldier or officer;

3. economic security and complete freedom from economic concerns, all productive and ancillary services being provided by two distinct categories of dependents, helots and *perioeci*;

* All references in this chapter to Xenophon, unless otherwise indicated, are to his pamphlet which goes under the inaccurate title, *Constitution of Sparta*.

4. a public (rather than private) life in an all-male community, with maximum conformity and anti-individualism.

Structurally, however, the system then generated two further, unavoidable, closely interrelated inequalities apart from those inherent in each child at birth. One was the inequality, not very tangible but none the less real, that followed from inequality of performance, whether in the *agoge* or in games and hunting or in war. The other arose from the need for leadership and élites, not only at the top (kings, ephors and council of elders), but also in the smaller military units, and, because of the Spartan *agoge*, in the age-classes beginning at a remarkably early age. Xenophon's 'love of victory' (*philonikia*) produced losers as well as winners (4.4.), a self-evident fact which is often overlooked by modern scholars, who then write as if everyone passed through every stage a prizewinner.

All this was massively buttressed, psychologically and institutionally. Living in public for so much of their lives, the Spartans were more strongly susceptible than most people to the pressures of public opinion and of the network of rewards and punishments, with its great stress in childhood on corporal punishment, and in adulthood on a rich and imaginative variety of expressions of social disfavour or even ostracism. Everything was harnessed into service, including piety and *rites de passage*. Perhaps the most dramatic example is the transformation of the *krypteia*. This ancient rite of initiation at the age of eighteen became rationalized, that is, re-institutionalized, by being tied to a new police function assigned to an élite youth corps. Significantly, policing the helots was one of their duties.[9]

An important part of the buttressing was negative, so to speak, the reduction to the barest minimum of the disruptive, centrifugal effects of property and the family. We may permit ourselves to be more 'sociological' and less moralistic than Xenophon, for example, in analysing the functions of the Spartan regime of property and family.

Property–extensive comment is unnecessary at this point, though I shall have to return in the next section to the inequality in wealth. The total withdrawal from economic (and not merely banausic) activity, the austerity, the sharing were meant to be cohesive factors, and they were.

Family–a mere enumeration of certain rites and institutions is sufficient to reveal the scale of the effort to transfer allegiance away from the family or kinship group to various male groups: the steps taken to insure procreation, with which Xenophon opens his *Constitution of Sparta*; the right of any father or indeed of any adult

Spartiate to exercise authority over any child; the singularly joyless marriage ceremony with its rare transvestite ritual; the barrack life. The family, in sum, was minimized as a unit of either affection or authority, and replaced by overlapping male groupings – the age-classes, the homosexual pairings between younger and older men (whether 'Platonic' or not), the élite corps, the *syssitia*. Two details are perhaps worth mentioning here, though I shall have to return to them at the end.

1. The age-class system was unusually ramified. I have no precise idea of what its effects were, but at least the complexity greatly increased the occasions for ritual reinforcement.

2. On entry into adulthood, the Spartiate was at least partly divorced from his age-class by the practice of individual co-optation into a *syssition*. Any device which cuts across a 'natural' grouping, whether family or age-class, can be seen as one more way of strengthening the structure as a whole against its individual parts.

So much buttressing was necessary, in part at least, because the Equals turned out, in the end, to be meshed in a complex of inequalities. There were leaders, élites, at all levels, and the primary principles of selection were appointment and cooptation; never, it should be stressed, selection by lot, the standard Greek device for imposing equality. All *homoioi* were eligible in principle and that fact differentiated the Spartan army from those, like the Prussian, which had an officer corps drawn solely from a pre-existing and exclusive élite. The end-result, however, was the same in one respect: there was a chain of command in which the authority-obedience syndrome moved in one direction only, from the top down. To be sure, there were two exceptions in the method of selection: the council of elders and the ephors were elected in open competition. It is a pity that we know virtually nothing about this procedure or about the men elected. Were they usually the same men who had already come out on top through cooptation? That is what I should expect in this society, and I shall come back to the question shortly.

In so far as the success of the system is to be measured by its military successes, the verdict must, of course, be favourable. The Spartan army was better than any other, with more stamina and greater manœuvrability, thanks to superior physical condition, better training and discipline, more obedience. Thought seems to have been given to military organization; at least the not infrequent changes in organization suggest that. On the other hand, there is no evidence of interest in tactics or weaponry beyond the maintenance of both at the best traditional level.

The production and distribution of weapons remain something of a puzzle. I think we can take it that the procurement of metals and the manufacture of arms were the responsibility (and also the privilege) of the *perioeci*. But how did the individual Spartiate obtain his arms and armour? The traditional Greek conception of the hoplite as by definition the citizen (or metic) rich enough to equip himself, does not apply. All Spartiates were 'rich' enough, but none had the proper market mechanism. The choice lies between (a) individual procurement from *perioeci* by payment in kind (or, conceivably, iron spits), and (b) procurement and distribution by the state. I know of no ancient text which gives the answer. Nor does archaeology help in the absence of systematic excavation of any perioecic community. One can argue either way from the shields, all of which were required to have a Lambda inscribed on them, but many (if not all) of which also had a personal blazon. My own preference is for the public supply system, because the other seems insufficiently reliable and because we do have textual evidence that once the army had marched off, the state took responsibility for repair and replacement (as it must have done for the initial procurement even at home when helots were enrolled as hoplites).[10]

III

So much for the ideal type. In actual practice the system was filled with tensions and anomie.

1. To begin with, the Spartan army was not always big enough for its needs–needs which were more cause of the system than consequence. *Perioeci* were an integral part of the hoplite army, and, at least on major occasions such as the Peloponnesian War, substantial numbers of helots and ex-helots (*neodamodeis*) were also enlisted. I have no answer to the very important question of how helots were selected and trained for hoplite fighting (or to any possible connection with the mysterious *mothakes*). Spartans were regularly accompanied by helot orderlies or batmen and there is no particular problem in using such people as light-armed auxiliaries. Hoplite training, however, could not be achieved casually; the essence was movement in formation, and it was for their unique skills at this in particular that the Spartans were commended by ancient writers. That helot and ex-helot hoplites were a serious flaw in the system is self-evident, psychologically as well as in its overt functioning.

2. For Aristotle the greatest vice was financial corruption. Perhaps he was thinking primarily of the changed Sparta of the later fourth century, but bribery is already a major theme in Herodotus.[11] The infrastructure was flawed. The regime of property and inheritance, like the political system, was a compromise. Heavy as the

pressures of austerity and withdrawal from all economic activity may have been, they were insufficient to overcome completely the counter-pressures of inequalities in wealth, or the fears of impoverishment whether through large families or otherwise. The prohibition of business activity (*chrematismos* is Xenophon's carefully chosen word) does not eliminate a desire for–and an ability to employ–wealth, not even if the prohibition can be perfectly enforced. Xenophon's statement (7.6) that the possession of gold and silver was prohibited must be understood, in my opinion, to refer only to coin, as his context implies. But gold and silver have other functions, revealed by Herodotus, perhaps unconsciously, when he employs the good old Homeric word *keimelion* (treasure) in his story (6.62) of how King Ariston acquired his third wife, the mother of Damaratus. Coined money is not essential for exchange, and there were exchanges in Sparta. Even if one were for some reason unwilling to accept the accuracy of Thucydides' inclusion of buying and selling among the activities forbidden to a Spartiate when he suffered loss of civil rights (5.34.2), there is no getting away from the sportsmen Damonon and his son Enymakritidas, who made a dedication to Athena Chalkioikos, probably in the middle of the fifth century B.C., recording twenty or more victories.[12] The text stresses that they won with their own horses and their own chariots, and the latter had to be acquired by the exchange of wealth in some form.

Presumably a sufficient equilibrium could be maintained despite the pressures so long as the Spartans remained safely cocooned within their own world. But not when they were drawn abroad.

3. There was structural tension within and about the leadership. I am not concerned with disagreements over policy which are inevitable whenever there is shared leadership–examples are abundant, as with respect to the situation in Athens after the overthrow of the Pisistratids, or whether to go to war with Athens in 431–but with the tensions inherent in the positions themselves, in the efforts to attain and then to maintain and enhance positions of leadership. We must not allow ourselves to be bemused by the Greek obsession with the 'lawgiver': the sixth-century revolution had to strike some sort of balance among the social elements that were then in existence, and this balance meant failure to institute a unified leadership principle. Hence there were hereditary kings, elected elders and ephors, and appointed leaders at other levels. Again we must not be bemused by a Greek obsession, this time with the 'mixed constitution'. Instead of an equilibrium there was permanent conflict, which could not be cushioned by the self-confidence and stability which are generated, for example, by an exclusive leader-

ship caste. Even the kings, in Aristotle's words, were compelled to court (*demagogein*) the ephors (*Politics* 1270b14).

The leitmotif, I think, was not so much a conflict between kings and ephors, as such, as between men of energy and ambition–the men imbued with excessive 'love of victory', a Lysander as well as a Cleomenes, actual and potential–and the rest. One source of *stasis*, Aristotle noted (*Politics* 1306b31–33), was the dishonourable treatment of men of virtue by others whose virtue was no greater but who had more honour, and the specific example he gave was the treatment of Lysander by the kings. That the kings were a persistently disruptive force of a special kind and magnitude in classical Spartan history needs no demonstration. What deserves notice, however, is that they were potentially disruptive by definition, so to speak, that their very existence was a contradiction of the ideal type of Spartan equality. Cleomenes I, wrote Herodotus (5.39), reigned not because of his own manliness but by heredity. That sums it up. Given the psychological underpinning of being born to high office and the various charismatic practices and institutions attached to Spartan kingship–Herodotus knew what he was saying when he called the royal funeral rites 'barbarian'–it depended solely on the personality of the individual king whether he was a force for civic peace or for strife, or no force at all.

The hereditary principle also injected the family into the picture, again in violation of the Spartan ideal. The various recorded manœuvres on behalf of younger sons and other kin of kings, including the classic employment of allegations of illegitimacy, belong to the courts of tyrants and barbarian monarchs, not to a Greek *polis*. It then becomes necessary to consider whether kinship did not also play some part in the leadership struggles outside the kingship. I have already said that it is my guess that the men chosen for the council of elders, the ephorate and the magistracies were those who had earlier come out on top through the appointment procedures. All *homoioi* were, in a formal sense, equally eligible. But were they in practice? Who, then, were the men whom Herodotus called 'among the first by birth' (7.134); and what did Aristotle mean when he said that election to the council was 'oligarchical' (*dynasteutikos*, which implies manipulation as well), whereas everyone was eligible for the ephorate (*Politics* 1306a18, 1294b29–31)? It is true that such texts are very rare: the more common reference is to individuals being or wishing to be 'first' or 'among the most powerful', which need mean nothing more than to achieve leadership by their own efforts. But the few texts remain, and they say what we should have guessed without them, namely, that there were families who were able to influence the appointment procedures in favour of their own members, beginning at the first opportunity, among the children. That means, in effect, that there developed an element of hereditary aristocracy within the system, far from closed, but not without considerable influence nevertheless. And I have no doubt that wealth played its part here (as Herodotus 7.134 implies). There were others, in sum, besides Cleomenes who achieved positions, lower or higher in the ranking, by birth rather than by manliness.

Inevitably when there is struggle for leadership, disagreements over policy reflect calculations of personal advantage in the struggle alongside, and confused with, calculations about the desirability of a proposed policy as such. Sometimes these differences were brought before the people in assembly, and that raises one further question respecting equals and unequals. The time has long passed when any serious historian or political scientist thinks in nineteenth-century liberal terms about voting behaviour, with its image of the 'reasonable man' weighing the issues 'rationally' and free from all prejudices, pressures and emotions. It is nevertheless legitimate to ask whether there was something in the Spartan structure which makes the 'reasonable man' approach even less applicable, even more of a caricature, than, say, for the Athenian assembly. I will put the question very bluntly. Can we imagine that the obedient, disciplined Spartan soldier dropped his normal habits on those occasions when he was assembled not as a soldier but as a citizen, while he listened to debates among those from whom he otherwise was taught to take orders without questioning or hesitation?[13] I do not think we have any evidence from which to answer concretely, but my guess is that the Spartan assembly was much closer to the Homeric than to the Athenian in function and psychology. Archidamus and Sthenelaidas harangued each other before the assembled people as Agamemnon and Achilles did. That is not open discussion. But neither is it mere puppetry: when the leadership divided over policy, someone had to make the decision, and that was the people in assembly.[14]

4. There was too much social mobility in both directions, too much, that is, for a society which in principle was completely closed and rigid, and which therefore lacked the mechanism (and the psychology) necessary to adjust the mobile elements properly in their new statuses:

(a) There were Spartiates who lost status, yet somehow remained within the community in a curiously inferior position (as distinct from exiles). These were not always economic failures (men who could not maintain their *syssition* quotas); a depreciation in status could also follow from failure at some stage in the *agoge*, failure in battle, loss of civic rights, or the like.

(b) There were helots who rose in status, many even achieving membership in the *damos*, the citizenry (for that is what *neodamodeis* has to mean, whatever inferior shading it may imply).

I am frankly unable to visualize these people, how they lived or even, in many cases, where they lived. The helots who fought under Brasidas, says Thucydides (5.34.1), were first given permission to reside where they wished, but then they were settled with the *neodamodeis* at Lepreon on the Elean border to help serve as buffers against the hostile Eleans. Neither Thucydides nor anyone else explains what it meant in practice to be 'settled' or to reside where they wished, or where and how the degraded Spartiates lived. That all these groups were an undigested lump within the system is self-evident; the Spartan prisoners who had surrendered to the Athenians at Sphacteria were on their release treated as such by the regime, too, simply because they could anticipate loss of civic rights. Interestingly enough, this particular group came from the first families.[15]

Yet it must be recorded that neither separately nor together were the misplaced elements able to destroy the system directly. We are told of only one actual attempt, and that a failure, the abortive revolt led by Cinadon in 397 B.C. Several aspects of that revolt are neatly symbolic. Cinadon himself had been employed by the ephors on secret missions. Aristotle (*Politics* 1306b34) described him as 'manly' (*androdes*), and it would be nice to know whether Aristotle had any more information than we have on which to base that perhaps surprising adjective. When asked why he had conspired, Cinadon's reply was, 'In order to be inferior to no one in Sparta' (Xenophon, *Hellenica* 3.3.11). Appropriately, the chief agents in suppressing the revolt before it started were drawn from the élite youth corps.

5. For the sake of completeness, I record without discussion two further sources of tension: (a) the women, if Plato and Aristotle are to be believed; and (b) experience abroad.

IV

I have said very little so far about war or warriors. The paradox is that militarism in Sparta was in a low key. Among the more than 100,000 lead figurines found in the ruins of Artemis Orthia, neither soldiers nor arms are particularly prominent (though they exist). There were no war games, no warrior-graves. The latter disappeared abruptly throughout the Greek world, save for strikingly few exceptions on the fringes, more or less at the same time as the appearance of the hoplite, that is, with the extension of the military role from the 'heroic' aristocrat to a broader sector of the population. Sparta was no exception. Sparta seems not even to have included removal from the army among the punishments for military disgrace. At least that is the implication in Herodotus' story (7.229–31 + 9.71) about Aristodamos, the survivor of Thermopylae who was permitted to die a glorious death (though officially not recognized as such) at Plataea. And the men who surrendered at Sphacteria, temporarily deprived of civic rights though they were, soon found their rights restored. There is also no trace of the 'war habit' characteristic, for example, of the Assyrians, the tendency to go out and fight simply because that is what warriors are for. After the Second Messenian War and the sixth-century revolution, Sparta was, if anything, less quick to join battle than many other Greek states. The Corinthians were not wrong when, in Thucydides' account in his first book, they made a special point of that.[16]

If we look on the whole of Laconia and Messenia as a unit, then of course there was a pyramidal social structure with the Spartiates as a military élite at the top. However, it was not a military élite in the sense of the Prussian Junkers or even of the Theban Sacred Band. Instead we must think of a (conceptually) closed system as a whole, which had a military function but not a wholly militaristic stamp. I am using these words as they are distinguished by Alfred Vagts: 'The military way is marked by a primary concentration of men and materials on winning specific objectives of power with the utmost efficiency. . . . Militarism, on the other hand, presents a vast array of customs, interests, prestige, actions and thought associated with armies and wars and yet transcending true military purposes.' In a sense both are of course visible in Sparta, but a further quotation from Vagts's book will show why I said 'not a wholly militaristic stamp'. Vagts continues: 'An army so built that it serves military men, not war, is militaristic; so is everything in any army which is not preparation for fighting, but merely exists for diversion or to satisfy peace-time whims like the long anachronistic cavalry today . . . enterprises for sheer glory or the reputation of leaders, which reduce the fighting strength of armies and wreck them from within, come under that head.'[17]

That may conceivably describe a Cleomenes I, for example, but he was rejected. It is not until the fourth century B.C. that the refrain becomes insistent in Greek writers that the Spartan state was like an army camp;[18] that the sole aim of the lawgiver was war; that in consequence Spartans were too underdeveloped in all other human aspects (or, contrariwise, that they were praised for precisely those narrow qualities which Plato and Aristotle condemned); that, in sum, they were not only efficiently military but also excessively militaristic. All this is well known and requires no elaboration. But it is not unnecessary or out of place to say that this was not the whole picture even in fourth-century writers. Why did Plato, who criticized Sparta so brutally in the eighth book of the *Republic* (547D–549A), not simply dismiss her? Why did he instead select a Spartan to be one of the trio who were to set up the new state of the *Laws*?

The answer, of course, is that for Plato Sparta had much to offer despite her one-sidedness, not in her laws or institutions narrowly conceived (which are hardly reflected in Plato's book) but in her fundamental conception of a total community, in her *eunomia* as a way of life, one which he wished to strip of its militaristic side (but not of its military function). Sparta had long been a bulwark against tyranny, after all, both at home and abroad; that may not be very true, especially not about Sparta's activities abroad, but it was firmly believed to be true by many Greeks, and it was repeated *ad nauseam*. Pindar believed it. There are not many references to Sparta in Pindar's surviving poems, but they are more significant than their rarity might imply precisely because they are all gratuitous. Pindar wrote no odes for Spartan victors and he did not have to drag Sparta in at all. In the *First Pythian*, celebrating a victory by Hiero I of Syracuse, the poet comments in these words on Hiero's new foundation at Etna (lines 61–70):

> that city in liberty built
> of gods, and ordinances of Hyllos' rule, and the
> descendants of Pamphylos,
> those, too, of Heracles' seed,
> who dwell beside Taygetos' slopes, are minded to abide
> for ever in the decrees of Aigimios,
> Dorians. . . .
> By your [Zeus's] aid, this leader of men,
> enjoining it upon his son also, might glorify his people
> and turn them to peace and harmony.[19]

Some quite remarkable nonsense has been, and is still being, written about those lines. The absurd suggestion is offered that Hiero, following a brutal expulsion of population of the type so familiar in Sicilian history, actually planned to introduce the Spartan constitution and *agoge* at Etna under the kingship of his son Deinomenes.[20] If it is not obvious that all Pindar had in mind was a traditional royal and aristocratic set-up, in which the people would find its freedom in discipline, piety and honourable rule by their betters, then Edouard Will has settled the point by drawing attention to the remarkably parallel lines in a fragment about Aegina.[21] If there was anything political, in the narrow sense, in Pindar's mind, then it was to whisper a reminder of Sparta's anti-tyrant tradition. There is never anything more in Pindar, never a suggestion that Sparta was somehow peculiar or unique; in particular, not that Sparta was militaristic in a way that set it apart from the states and the aristocracies of the old school in which the values he accepted were to be found.

> There they surpass in counsels of elders,
> And in the spears of young men,
> And in choirs, and the Muse, and Glory.[22]

That was sung about Sparta in another fragment; it could as well have been used for Thebes, Thessaly, Aegina or Cyrene, or even for the kind of Athens that Miltiades and Cimon stood for in his eyes.

Nor is the picture in Herodotus very different on the essential question. Given his subject-matter, Herodotus was bound to stress the military skill of the Spartans and their unfailing obedience to the rule never to retreat in battle. Being Herodotus, he was also bound to dwell on certain oddities, such as the honours and rituals surrounding the kings or the penalties meted out to cowards. Herodotus was alert to, and often very subtle about, nuances differentiating Greek states from one another. But that was still some way from the altogether odd Sparta of the fourth-century mirage. For him the Greek world was divided into two kinds of communities, those ruled by tyrants, which were a bad thing, and those ruled by themselves. The latter in turn were either fully democratic or they were not, and Sparta was the most important, the most powerful and the most interesting of those which were not.

I have gone on at some length about the way in which Sparta was classed with a whole category of Greek *poleis* because it is essential to be clear on what was really different and unique about Sparta. At the beginning I made the point that we must not think of the various strands in the Spartan structure as monolithic in their history and movement. If we look at these elements again, this time from the point of view of their uniqueness or familiarity, we find the following (details apart):

1. Helotage was not altogether rare; it was found in Thessaly, in Crete, in Sicily, and probably throughout the Danubian and Black Sea areas of Greek settlement.*

* I do not ignore the probability that the proportion, and therefore the potential menace, of helots to citizens was greater in Sparta than elsewhere, as will be evident shortly.

2. The Spartan governmental machinery had its peculiarities to be sure, but not a single feature of significance other than the kings that can legitimately be called unique among the Greeks.

3. Every Greek community had its *rites de passage*—at birth, on entering adulthood, at marriage, at death. The variations were endless, and, looked at in isolation, the only things that stand out about the Spartan rites were their perhaps greater frequency and their apparently greater stress on physical punishment and brutality.

4. There is absolutely nothing to my knowledge in Spartan cults or cult practices deserving of notice in our context.

5. Not even the *syssitia* or the age-classes were of themselves unique.

This last point requires elaboration. Some form of table fellowship can be found in all human societies. The association of *syssitia* with age-classes is specifically attested in several Greek communities, and there is every reason to suspect that our information is fragmentary and incomplete. Age-classes, in turn, are common under a great diversity of circumstances. Armies regularly employ them whenever there is conscription, both for the initial training and for call-up when their services are required. On the other hand, there was a proliferation of societies of the youths in Hellenistic and Roman times, precisely the period when they had lost all military function and turned instead to the gymnasium and the palaestra.[23] Love of victory could take a sporting form just as well as a military—as Pindar bears witness.

What was unique about Sparta was the way all these elements were combined into a coherent structure, and the pivotal organizing mechanism, the *agoge*. I must insist that there is nothing inherent in age-classes which has to end in the Spartan *agoge*, or even in its ethos of obedience and self-effacement before the interests of the state. There is no self-evident reason why an organizational division into young and old should evolve into the complexity of the Spartan age-class system. It is the complexity and the function that are unique in Sparta, not the division into confraternities of the old and the young. Nor is there any inherent reason why helotage should have led precisely to the Spartan system; and so on through each of the elements. But when the system finally emerged, each element was re-institutionalized in a process that never quite came to an end. And the *agoge* was invented. That last is a pure speculation, of course, but of all the elements in Sparta the *agoge* is the one of which it is most impossible to find traces in our earliest Greek record or traditions, the one which alone 'makes' the Spartan system, so to speak. Therefore I am driven to the inference that, as a pattern of life for the young and as an attempt to fix the individual Spartan's behaviour and ideology for a lifetime, the *agoge* was a late invention, however old some of the initiation rites and other external aspects of it may have been. It was the *agoge*, finally, and the *eunomia* it was held responsible for, which in the end caught the Greek fancy and lay at the heart of the Spartan mirage. 'One of the finest of your laws', said Plato's Athenian (*Laws* 634D), 'is the one absolutely prohibiting any of the young men from inquiring whether any of the laws is good nor not.'

The one phenomenon which remains a complete puzzle is the survival of kingship, worse still, of a dual kingship. I have no explanation to put forward, but I will suggest that 'survival' may not be the precisely correct word. What do we know about Spartan kings or kingship between the legendary Menelaus and Leon (or Cleomenes I for that matter)? Genealogies and stories told by Plutarch add up to very little history. Prerogatives in sacrifice and the like were commonplace in Greece whenever anyone exercised the priestly function, whatever his title; guards of honour are so obvious that they can, and have been, thought up time and again in history; double rations in the *syssitia* are really not the same as the Homeric prerogatives, no matter how often they are said to be; and above all, the funeral rites–which Herodotus found to be the most striking thing of all about the Spartan kings–cannot be survivals in any sense, since we know of no precedent in the Greek tradition, nor did Herodotus, who called them 'barbarian'. It is at least a defensible hypothesis that the Spartan kingship in the institutional form that we know was as much, or more, a product of the sixth-century revolution, stimulated by the failures of the Second Messenian War, as of inertia, which, in the absence of an explanation, we have the habit of calling 'survival'.

There remains, finally, to look at one other unusual feature of Sparta. No other Greek state was a territorial state like her, in which *polis* and territory were not synonymous, so to speak (as they were between Athens and Attica); in which the *polis*, at least ideally, consisted of a single class of Equals ruling over a relatively vast subject population. The Second Messenian War was decisive in this respect, too. Thereafter the military function became primarily a police function, aimed against an enemy within rather than at enemies real or potential without. To preserve the difficult position of a ruling class in those special circumstances, the whole society was structured to fulfil the police function. Even the efforts expended to found and maintain the Peloponnesian League, though they required repeated warfare, may be accurately described as part of the police function. Sparta's tragedy thereafter stemmed from a familiar cause: she did not live in a vacuum. The Persian invasions foreshadowed what was to come in the Peloponnesian War. Against her will almost, Sparta was drawn into extensive military activity, genuinely military. That entailed severe pressure on manpower and a dangerously extensive incorporation of non-equals into the army if not into the ruling class, unprecedented opportunities for ambitious individuals, extensive travel abroad and a breach in the traditional xenophobia, the impossibility of holding the line against the seductions of wealth. The system could not and did not long survive. And so the final paradox is that her greatest military success destroyed the model military state.

II

UTOPIANISM ANCIENT AND MODERN*

I

EVER since Thomas More gave the world the word Utopia early in the sixteenth century, a semantic cluster has grown round it, or perhaps I should say a spectrum of meanings, of great range and complexity, and of no little confusion. I shall not attempt a formal definition, but a certain amount of narrowing of the field of discourse is an unavoidable preliminary. To begin with, there is an inherent pun in the word itself, which is normally and mistakenly overlooked. The initial letter 'u' stands for the Greek *ou* ('no', 'not') and hence Utopia is Nowhere. But by the exercise of a little imagination the 'u' can also stand for the Greek prefix *eu* ('good', 'well') and then we get 'good place', 'ideal place'. That this alternative is not wholly fanciful is proved by two lines of the 'Meter of IV Verses in the Utopian Tongue' appended to More's work, which read, in the sixteenth-century English translation: 'Wherfore not Utopie, but rather rightely / My name is Eutopie: a place of felicitie.'

All Utopian thinking has an element of fantasy, of dreaming, or at least of yearning, for a better life and a better world. And all men dream in this way, about themselves and their families if not about society in general or the world at large. A poem by Cercidas of Megalopolis, at the end of the third century B.C., begins, 'I blame Zeus because he did not turn that fellow Xenon who is packed with malice and a mass of incontinence, into a child of poverty, thereby giving *us* a flood of silver that now runs to waste.' Then he goes on to

* Originally presented to the Congressus Internationalis Antiquitas Graeco-Romana ac Tempora Nostra in Brno on 14 April 1966, this essay was then published, in a much enlarged and revised version, in *The Critical Spirit. Essays in Honor of Herbert Marcuse*, ed. K. H. Wolff and B. Moore, Jr. (Boston 1967) pp. 3–20. I have made a few further revisions now, chiefly to take note of discussions the essay has stimulated. I am grateful to W. K. C. Guthrie, Jan Pečírka, J.-P. Vernant and Pierre Vidal-Naquet for criticisms and suggestions.

Copyright © 1967 by Beacon Press, and reprinted with their permission.

a generalized lamentation, 'To what sort of sovereign, then, or to which of the sons of Heaven, can one turn in order to discover how to get one's desert–when the Son of Cronos, who begat us all and gave us all birth, shows himself a mere stepfather to some and a real father to others?'[1]

Cercidas was a Cynic philosopher, but that fact is not relevant in the present context. Such sentiments decrying one aspect of the human condition could have been expressed, and have been, by millions of despairing individuals in many different societies. They are only one step removed from the imprecatory lead tablets (*tabellae defixionum*) buried in the ground by Athenian peasants in the fourth century B.C., calling upon various demons and evil spirits to destroy a neighbour's crops and render his flocks sterile, and his wife, too. One further step carries us to the fantasies and projects characteristic of the opium or hashish addict or of the victim of schizophrenia or paranoia. Frank Manuel has pointed out that the *Description of a New World, Called the Blazing World*, by Margaret Cavendish, Duchess of Newcastle, published in 1666, 'has much in common with the delusions of Dr. Schreber which Sigmund Freud analysed in a famous paper'.[2] We must not be too quick to rule all this out as irrelevant. Let us remember that Fourier also had schemes for heating the North Pole and sweetening the ocean which are not really distinguishable from the projects of a paranoiac–and Fourier was an influential 'Utopian socialist'.[3] Let us also remember that in ordinary speech 'utopian' has not only a positive connotation but even more commonly a negative, pejorative one: 'impractical', therefore useless and even dangerous because it diverts attention and effort from the realizable.

Yet, for purposes of the present analysis, we must divide the spectrum at some point, and the obvious step is to draw the distinction formulated by Northrop Frye: '. . . we should expect to find that the more penetrating the utopian writer's mind is, the more clearly he understands that he is communicating a vision to his readers, not sharing a power or fantasy dream with them', a vision that derives from 'an analysis of the writer's present society'.[4] That element of analysis, of criticism, is what brings the important Utopias back from Nowhere to reality in a way that the purely private, not to mention the lunatic, fantasies do not. That is what makes them a worthy subject of historical analysis, as distinct from a purely Freudian or other analysis proper to individual psychology. Much as the two kinds of analysis may overlap, the distinction remains valid and fundamental.

We are largely restricted to literary formulations, and we run a risk thereby. Ancient writers, virtually without exception, reflect the views and sentiments and prejudices of the educated classes, which means the upper classes. So do most writers throughout modern history. An awareness of that familiar bias does not get us very far in trying to reconstruct what the submerged classes thought, but it should warn us against the common intellectualist fallacy of seeking some particular book behind every popular idea or popular action. The way in which scholars persistently took it for granted that a book by Iambulus provided the inspiration for the Sun State of the followers of Aristonicus in Asia Minor towards the end of the second century B.C. is perhaps the best example of this fallacy at work in the study of ancient history, as we shall soon see.

By 'Utopian writer' I do not wish to restrict myself to the formal constructors of Utopias (although the emergence of that particular kind of writing in different historical periods is itself an important aspect of the whole question). One must look at the Phaeacian section of the *Odyssey* as well as at Plato's *Republic* or at Iambulus. There is an unfortunate convention among historians of Graeco-Roman antiquity to throw much of this writing into the loose category of the 'novel', and by implication (or sometimes explicitly) to denigrate it as something second-rate, not really deserving the same serious attention as something else called 'philosophy'.[5] Of course there is a valid distinction, and of course Iambulus was no Plato, but just as a modern novelist may be a better analyst and a more profound critic of his society, so the possibility cannot be rejected *a priori* that even an Iambulus may in some respects teach us as much about ancient society as a Plato.

Utopian ideas and fantasies, like all ideas and fantasies, grow out of the society to which they are a response. Neither the ancient world nor the modern world is an unchanging entity, and any analysis of Utopian thinking which neglects social changes in the course of the history of either antiquity or modern times is likely at some point to go badly wrong. Nevertheless, a conceptual analysis which treats all western Utopian thought *en bloc* to begin with, may be useful. This is what I shall do in much of my essay, moving freely in time and in both directions, accepting the risk for the moment of being over-schematic and unhistorical. Before I have finished, I hope to bring the analysis back to a proper historical one.

II

The very word Utopia suggests that the ideal society is not actually or wholly attainable. Nevertheless, every significant Utopia is conceived as a goal towards which one may legitimately and hopefully strive, a goal not in some shadowy state of perfection but with specific institutional criticisms and proposals. Utopia transcends the given social reality; it is not transcendental in a metaphysical sense. All this sets the social Utopias apart from the Garden of Eden, under which I subsume the various primitivistic images, whether the perfect, simple, innocent society is located in the distant past, in a Golden Age, or in a far-off place.[6]

There is a sense in which a Garden of Eden shares a quality of criticism with Utopia, specifically in the idea, explicit or implicit, that a world without evil is not even conceivable, let alone possible, so long as the two chief roots of evil are present, namely, strife over wealth and property and strife arising from sexual drives. But such primitivistic dreams immediately depart from social Utopias in their fabulous, magical quality. 'The golden race', says Hesiod in his *Works and Days* (lines 116–18), 'had all good things; for the fruitful earth unforced bare them fruit abundantly and without toil.' In the Garden of Eden fantasies, animals are well-behaved and kindly, men live far beyond the mortal span, disease is unknown, so that wealth and sexual rivalry and strife of every kind automatically disappear because they are utterly meaningless and pointless. Innocence becomes the only quality of life. Nature takes care of everything.

Understandably human as all this is, it cannot serve either as a goal or as a paradigm. Nor was it meant to. One need only compare Hesiod's account of the Golden Age with his prescriptions for the Iron Age. There is no escape from the latter; the sole hope is to toil and to be honest and thus, with the help of the gods, one may ease one's burdens. No more. There is not a whisper in Hesiod of a way by which to change or transcend the present state, to re-approach the Golden Age. The Golden Age is firmly located in myth and in mythical time. It serves to define the Iron Age by its opposite, to define and in a sense to explain the evil that man is eternally doomed to live with, above all, to die. The question posed at the very beginning of the *Works and Days* is just that, Why is the world so full of evil? The first answer is traditional, the myths of Prometheus and Pandora. Hesiod tells them very briefly and then continues, without a pause, 'I will sum up to you another tale', the tale of the ages ('races', strictly) of man.[7]

In one important respect, of course, I should not have used 'Garden of Eden' as the generic term. In Judaeo-Christian religious thinking the myth of the Golden Age was tied to life on earth in a new way; myth and history, mythical time and historical time met together. The notion became central that some men can look forward to a return to the Golden Age, to the Last Judgment and the Resurrection. That will come about by act of grace and not by social action, and it will be a Golden Age only for the elect. One may prepare for it, but only ritually or by martyrdom and not by changing society. Hence not even within this conceptual framework is the Golden Age a Utopia. The history of Christianity has produced examples enough of men and movements who insisted that social reform and Utopianism are irrelevant and even misleading. It has also produced impatient men and movements, unwilling to wait for ever for the final triumph, and to these I shall return shortly.

The Graeco-Roman world never achieved a successful image of the Kingdom of Heaven, and therefore the Greeks and Romans were not faced with either the prospects or the alternatives available to the Christian. Some of the philosophical schools provide a thin analogy: when the early Cynics, for example, argued that everything external to man's inner virtue is irrelevant, they rejected social reform, and *a fortiori* Utopianism, in a way that is reminiscent of certain Christian thinkers. Crates of Thebes, in the late fourth century B.C., wrote a poem to the 'city Pera' which is 'fair, fruitful, squalid, owning nought' and over which men do not go to war.[8] (*Pera* is the Greek word for a leather food-pouch.) But for the bulk of the population there was little consolation in doctrines which demanded unrelenting austerity, self-restraint and self-discipline without the reward of eternal salvation. Private fantasies and magical practices flourished; at least on earth one could both dream and try to help oneself privately in mundane matters. Examples could already be found in Homer which they all knew by heart. In the *Odyssey* Phaeacia has Utopian overtones–it exists in isolation, it is luxuriously rich, it offers boundless hospitality–but it is also fabulous: the Phaeacians are the ideal seafarers, for they 'have no pilots and no rudders . . .; but [the ships] themselves understand the thoughts and intents of men' (8.557–59).

Not even the later Utopian writers could all escape these pulls. Both Euhemerus slightly and Iambulus rather massively mixed the fabulous with the critical. Euhemerus, writing about 300 B.C., described a Sacred Isle in which spices grew virtually without human effort and in which a single plant, the *poliuros*, sufficed for food, drink and medicine. Iambulus, whose date is unknown though it must fall somewhere between Alexander and Augustus, visited an island in the Indian Ocean where men had rubbery bones as well as forked tongues which permitted them to carry on two conversations simultaneously, and where they lived to the age of 150 without illness, when they lay down and slept eternally. At the end,

Iambulus concedes that it is all a fable: after a stay of seven years, he says, he and his companions were expelled as 'evildoers'.[9]

For all the criticism implicit in the social and political arrangements, we are nevertheless in Cloudcuckooland, as the satirists were quick to point out. We are back to personal fantasies dressed in community form. They were common fantasies in antiquity, judging from the proverbial contexts in which the phrase 'life under Cronos' (or 'under Saturn' in the Roman equivalent) recurs in the literature.[10] Even the educated enjoyed them. Herodotus is a quarry of relevant tales, intermixed with his Scythians and Amazons and Hyperboreans. Alexander's campaign in India produced a new outcropping (as did the great explorations at the beginning of the modern era). Euhemerus even borrowed the idea of a priestly caste from India and introduced it into his social structure, a very strange idea indeed for a Greek Utopia. But the only expression of these dreams in action known to me was in the Saturnalian type of festival, widely spread in Greece as well as in Rome, under various names including the Cronia, when the slaves sat at table and their masters waited on them.[11] Nothing, I suggest, could more perfectly symbolize the fantasy aspect, the reduction of the element of genuine criticism to an Aristophanic joke. The joke became a cruel one when late Roman emperors proclaimed their reigns as a Golden Age, when the court poet Claudian in A.D. 396 predicted (*In Rufinum* 1.372–87) the glories of a reign about to begin, employing language consciously reminiscent of the Sibyl, who had written: 'For the all-bearing earth will give her best fruit without end to mortals, bread, wine and wild olive. . . . And streams will flow with sweet white milk, and cities will be full of goods and the fields will be fat; nor will there be swords nor the din of battle on the face of the earth. . . .'[12] Claudian and his imperial patrons, like Virgil before him, were trading on – I should even say mocking – the traditional dream-fantasies of the oppressed.[13]

One specific situation within the Graeco-Roman orbit seems to have been exceptional and it is interesting enough to warrant a digression. I refer to the Heliopolis, the Sun-State to which a certain Aristonicus summoned the slaves and oppressed poor of Asia Minor in 132 or 131 B.C. The background is as follows. In 133, King Attalus III of Pergamum bequeathed his kingdom to Rome in his will. Aristonicus, a bastard member of the royal family, challenged the bequest, laid claim to the throne, and started a civil war. When the normal methods of usurpation proved unsuccessful, he turned as a last resort to the slaves and half-free peasants, promising them the Sun-State. The movement was crushed, with no little difficulty, by the Romans, the kings of Bithynia and Cappadocia, and the Greek cities of Asia Minor acting in concert against a common threat. Our sources, which are very brief anyway, concentrate on the military side of the uprising. They tell us absolutely nothing about Aristonicus' promises, apart from emancipation from bondage, and only once is there a mention of the Sun-State. 'Going into the interior,' writes the geographer Strabo (14.1.38), 'he quickly assembled a multitude of poor men and slaves, whom he won over by a promise of freedom and whom he called Heliopolitans.' That statement, which I have quoted in full, is not exactly informative. Yet that, together with the additional fact that Aristonicus was joined by the Stoic philosopher, Blossius of Cumae, the former mentor of the Gracchi, is the sole basis for the once common assumption that Aristonicus proposed to introduce in real life in Asia Minor the social and political regime projected by the Utopian writer Iambulus, who said of his islanders that above all other gods they honour the sun, 'after whom they name both the islands and themselves'.[14]

It has in recent years been demonstrated that the supposed connection between Aristonicus and Iambulus, a modern idea not mentioned in any existing ancient source, is without foundation.[15] Nevertheless, Strabo's reference to the Sun-State, for all its emptiness, is unlikely to be something he invented and therefore some explanation is required. It is just possible that both Iambulus and Aristonicus shared a common tradition in one respect, and that is my reason for this digression. There was nothing in the inherited Greek myths or rituals to warrant the patronage of the very insignificant sun-god Helios. But there is evidence of a long-standing link in Near Eastern religions between the divine sun and justice, and in Asia Minor in the second century B.C. there was a strong infusion of Near Eastern religions, especially among the slaves and lower classes. I am therefore tempted to wonder whether there is not a parallel here, in the link between a kind of Messianism and social revolution, in particular with the millenarian or chiliastic movements that emerged in Europe during the later Middle Ages and again in the nineteenth century.[16] These were movements which took seriously the Christian promise that one day the two streams, the mythical and the earthly, would come together in the final triumph of justice. Salvation, the return to the Garden of Eden, was declared by prophetic voices to be at hand.

If my guess about the Sun-State of Aristonicus should prove to have merit–and I know of no evidence from which to test it–it would take us outside the Graeco-Roman orbit for all meaningful purposes. The other slave and peasant revolts of antiquity were neither salvationist nor Utopian. Their aims were to obtain freedom for themselves at the minimum, to turn the social relations upside down at the maximum; to turn themselves into masters and their former masters into slaves, but not to alter the fundamental structure of society. In so far as religion played a role it was purely ancillary, for example, to give the leader a charisma, which has nothing to do with bringing about a return to Paradise or a Golden Age.[17] Millenarian movements, by contrast, are not only salvationist in the religious sense; they are also wholly vague about their social aims, about the structure of the society to be achieved or even about how it is to be brought about. 'The movement', Kaminsky has pointed out, 'always subscribes to an ideology that empties the existing social order of all value; it also invariably takes the form of a physical movement–a withdrawal from the existing order. Thus on the one hand its ideology is arbitrary, extravagant, and fantastic; on the other hand its social structure is all but non-existent: it is a perfectly plastic mass, without the solidity that comes from a practical, working relationship with reality.'[18] These are the responses of 'pre-political people', in Eric Hobsbawm's phrase. Like all Garden of Eden conceptions, millenarian visions must in a strict analysis be distinguished from Utopia. The latter may be Nowhere, it may be extravagant and unattainable, but its protagonists are decidedly neither pre-political nor without 'a practical, working relationship with reality'.

III

As a framework for the analysis of Utopia, I suggest two antithetical pairs of elements, which may also serve as a kind of definition by specification. The first antithesis is between a static and a dynamic Utopia, or, phrased differently, between an ascetic and a want-satisfying Utopia. The second antithesis is between an egalitarian and a hierarchical Utopia.

Since Utopia belongs to the realm of the real world, not of myth, it can never, strictly speaking, start from the natural sufficiency of goods which characterizes the Garden of Eden. There the sheer abundance, always renewed and never exhausted, eliminates greed, gluttony, licentiousness, and the conflicts they generate. The real world, in contrast, had long been faced not by abundance but by an absolute insufficiency of resources. My first antithesis then divides neatly into two chronological periods separated by the Industrial Revolution. Ancient or early modern Utopias had perforce to accept scarcity of goods as a datum, and therefore to stress simplicity, the curbing of wants, asceticism, and a static society. Then came the release of new sources of energy and with it a flood of technological Utopian imagination, from Condorcet and Fourier through Jules Verne to H. G. Wells. They grasped that for the first time in history the technical possibilities had been created for a new kind of Utopia, one in which abundance replaced scarcity, in which human and social possibilities had taken a leap forward to something previously unthinkable outside the world of myth.

The new possibilities also created new doubts. Not all nineteenth-century Utopians shared the new dynamic, want-satisfying vision. There was concurrently an ascetic trend, to be seen in the Owenite and Fourierist colonies in the United States, in Thoreau and in William Morris. There were now, in other words, alternative and conflicting proposals growing out of the examination and critique of industrial society. Earlier these choices simply did not exist. As Hexter has said of More's *Utopia*, 'The Utopian economy does not justify itself as modern economies do by claiming to give men in the fullest measure the things they want. . . . The justification for the Utopian system in all its aspects, economic and other, is that it provides all men with what they need in the measure that they need it; and while men ought to have what they need, they certainly do not need and ought not to have in full, or any other measure, whatever they happen to want.'[19] Modern critics of excessive materialism may say that, too, but Thomas More and his predecessors had to say it, unless they wished to flee to Cloudcuckooland. Even some of the fabulous Utopians, such as Iambulus, writing in a more sophisticated climate than that of Hesiod and with something of a background of philosophical inquiry in the intellectual atmosphere, introduced a very considerable ascetic element. His case is especially interesting because he admitted that in his island material conditions did not require this. The restrictions on, and controls of, the diet which he proposed, for example, constituted a consciously disciplinary device; they performed a moral function, not an economic or hygienic one.

The matter of moral discipline and reform is implicit in the phrase I have just quoted about Thomas More–men 'certainly do not need and ought not to have . . . whatever they happen to want'. All social Utopias base themselves on some more-or-less radical social changes –in the property regime, with respect to trade, and so on–but then even the static, ascetic ones begin to diverge on the extent to which these social changes would be sufficient in themselves to produce moral behaviour (and not merely necessary conditions). The so-called 'communist colonies' of the nineteenth century tended to the rather Arcadian view that on the whole the quiet, non-competitive life would bring about the desired moral transformation. The model of the monastery comes to mind. At the other extreme there is of course Plato, for whom even his very radical social reorganization would accomplish little or nothing without the elaborate educational programme and who believed that the whole moulding process would have to be repeated in every generation in order to hold the Republic intact. In his own way, Thomas More was on Plato's side on this question, but they then broke sharply on my second antithesis: the one constructed an almost completely egalitarian Utopia, the other a strictly hierarchical one.

IV

In antiquity it is hard to find any Utopian thinking which is not hierarchical.[20] 'It was easier', wrote Mumford, 'for these Greek utopians to conceive of abolishing marriage or private property than of ridding utopia of slavery, class domination and war.'[21] This is sharply underscored by the ancient satirists of Utopia: witness Aristophanes in the *Ecclesiazusae*. That play ends in a comic riot ridiculing the sexual ideas of the Utopians (which, it should be stressed, does not deprive the criticism of its seriousness), but the heart of the attack lies in nine words in the Greek (lines 651–52): Question–Who then will till the soil? Answer–The slaves. The interchange goes on to develop a number of half-serious and half-ridiculous corollaries but we need not pursue it further.

It is a pity that we are so ill-informed about the men and ideas who were the butt of Aristophanes and the other comic writers of his day,[22] or about their successors. Phaleas of Chalcedon and Hippodamus of Miletus are known only from Aristotle's criticisms of them in the second book of the *Politics*, which reveal little more than that Phaleas, who may have been only marginally a Utopian anyway, wished to bring about equality of private property in land (but not in other forms of wealth) among a small body of citizens, while all craftsmen were to be reduced to public slaves; that Hippodamus projected another small community with a formal three-class structure in which the farmers alone possessed land, the warriors arms, the artisans nothing. Clearly neither was an egalitarian, despite the assertions of some modern commentators who confuse the right to vote with equality. The model was Sparta, the most rigidly hierarchical society in the Greek world.

What is left of the work of Euhemerus is abridged and garbled, but Diodorus leaves no doubt that his Sacred Isle was divided into castes; whether three or five castes remains an open question, but that is not of any importance in the present context.[23] Diodorus also has a brief story (5.9) about the tiny Lipari Islands off Sicily where for a time land was held in common in the sixth century B.C. However, this was an emergency measure–half the small community cultivated the land while the other half waged a piratical conflict with the Etruscans–and gives no insights into ancient Utopian thinking.[24] Of Aristonicus' Heliopolis, as I have already said, we know absolutely nothing. Nearly two centuries earlier, Alexarchus, younger brother of the Cassander who ruled Macedonia for a time after the death of Alexander the Great, founded an Ouranopolis, a City of Heaven, on Mt Athos, called himself the Sun and invented a secret language. And Alexarchus carries us all the way back to lunacy and its personal fantasies.

We are therefore left only with the Republic as a subject for detailed analysis. Plato's attitude to class and labour is a heavily nuanced one. His Guardians may live off the involuntary labour of others but they do not exploit anyone for their own enrichment or even, strictly speaking, for their own benefit, and they, of all men, live a life of ascetism and strict discipline. Nor is labour merely dismissed as an activity fit only for slaves (nor as a punishment for sin). Labour is a necessity; more than that, it has positive qualities: there is legitimate pride in skill and craftsmanship, there is the moral discipline it induces, there is even a sense in which one may speak of a vocation of labour. But there is also an immutable hierarchy of values, in which labour occupies the lowest rank of acceptable and necessary activities, and this is matched by a hierarchy of social classes and backed by a metaphysical doctrine of the nature of the soul.

For all his radicalism, in sum, Plato, like the other ancient Utopians, could never depart from the notion of the natural inequality of men. Nor could Zeno: he simply cut the Gordian knot in his Republic by excluding all men who were not virtuous, not morally good.* The real world was a chaos. The function of the Utopians was to remedy it through order, regularity and virtue. They differed in their remedies and their explanations, in the depth and breadth of their thinking, but they agreed that inequality had to remain, re-structured, so to speak, but not abolished. And on that

* The key passage is Diogenes Laertius, *Lives of the Philosophers* 7.32–33. Although Zeno's *Politeia*, an early and perhaps his earliest work, has been taken as a Utopia, that is an illusion in my opinion. Its form can be explained by its explicit purpose, an attack on Plato's *Republic*. Zeno proposed to cure the ills of society by ignoring all but the good men and by abolishing social institutions, not by changing them, just as the later Stoics preached the equality and universal brotherhood of all men as an ideological justification for the preservation in real life of the grossest inequalities, ending with absolute monarchy.

absolutely fundamental nexus of ideas the modern world broke dramatically with Thomas More. It must be remembered that *Utopia* was first published in Latin as early as 1516, in a posthumous English translation in 1551, and in translations into all the major European languages by the end of the sixteenth century. I shall quote one sentence: 'Husbandry is a science common to them all in general, both men and women, wherein they be all expert and cunning.' One can almost match that in Iambulus, but he was at least half in the world of myth and Thomas More decidedly was not. 'Equality is justice. That is the cutting edge of More's thought in *Utopia*.'[25] More's egalitarianism did not win the day by any means. The authoritarians, those whose Utopia was to be imposed from above and maintained by domination, were perhaps in the majority, from Campanella to Wells. But More was nonetheless explosive in his conception: a new possibility was opened up, though at first only for Utopia, and no opposition could again remove that possibility from men's consciousness.

From the sixteenth century on, the history of the role and psychology of labour is a corollary and equally complex part of the complex history of modern society, with its class structure and its value systems. I cannot even begin on that subject, but I cannot resist one pathetic quotation from Nathaniel Hawthorne's *Blithedale Romance*, published in 1852 and based on the experiences of the Utopian colony called Brook Farm a few miles outside Boston, which existed from 1841 to 1846. Hawthorne wrote as follows:

'The peril of our new way of life was not lest we should fail in becoming practical agriculturalists but that we should probably cease to be anything else. While our enterprise lay all in theory, we had pleased ourselves with delectable visions of the spiritualization of labour. It was to be one form of prayer and ceremonial of worship. Each stroke of the hoe was to uncover some aromatic root of wisdom heretofore hidden from the sun. Pausing in the field, to let the wind exhale the moisture from our foreheads, we were to look upward and catch glimpses into the far-off soul of truth. In this point of view, matters did not turn out quite so well as we had anticipated. . . . The clods of earth, which we so constantly belaboured and turned over and over, were never etherealized into thought. Our Thoughts, on the contrary, were fast becoming cloddish. Our labour symbolized nothing. Intellectual activity is incompatible with any large amount of bodily exercise. The yeoman and the scholar – the yeoman and the man of finesse and moral culture . . . – are two distinct individuals, and can never be melted or wedded into one substance.'

V

Ancient writers would have agreed with Hawthorne's conclusion, despite their Arcadian glorification of the rustic life, and they would have been completely puzzled why he had to suffer his Arcadian failure before he discovered so obvious a truth. Neither Xenophon nor Virgil went to his villa to labour. Brook Farm was no doubt a pathetic and melancholy experience, yet the very attempt reveals the unbridgeable gap that exists between us and antiquity. I have already indicated two reasons for saying that: first, the fact that it was not possible by any means to bring about an equitable society in antiquity, given the poor resources, the low level of technology, the absence of growth possibilities (other than conquest) in the economy, and the absence of the very idea of progress; second, the acceptance of human inequality, and therefore of the necessity of domination, as natural and immutable. I must now add a third element, and that is the smallness of scale on which men operated and in which they thought. For ancient Utopians it was axiomatic that Utopia was possible only in a small, face-to-face community. Contrariwise, those who looked to mankind in general, to the universe–the Cynics with their *cosmopolis*, the Stoics with their brotherhood of all men–were precisely the thinkers who, in so far as they remained consistent and rigorous in their thinking, turned their backs on society altogether.

In the present day, and for the first time in history, all problems are technically soluble; there is widespread acceptance, no matter how superficially or with whatever reservations, of the idea that equality and freedom (however defined) are necessary elements in justice and a just society; and everything is on a gigantic, even terrifying, scale. This last is a fairly new element in the situation, and one of the highest importance. By scale I refer not only to geography or technology or national territory but to the scale of organization which modern life requires. Even if we and the ancients did not differ on the other two issues, this matter of scale would of itself be sufficient to render their social Utopias irrelevant today.

What, then, is the present position with regard to Utopian writing and thinking? The answer is that we seem to have turned the whole tradition upside down. In western literature today, at least outside the socialist sphere, satires on Utopia have become very prominent, as Northrop Frye noted, while there is a paralysis of genuine Utopian thought.[26] Another commentator said this more brutally when he entitled a course of lectures *From Utopia to Nightmare*.[27] 'If alert readers once sat down with Bellamy's *Looking Backward* or Wells's

A Modern Utopia,' today they 'seem more likely to meditate upon Huxley's *Brave New World* or Orwell's *Nineteen Eighty-Four*.'[28] (I take no responsibility for the word 'alert'.) This newer kind of satire is radically different from the ancient, that of Aristophanes, for example, in the *Birds* or the *Ecclesiazusae*. For the latter the joke about Utopianism was its absurdity, its impracticality, its impossibility. For our own satirists, however, there is no joke at all; on the contrary, they attack Utopia because it is in fact possible and achievable, and because it then turns out to be Dystopia for them, the opposite of Eutopia. Huxley prefaced *Brave New World* with a quotation from Berdyaev: 'Les utopies apparaissent comme bien plus réalisables qu'on ne le croyait autrefois. Et nous nous trouvons actuellement devant une question bien autrement angoissante: Comment éviter leur réalisation définitive?'*

All major movements for social reform and of course all revolutions (and not a few wars) have been animated by a spirit of Utopianism (though not necessarily by a specific blueprint for Utopia). They then turn out not to have attained Utopia, even at their best, and there is an inevitable let-down. Voices are raised against both the social changes and the underlying Utopianism, against the possibility of human progress, against man's potentiality for good. Contemporary Dystopias seem but another example. But they are a special kind of example. The fact that in principle the technological, economic and political problems are now soluble has had a powerful impact for at least two reasons. First, it has concentrated the attention so completely on practical and immediately available solutions that it has narrowed the field in which the traditional kind of Utopian imagination can play, when it has not barred the door to it altogether. Second, the solutions require constant enlargement of the already enormous scale of operations. That element of scale takes us further and further from traditional Utopianism, ancient or modern. It generates its own tensions and fears; in traditional terms, the fear that the age-old struggle to achieve a balance between freedom and order has finally been lost for ever. 'The capabilities (intellectual and material) of contemporary society are immeasurably greater than ever before–which means that the scope of society's domination over the individual is immeasurably greater than ever before.'[29]

If Utopian thinking is to recover from its present state of paralysis, it will have to break with its past. Social and political engineering

* 'Utopias appear to be much more realizable than was once believed. Today we are therefore faced with a no less agonizing question: How shall we escape their final realization?'

has been given over to the practical imagination. Utopia must therefore take the next transcending step. After the elimination of the burdens of want and struggle and war there would still remain the burdens of fear and guilt, of domination. What Oscar Wilde said in *The Soul of Man under Socialism* has lost none of its force: 'A map of the world that does not include Utopia is not worth even glancing at. . . . Progress is the realization of Utopia.'

12

THE HERITAGE OF ISOCRATES*

I

OURS is 'a time of despair, with its total hopelessness, its fatal lassitude, its mortifying memories of song and saga and beauty from older epochs which it hardly dares to summon any longer. It turns all greatness into grimacing vulgarity. It believes it can elevate itself to heroism in war, but the outcome is the banality and hatefulness of daily life to which the demobilized veterans return.' It is, in short, a world of 'triviality', of 'tragicomic marionettes', a waste land.[1]

That jeremiad by a renowned German literary scholar and critic, Ernst Robert Curtius, appeared in an essay on Eliot in 1927. In the same year Curtius published his translation of *The Waste Land*, a most remarkable thing for a German professor to have done, and a Professor of Romance Philology at that. But then, Curtius was an altogether remarkable figure in European literary studies. An American scholar has recently said of him that in 'urbanity of style and outlook, range of interest, volatile curiosity and intensity of historical consciousness, only such patricians of the mind as Croce or Edmund Wilson are his equals'.[2] Odd though this formulation may be, it does register the intellectual status of the man, and that is important for my argument.

Curtius came from an old Hanseatic family that had settled in German-ruled Alsace and included distinguished men in the worlds of learning, public affairs and the Lutheran Church. Among the major influences in his own development he counted Nietzsche, Bergson, Max Scheler, Friedrich Gundolf and Stefan George, all

* The Encyclopaedia Britannica Lecture, University of Edinburgh, 23 November 1972, published in somewhat revised and elaborated form by the Edinburgh University Press under the title, *Knowledge for What?*, and now re-published with only a few minor changes. I am grateful to P. H. Hirst and G. G. N. Mackenzie for their help.

Copyright © 1972 by the University of Edinburgh, and reprinted by permission of the University.

powerful personalities with a mystical, anti-rationalist stamp, and the Germans among them strongly nationalist in a complicated way, as was Curtius himself. Predictably, he rejected Nazism and spent the years 1933–45 in what has been called the conservative 'inner emigration' within Germany, dedicating himself to the study which emerged in 1948 in a monumental work, *European Literature and the Latin Middle Ages*,[3] preceded by twenty-two articles in learned journals, all published between 1938 and 1944, a scholarly output he himself later called his 'welcome spiritual alibi'.[4]

'Alibi' is not to be misunderstood: this demonic labour was no retreat to an ivory tower. Quite the contrary, 'it grew out of vital urges and under the pressure of a concrete historical situation,'[5] created not by the Nazis but by modern society itself ever since the Industrial Revolution. The description of our world as one of 'grimacing vulgarity' and 'triviality', it is essential to remember, was published in 1927, in the heyday of the Weimar Republic. By 1932 Curtius had made his decision. 'If it is true', he wrote then, 'that dark centuries lie before us, and later bright renaissances, it follows that the humanism of today must link itself neither to antiquity nor to the Renaissance but to the Middle Ages. The new humanism must be not classicism but medievalism and a sense of restoration (*Restaurationsgesinnung*).'[6] Hence the affinity with Eliot, and, though unexpressed on either side, with Dr Leavis.

In the preface to a volume of essays published in 1943, during the war, under the title *Education and the University*, Leavis wrote: 'This is clearly a critical time. It is still possible to say that "post-war reconstruction" represents opportunities as well as depressing probabilities.' To be sure, he located 'traditional wisdom' neither in the Middle Ages nor in Latin but in England, but that is a secondary matter. Seventeenth-century England was to be the centrepiece of the 'English School', the new queen of the sciences, because it was 'a key phase, or passage, in the history of civilization . . . at one end in direct and substantial continuity with the world of Dante, . . . at the other a world that has broken irretrievably with the medieval order and committed itself completely to the process leading directly and rapidly to what we live in now.'[7] For Curtius, too, the Industrial Revolution was the beginning of the end: it saw 'the first powerful revolt against cultural tradition, which was marked by Rousseau. The tradition was restated by the universal genius of Goethe. But it was restated for the last time. Goethe has not been succeeded by another universal genius. . . . He is the last link of that golden chain.'[8]

Moral regeneration through literature of the past, specific and selected literatures, is thus the central affinity between Curtius and Leavis. In the words of the former, Goethe 'is not too remote from us. We can still grasp that link.'[9] But there is a further affinity. Leavis's 'English School'–he was quite explicit about this–'would be essentially designed for an élite'; 'this would be a condition of its influence and importance'.[10] And elsewhere in the volume he quoted with approval the following from an American classical scholar, Brooks Otis: the central task is to restore 'the unity of the Educated Class, and the unity of the Educated Mind in terms of the ideas of its own age', for this class in the past 'may be said to have definitely represented and been responsible for civilization in their time'.[11] Curtius, for his part, in a footnote on the first page of his *European Literature and the Latin Middle Ages* quoted the following 'warning', written in 1926 by his philosopher-guide Max Scheler:

'The expansion of democracy, once the ally of free scholarship and philosophy against the supremacy of the ecclesiastically restricted mind, is slowly becoming the greatest danger to intellectual freedom. The type of democracy which condemned Socrates and Anaxagoras in Athens is slowly reappearing in the West and perhaps in North America too. Only the struggling, predominantly liberal democracy of relatively "small élites"–so the facts already teach us–is an ally of science and philosophy. The democracy now dominant, and finally extended to women and half-children, is not the friend but rather the enemy of reason and science.'

And so we see, on the highest academic authority, two interlocking uses of the past, regeneration, salvation, through an immersion in past culture, and specifically in literary culture–it is not too forced a metaphor to speak of a cult of the past–and, second, the education in this fashion of a pre-selected élite.* Both these uses and, indeed, fundamental presuppositions of an important sector of our higher education, have their roots in ancient Greece. Certain aspects of that Greek experience are worth looking at, if for no other reason as a paradigm of how a cultural institution can continue, with some modification and distortion, long after its social base has disappeared.

II

The Greek word *scholē*, with its root-meaning of 'ease', 'idleness', 'leisure', is the ancestor of the word for 'school' in virtually all European languages–that well-worn bit of information is always

* Throughout I shall use the word 'culture' to mean 'high culture', 'humanistic culture', in the sense in which we speak of a 'cultured person', and not in the descriptive, non-normative sense in which an archaeologist speaks of 'material cultures', an anthropologist of the 'culture of the Chippewa Indians'.

good for a laugh in opening a course in the history of education; an ill-judged laugh, for a fundamental quality that has survived throughout the history of higher education in the West has its kernel in that simple etymology. In a passage in Book VII of the *Politics* (1328b24–29a39), where he is discussing the ideal state, Aristotle summed it up briefly and categorically: working craftsmen, shopkeepers and farmers, he wrote, are disqualified for higher education; property, wealth, is a necessary condition, 'since *scholē* is essential both for the creation of virtue and for civic (political) activities'. Obviously Aristotle equated leisure not with idleness, but, as a modern commentator has phrased it, with 'the possibility of disposing of one's own time',[12] whether for purposes of philosophical study or for civic leadership, the two activities, and the only two, appropriate to members of the leisure class (I use the term in Veblen's sense) if they are to fulfil their natural functions in life.

Two points are to be underlined. The first is that Aristotle lived in a slave society in which the leisure class, the gentlemen, were in principle rentiers and therefore free from managerial concerns as well as from work in the narrow sense. Free labour and slave labour were, in this context, jumbled together: 'Illiberal, too, and mean', said Cicero (*De officiis* 1.150), 'are the employments of all who work for wages, . . . for in their case their very wages are the warrant of their slavery.' The second point is that each new generation within the leisure class had a claim on higher education because of membership in the class, not the other way round, that education provided an entry into the ranks of the virtuous (the 'good people', *boni*, the 'best people', *optimi*, as Romans like Cicero called them) and of those qualified for civic leadership. Although Aristotle was discussing the ideal state, on these two points he was registering actual practice, as it existed from his day, the late fourth century B.C., to the end of antiquity and beyond. There were exceptions. There were the two ambiguous professions, medicine among the Greeks, law among the Romans, for which centres of advanced education and research were created. There were also, largely concentrated in the later Roman Empire, men who climbed the social ladder, sometimes to, or very close to, the highest rungs through their educational, pedagogical and rhetorical accomplishments.[13]

Exceptions, however, are exceptions, and we may include in that category those intellectuals, of whom Diogenes the Cynic is the famous exemplar as well as the caricature, who pushed the idea of the inwardness of virtue to the extreme and rejected the twin ideal of virtue *and* public leadership.[14] The leisure class as a whole accepted the doctrine, no matter how many or how few tried to practise it at any given time, that membership of the class entailed the duty to prepare to rule and then to do so in the light of a proper education. What was debated, at least among the more articulate intellectuals in the dominant strain, was only the means to achieve the accepted end. And there was no prolonged serious debate. Disagreement over details never ceased, but fundamental argument over meaningful alternatives occurred only in the fourth century B.C., centred in Athens, and the debate ended with the total victory of Isocrates over Plato.

Plato developed an elaborate scheme for a mathematico-philosophical training, increasing in its abstraction as it progressed, which, in an ideal world, would produce an élite of perfect and perfectly rational rulers. At the foundation of the programme lay not only a metaphysic and an ethical doctrine but also a psychology. The human *psyche*, 'soul' as we conventionally translate it, has three distinct and competing elements, unequally distributed among individuals and thus responsible for a natural inequality among men. Society should ideally also be divided into three sections, corresponding to the three parts of the soul, and for each Plato proposed an appropriate kind of education, the highest form being reserved for the naturally qualified few, whose *psyche* would be trained in a lengthy, difficult process, until they were capable of apprehending the Absolutes, and then of ruling with absolute justice.

The argument is a unified one. The psychology and the metaphysics are inseparable from the educational proposals. The nineteenth century understood that clearly, and its implications: 'whatever we may think of his analysis of the soul in its details,' wrote Nettleship in what used to be the standard exposition in English of Plato's theory of education, 'we shall hardly escape the conclusion that some such analysis is an indispensable condition of a really rational theory of education . . . the most fatally unpractical thing in the world is to go on testing methods by results which take every factor into account except the one upon which the whole result ultimately depends.'[15]

Mid-nineteenth-century Balliol thought highly of Plato's psychology, even if not in all its details, and logically proceeded accordingly. But what if, with Gilbert Ryle, we hold that there is a long list of 'reasons given by Plato for . . . quite important doctrines' which 'no tutor would accept from a pupil', among them, 'that the Soul is tripartite; that if the Soul is tripartite, the ideal society would be a three-class state; . . . that one and only one of the classes should be taught to reason; that membership of a class should normally be determined by pedigree; ... that political institutions must degenerate unless there are rulers who have had the sort of higher education described'? The only permissible conclusion would then be, in Ryle's moderate formulation, that 'if any one of these propositions is dubitable, the positive recommendations of the *Republic* are unestablished'.[16] Yet the powerful spirit of Plato continues to darken reason. It is remarkable how contemporary histories of education are filled with admiration of Plato, achieved by politely passing over the psychological propositions; remarkable, too, how the humanities divisions of universities remain partially Platonic in spirit.

To be sure, the formal abstractness of the Platonic curriculum has been rejected; it was in fact successfully dismissed in his own day by Isocrates, 'the master of all rhetoricians' as Cicero (*On Oratory* 2.94) called him. In a continuous and conscious attack on the Platonic conception, Isocrates, whose own school turned out an entire Who's Who of Greek intellectuals and public figures, argued that higher education must be a training for life, for the good life of the citizen élite. Just what these broad, emotionally charged categories mean is not easy to discover: Isocrates was not a systematic thinker and one is driven to picking out statements here and there, not always consistent, and never more than vague on the ultimate goals. However, in what was the nearest he came to a full statement of his educational ideas, written in 354 or 353 B.C., when he was eighty-two years old (and he still had an active fifteen or sixteen years ahead of him), he stated the following principles (15.266–75). First, mathematics, grammar and music (terms to which I shall return) are important only as a 'gymnastic of the *psyche*', a metaphor that identifies Isocrates as a forerunner of 'faculty psychology', of the notion that the faculties, like muscles, are strengthened by exercise; these studies are therefore just a 'preparation for "philosophy"' (in inverted commas, since Isocrates' use of the word *philosophia* was loose, not technical, meaning no more than 'a virtuous, therefore wise, way of life'). Second, virtue cannot be taught, though virtue is the aim of life. Third, anyone with a predisposition to virtue *and a proper station in life* can become 'better and worthier' if he is eager to speak well and to persuade, and that can be taught.

It may or may not be wholly fair to Isocrates, it may not even be true, but it was fitting that later antiquity believed that a large siren had been carved on Isocrates' tombstone.[17] For Isocrates 'has had to bear the blame for more than two thousand years as the man who anchored the rhetorical viewpoint ... in politics, in education and in historiography'.[18] Thereafter rhetoric occupied pride of place in higher education, in a scheme that soon became canonized into what the Romans called the seven 'liberal arts' (studies, disciplines).[19] The four preliminary studies comprised what Isocrates had called the 'gymnastic of the *psyche*', mathematics subdivided into arithmetic, geometry, music (that is, harmonics) and astronomy. The three advanced disciplines then gave the training in speaking well and in persuading: grammar, which was a combination of linguistic study and literary history, rhetoric and dialectic. This canon eventually passed from the ancient Greeks to the Byzantine world, from the Romans to the Latin west.

The total victory of rhetoric has to be understood accurately and in its full implication. The philosophers resisted; schools of philosophy continued in existence, but they attracted only philosophers or would-be philosophers, not the youth of the leisure class in general. The philosophical knowledge to which the second-century B.C. historian Polybius pretended, for example, is patently what he had learned in his study of grammar (and perhaps also of dialectic) in a rhetorical school, odd tags and generalizations, limited in range, neither profound nor accurate. And the eventually dominant philosophical tradition, Stoicism, itself capitulated in the end. Zeno, the founder of Stoicism in the generation after Aristotle, was a dedicated believer in the life of contemplation, and accordingly, we are told (Diogenes Laertius 7.32), at the beginning of his *Republic*, an anti-Platonic work now lost, he dismissed liberal-arts education as 'useless'. But by the time Stoicism came to Rome nearly two centuries later, eventually to become in effect the official philosophy of the Roman aristocracy, it had abandoned Zeno's quietism and accepted the role of educator for the ruling class, and it therefore accepted the liberal arts as well. To be sure, one can read in Seneca (*Moral Epistles* 88), who was Nero's tutor, a Roman senator and perhaps the wealthiest man of his time, that the liberal arts only prepare a young man for virtue, they do not teach virtue itself. How that last, critical step is to be taken is never made clear, as Seneca dispenses a cloud of Isocratean verbiage. As for what remained of genuine philosophy in Roman Stoicism, that was summed up by Hegel in a single sentence in his *Lectures on the History of Philosophy*: '. . . all speculative interest was really lost, and a rhetorical or hortatory disposition shown, of which mention cannot be made in a history of philosophy any more than of our sermons.'[20]

Nor did the technical and professional subjects escape the rhetorical take-over. Mostly they do not enter into consideration at all: with the two exceptions of law and medicine, all techniques ranked as crafts and were taught and transmitted through apprenticeship. There were no schools for them, not even for engineering or architecture. There were some medical schools, at least from the time of Hippocrates late in the fifth century B.C.; schools of law did not emerge until late in the Roman Empire (for reasons implicit in the way Roman law developed). And even those professions resorted to apprenticeship, rather than the school, with considerable frequency. Technical and professional men lacked *scholē*, after all; only the law and farming, gentleman-farming, were permissible vocations in the leisure class to whom higher education was directed. Nothing more was required in a civilization that was neither industrial nor scribal nor priestly.

However, a vast body of technical literature arose (most of it now lost) and it is there that rhetoric intervened.[21] The earliest surviving manual, written by Anaximenes of Lampsacus about 340 B.C.,[22] is, appropriately enough, devoted to rhetoric itself and it already revealed the essential characteristic that its numerous successors extended to a *reductio ad absurdum*, namely, 'an almost morbid tendency towards systems and rules',[23] a passion for taxonomy, for classes, sub-classes and sub-sub-classes, more than a touch of which seeped into manuals on music, agriculture and military science. The rhetorical 'manuals' were utilitarian in the strict sense, they were textbooks in the rhetorical schools, but one wonders how many Roman landowners turned to Varro's *De re rustica* for practical instructions. In the preface to his *De architectura*, Vitruvius included his having been through the liberal arts curriculum among his qualifications for writing his manual, and he suggested that history be added as another subject; Galen proposed the introduction of law and medicine.[24] No one paid the slightest attention. Education retained the predominantly literary tone Isocrates had demanded.

The origins of Greek oratory, as of its later transmittal to the Romans, has a simple explanation well known to the ancients: it met the need created by the emergence of the popular assembly and the popular courts. The remarkable paradox, then, is that rhetoric achieved its cultural dominance in a society in which the original political impetus had disappeared. The death of Isocrates coincided with the defeat of Athens by Philip II of Macedon, father of Alexander the Great, and with the imminent demise of popular government among the Greeks. In Rome, after the death of Cicero, oratory retained a purpose, though a steadily dwindling one, in the Senate for perhaps a century and then no more. Of the three types of oration defined by Isocrates, two were dead, the political and the forensic; only the third remained, the epideictic, which means literally a 'display piece', a declamation. Cities, wealthy patrons, even kings and emperors encouraged, and offered considerable emoluments to, skilled practitioners of epideictic oratory. Occasionally, outstanding orators appeared who were serious and courageous enough, and their best pieces are still worth reading for what they say. But the overwhelming majority were as empty, as boring, as meaningless, as subservient to authority, to conventional values and the status quo as the very title, display piece, implies.

They were also often learned, in a specific way, thanks to the liberal arts education through which the orators had passed. The Latin adjective *liberalis* lends itself to a play on words. Seneca was still deriving it correctly from *līber*, free, but the later writers, Cassiodorus and Isidore of Seville, who were the chief transmitters to the Middle Ages, linked *līberalis* with *liber*, a book, and they were right in reality if not in etymology.[25] Not only did the liberal arts rapidly become book study, they became a study of a restricted, canonical list of books, and even of parts of books (as anthologies tended to take over in the schools). The liberal arts became frozen in the past, in a highly selected segment of the past at that, one which can be expressed statistically in some figures of book ownership.

Thanks to the soil and climate of Egypt, which became Greek in its high culture after Alexander the Great and remained so until the Arab conquest in A.D. 642, fragments of ancient books, written on papyrus, continue to see the light of day. Of all the fragments of Greek literary works rediscovered and published through 1963, there are 1,596 books by or about authors whose names are identifiable. Something less than half the total were copies of the *Iliad* or *Odyssey* or commentaries upon them. The second best represented author is the orator Demosthenes with 83 (again including commentaries), followed by Euripides with 77 and Hesiod with 72. The classical Athenian orators together reach a total of 154, close to three times that of the philosophical books of the same period.

The contrast with books written in the nearly 1,000 years that followed the death of Alexander the Great, in other words, with books by contemporaries of their owners in Graeco-Roman Egypt, cannot be overstated. The comic playwright Menander, writing in the generation immediately after Alexander, whose influence through the Romans Plautus and Terence made itself strongly felt in Renaissance Europe, is represented by 29 copies, the equally influential poet Callimachus by 51, the pastoral poet Theocritus by 10. Otherwise, there are not 50 copies of all the creative or imaginative literature of the thousand-year period. In historiography, the three great classical writers, Herodotus, Thucydides and Xenophon, are represented by 81 books, the second-century B.C.

Polybius by one, the second-century A.D. Appian by one, the biographies of Plutarch by two. In philosophy, Plato has 42 (by a neat coincidence the identical number as Isocrates); thereafter the drop is sharp: Aristotle 8, his greatest pupil, Theophrastus, 4, the third-century B.C. Stoic Chrysippus 3, Philo of Alexandria 3, Zeno, founder of Stoicism, none, Epicurus none. But there are 56 copies of anonymous works of philosophy of the type dismissable along with yesterday's sermons.[26]

The rigid Graeco-Roman liberal arts education, in sum, with all its attention to 'gymnastic of the *psyche*' and to speaking (and writing) well and persuasively, pressed culture heavily with the dead hand of the past.

III

I do not propose to pursue the complicated, multilinear history of the liberal arts through the centuries. My reason for taking so long over the Greeks and Romans is not a merely antiquarian search for roots (which are well enough known anyway) but a prelude to asking what is the justification, if any, for the retention of the ancient heritage, however adjusted, in a wholly different society, with, one assumes, a different view of the human psyche. My concern is with higher education, in the broad sense of education above the age of sixteen or so, but in the narrow sense of non-vocational education, excluding training in vocational or professional skills, whether in schools of engineering or law, in trade schools or under the apprenticeship system, with which some aspects of higher education are more closely linked than is sometimes appreciated: the graduate student in the natural sciences, in particular, from the very start of his programme ' "works under" an established scientist who immediately becomes, as it were, master to the newly arrived apprentice'.[27]

The 'ancient heritage', as I see it, has three elements. First, there is a belief in the possibility and virtue of training the mind, however that notion is formulated. Second is the belief in the supreme value, for public life or the life of the citizen (not merely for future teachers or academics), of a fundamentally literary education, under which I include history and philosophy as well as languages and literature. A corollary is that such education should concentrate on the best literature, overwhelmingly, and in some schools of thought exclusively, past literature. Hence the third element is the identification of most non-vocational education with high culture, believed to be accessible only to a very small minority, an élite.

Considering the great diversity of contemporary systems of higher education, I shall concentrate on England, recognized to present the extreme case, and, before I proceed to discuss each of my three elements of the ancient heritage, I must briefly defend the position that this heritage is still a living one. The key fact in my argument here is the continuing tyranny of the one-subject degree, the extreme university specialization which reaches back to A-levels in the schools, and, to a not insignificant extent, even to O-levels, to boys and girls aged fourteen and fifteen.[28] Some university students transfer in mid-passage, some take joint honours degrees, but the total picture is, beyond any dispute, one of extreme specialization. As a result, a large proportion of university students and virtually all who do not attend the university are denied any formal contact with high culture, at least from the age when they first become sufficiently mature to study literature, history, philosophy meaningfully. Another large proportion are denied any formal contact with mathematics and the natural sciences after the same cut-off age. Among these latter are the majority of the leaders of our society (and future leaders so long as the present system of education continues), leaders in government, business, cultural and social institutions. It is this factual situation – and I insist that it is factual, not speculative – which lies behind my discourse.

Knowledge can be useful in a variety of ways. The activity of acquisition of knowledge may itself provide the learner with pleasure, like the acquisition of a stamp collection, and, though I do not underestimate the play element in man, I doubt that anyone will seriously claim that as a sufficient, or even as an important, ground for the expenditure of hundreds of millions of pounds of public funds on higher education, not even when the play element is translated to the 'higher' level of aesthetic satisfaction from music, mathematics or poetry. Knowledge may enhance social status: Dean Gaisford of Christ Church, who is supposed to have said early in the nineteenth century that a classical education 'enables us to look down with contempt on those who have not shared its advantages', was not simply silly, nor is he without later (and contemporary) analogues. I shall return to that point eventually. Third, knowledge may be useful in providing the skills necessary for earning one's livelihood or for advancing oneself socially; that is the popular sense of 'useful', a function of education I am not concerned with, as I have already explained. My interest is in the residue, in the general education a large fraction of our school and university population receives, and I trust that my failure to discuss the other uses will not be misunderstood as indifference to them or as a denial of their legitimacy.

What is the use, the function, of general education as now offered? What, in particular, is the justification for its extreme and early narrowing, in whatever direction, whether towards the physical sciences or towards literary studies with a strong bias for the past or towards any other single area of knowledge?

Implicit (and sometimes explicit) in all arguments for specialization, I believe, is a faith in the possibility of 'training the mind', a faith not shared by many psychologists today. With the abandonment of faculty psychology, of the mind-as-muscle concept, training the mind proves to be an ambiguous and unhelpful notion, except perhaps among extreme behaviourists who consider the rat in a maze to be a paradigm of all learning. The truism that all learning both depends on past learning and lays a basis for future learning is not the same thing, and anyway it offers no ground for specialization, or for claiming greater virtue as mind training for one subject over another. Such a claim requires a demonstration that, at the end of one course of study, the learner is better equipped not only in that particular study but in other, unrelated studies than he would be had he pursued another course.

The concept of transfer of training is then introduced. Some subjects, it is argued, offer a unique training which is transferable to other kinds of learning and action. There are several decisive objections. In the first place, attempts to test the claim have invariably been reduced to laboratory situations, not life situations, involving either very simple skills or very closely related ones.[29] With motor skills, at least, which are more meaningfully and readily tested, 'it is now recognized . . . that the effects of training are much more limited by the extent to which elements of skill learned actually form a component of other required achievements'; for example, 'if a man becomes proficient at tightening screws, this will transfer to other tasks which require the same sort of operation'.[30] Second, there is a persistent confusion between 'transfer of training' and 'prerequisite knowledge'. As an American psychologist recently said in a powerful plea for abandonment of the whole concept of transfer of training, the fact that algebra is necessary for calculus or that a knowledge of European history is advantageous for the study of American history is merely 'clouded by arguments about some kind of transfer'.[31] Third, although the study of Latin does help in the study of English, for example, the 'transfer' involves a very large, unnecessary expenditure of time and effort if the ultimate desideratum is knowledge of English. The same results can be achieved in a fraction of the time by concentration on English.[32] Transfer is therefore no argument that Latin is a more beneficial subject of study than English, and equally with all similar claims, for mathematics most obviously.

Cloudy arguments are by no means restricted to this one about transfer. In a public lecture that achieved considerable notoriety several years ago, a physicist complained that 'the universities are giving many more lectureships to the Arts departments than to science and technology . . . and not so much to those Arts departments that, whatever we may say about the classical languages, do earn our respect for the intellectual discipline they demand, as those where the discipline is less exact and therefore within the ability of the less able students'.[33] Putting aside the demonstrably false correlation between 'ability' and certain university subjects, we may ask what this rhetoric means. 'Discipline' is a word with a considerable semantic range, and it is tempting to see a touch of the penal connotation in the statement, what I may call the castor oil approach to education, that for the young unpleasantness is a necessary condition of benefit. If discipline means hard work and application, then I reply that it requires as much effort and application to *study* Plato or *The Waste Land* or the musical structure of *Der Rosenkavalier* as to learn calculus or Sanskrit.

There is, however, one genuine distinction covered by the rhetoric, the distinction between 'formal' and 'descriptive' subjects (to use John Hajnal's terminology), between those subjects, such as mathematics or a foreign language, in which each stage of the study is a prerequisite for the next stage, and subjects such as geography or history in which there is not that progression. Hajnal illustrates the distinction in this way: 'A student of history might find it troublesome to begin his studies with a scholarly volume about say the First World War, but–given ability and determination–he could make progress. On the other hand, . . . a student ignorant of calculus would be helpless when faced with a book on differential equations, no matter how brilliant he was.'[34]

But what are the practical conclusions? Is it seriously proposed that schooling is to be restricted to formal subjects to the very end of a university education?* In a study of research scientists who had taken their first degrees at Cambridge between 1920 and 1939, Liam Hudson showed that of those who were subsequently elected Fellows of the Royal Society, the proportion who had failed to achieve good class marks was almost identical with the proportion of those who were not elected to the Royal Society. The evidence, he commented, 'suggests not merely that original thinkers lack

* I take the precaution of adding that my rhetorical question does not imply the *exclusion* of formal subjects from school curricula below the university level.

intellectual discipline as students, but that this very lack of discipline, their erraticism, is an important progressive sign'.[35] There is that word 'discipline' again, and I have made the same kind of semantic slide to which I objected a few moments ago, but the point that the 'formal' subjects appeal to and encourage intellectual conformity–to which I shall return–is surely not irrelevant to the question of the place of those subjects in higher education. 'Learning' and 'knowledge' are umbrella words and all efforts to reduce them to the least common denominator or to a single explanatory model involve the elimination of a range of legitimate meanings of those two key words. Not even a young child learns only skills, only techniques and brute facts, and surely not a university student.[36] Otherwise the apprenticeship system would suffice, without our elaborate structure of schools and universities. It has been observed that an experienced craftsman in Greece, engaged in the reconstruction of ancient ruins, 'can gauge by eye the depth of the fluting of a column'.[37] No one will claim that achievement to be a paradigm of what we call education.

Practitioners of the descriptive subjects naturally do not let 'discipline' go by default. Leavis and his followers make endless claims for literary study as 'a discipline of intelligence and sensibility', 'a true discipline';[38] they assure us that 'literature has a logic of its own' and that criticism 'therefore requires a discipline of its own'.[39] Others overcome their sense of inferiority with respect to discipline by parading 'study in depth', a metaphor which often turns out to mean a study in greater detail, substituting the high-value word 'depth' for the low-value 'detail'. There is something truly Isocratean in this discussion: metaphors and other rhetorical devices take the place of reasoned argument. 'Criticism', wrote Curtius in a typical formulation, 'must always be chancy. Valuation cannot be grounded. The foundation is there, to be sure, but only as intuition. . . . Criticism is an act of creative spiritual freedom.'[40] And when Leavis was challenged by a friendly critic, 'If I may venture . . . some fundamental criticisms . . . I could wish you had stated your assumptions more explicitly and defended them systematically, . . . become conscious that large ethical, philosophical and, of course, ultimately, also aesthetic *choices* are involved',[41] he replied that this was not his business. As he never tires of asserting, there is 'a sufficient measure of agreement . . . about essential values to make it unnecessary to . . . provide a philosophy before starting to work'.[42] Such an *a priori* conviction may be comforting to the prophet and the seer; it provides no basis for rational discussion of the aims of education, or of anything else.

The scientist's counterpart, *his* rhetoric, so to speak, centres round the phrase, 'the scientific mode of thought', normally employed not as a merely descriptive phrase but as an evaluative and excluding one. In so far as the phrase implies respect for data, honesty in assessment and presentation, what is ambiguously called objectivity, it is equally applicable to every and any subject of study. No scientist has any claim to a monopoly in that respect, or even superiority. But it is also used, more loosely than is often allowed, as a symbol for the procedures characteristic of some, perhaps most but certainly not all, natural sciences, with physics the model. And then the implicit claim of superiority becomes pernicious. I will not waste time on the obvious point that scientists are not demonstrably more 'scientific' (or less) than historians, linguists or sociologists in their behaviour outside their professional work. There are more serious things to be said. In science the common habit, denounced by David Hume, of sliding from 'is' to 'ought' sentences and vice versa, is a legitimate and necessary procedure. The testing of theory by experiment is nothing less than an attempt to equate 'ought' and 'is', and the conclusions are either right or wrong, even if only in a limited and transient way. But in many other kinds of behaviour the 'scientific mode' is a stultifying goal, sometimes dangerous. On the one hand, the impossibility of attaining certain conclusions becomes an argument against introducing significant, desirable changes; on the other hand, efforts to convert 'ought' into 'is' in morals and social arrangements have not infrequently led to tyranny.

The popular association of science with exactness, with unqualified rightness and wrongness, also has important psychological implications. Hudson has shown how, in consequence, scientific studies at the school level more readily attract those he calls Convergers, youngsters who 'tend to plump for those routes through the academic system . . . in which the weight of accepted authority is greatest';[43] how, furthermore, their education and their subsequent careers help reinforce their predispositions. Independent confirmation comes from a routine questionnaire administered to university students, in which the inquiry about lectures and lecturers produced, apart from the familiar, boring replies, one revealing distinction: 'arts students were rather more likely to look for stimulus to their interest, and this seemed to relate to another quality which many of them stressed, but *which the scientists almost always ignored*–originality. They wanted a lecturer to give his own point of view, and to be controversial, to explore ideas which were not already in their books' (my italics).[44] Hudson of course adds the qualification that 'authoritarianism and convergence overlap; they do not coincide'.[45]

And I myself would add that the same overlapping will be found in other formal studies, such as grammar, and that this is yet another facet of that 'discipline' so much admired in some quarters. For those who believe authoritarianism in the young to be a contradiction of the aims of a liberal education, here is one more argument against current specialization.

IV

By now it may seem that I am working towards the conclusion that higher education has been a continuous functional absurdity for more than two thousand years. Not at all. What I have called the ancient heritage, the Isocratean rationale, was firmly grounded in the social structure and its institutional arrangements. Our word 'education' is ambiguous (as it is in most modern languages): for proper analysis, we require terminology such as suggested by Durkheim when he proposed to distinguish between 'pedagogy' and 'education', between formal schooling and the no less important education taking place all the time outside school.[46] Isocrates' programme was pedagogical, and it was designed for members of the ruling élite, a socially and culturally homogeneous group, whose common values were formed and repeatedly reinforced by their continuous association and shared experience, at first within the family and then outside, in the army, in the dining clubs, in their political activity. Higher education continued to be so based until the end of the nineteenth century; the structure and needs of society may have changed radically from one era to another, but not the fact that it was a homogeneous élite who received the pedagogy as one part of a larger common education. The link between school and *scholē* remained unbroken. A minority of outsiders were admitted, to be sure, but they were recruits into the élite, either as full members or as men to be admitted to the councils of the élite or, at the least, as their future retainers. The vaunted high correlation between the traditional English classical education (with a bit of mathematics thrown in) and achievement in later life is explained by the social situation, not by the intrinsic merits of the narrow pedagogical curriculum. It is normally and conveniently overlooked that the élite of Wilhelmine Germany were equally the products of the *humanistische Gymnasium*.[47]

Ever since Plato there have been voices raised in protest, some of them famous, none efficacious. But in the twentieth century the social ground itself has so altered as to compel a total re-examination of the educational procedures and their rationale. In the first place, the technological explosion requires a large number of men in public and private life who, though not themselves scientists or mathematicians, 'thoroughly understand what kind of knowledge scientific knowledge is',[48] as Mr Gladstone was not called upon to do. Second, the old social and political élite, self-confident and serene in the rightness of its values and its place at the head of a hierarchical society, is being transformed or replaced. Third, the entry into higher education has broadened accordingly, more so in some countries than in others but substantially everywhere. The student population is now heterogeneous in its culture and values, as in its career aspirations and possibilities (which are more nearly identical than is often appreciated).[49]

In every society, wrote Durkheim, the system of education is 'manifold'; one may say that 'there are as many different kinds of education as there are different milieux in a given society'.[50] Until our century that dictum was as true for pedagogy as for education, but now we have a large and growing student population who share the same system of pedagogy while not sharing the same education. The 'cultural capital' or 'repertoire' with which they come to higher studies is very different, even their language. Academic culture, high culture, is 'a common code enabling all those possessing that code to attach the same meaning to the same words, the same types of behaviour and the same works'; it is also 'a common set of previously assimilated master patterns from which . . . an infinite number of individual patterns directly applicable to specific situations are generated.'[51] Those who come to it from outside the élite normally come with an impoverished cultural capital, a different and inadequate 'set of master patterns', and their pedagogy is not reinforced by their continuing non-school associations unless, exceptionally, they become full recruits into the élite. They come to the academy, furthermore, in an era when, for the first time in history, youth has 'lost its social function'.[52] That is to say, as the age of biological maturity becomes lower, the age of social maturity, the age when one takes one's productive place in society, is postponed further and further; and the place eventually to be taken becomes increasingly problematical for many. It is hardly surprising that an unresolved conflict between education and pedagogy, during precisely these critical years missing a social function, generates flight if not rebellion, against accepted values, against the pedagogical system and all its works, against the intellect itself.

And how does the academy respond, that sector of the academy which is by definition concerned with general education, not with technological or vocational instruction? A common response is to wring one's hands in fatalistic pessimism. 'Art of integrity', John Vaizey has recently written, 'is never likely to be popular . . . it is an art of cultivation, not immediately accessible, for not only its appreciation but its simple, casual enjoyment depends upon a long apprenticeship.'[53] However, a brief historical consideration suggests an important qualification. Tragedy in fifth-century B.C. Athens was an art of integrity and it was popular; so has church music been in many places over long periods; even sermons, and I am thinking not of vulgar revivalist preachers but of the linguistically and intellectually complex sermons of Calvin and his followers, of John Donne, of other, perhaps lesser preachers to our own day. A long apprenticeship would no doubt have enhanced the understanding of these works, but the mass audiences had no formal training, no apprenticeship in that sense. What they had was a sharing in the myths, beliefs and values which were the stuff of such works, to which they could therefore respond with concentrated attention and with simple, casual enjoyment. If, as is hardly disputable, our world knows nothing like Greek tragedy or Bach masses, in this respect, the possibility must surely be considered that what has changed is not some existential popular taste but the groundwork itself; that high culture is no longer moored to a broad, common language and common value-system; that neither defeatism nor a rigid persistence with old pedagogical notions (which of course intensifies the defeatism) is the only possible response.

What is impossible is a return to the past, in any form: the cult of the past is an abuse of the past. When Curtius announced that 'continuity has become more important to me than present reality (*Aktualität*), Virgil and Dante more significant than all the moderns since the death of Goethe',[54] the crushing reply was given by a Harvard philosopher, Ralph Barton Perry: 'A man is no freer when imprisoned in the thirteenth century than when imprisoned in his own.'[55] Continuity is an empty container: what contents does one fill it with? T. S. Eliot had an answer that was logically defensible and coherent: 'Literary criticism should be completed by criticism from a definite ethical and theological standpoint. In so far as in any age there is common agreement on ethical and theological matters, so far can literary criticism be substantive.'[56]

The words 'definite' and 'substantive' are crucial. Eliot himself had a definite ethical and theological standpoint, but in our age, as he went on to say correctly, 'there is no such common agreement'. For those who do not share Eliot's theology, can there be an alternative *definite* standpoint for substantive criticism, not only of literature but also of society, of ethics, of politics? The question has to be asked because affirmative answers are in fact being offered precisely by those in the humanities who defend the tyranny of the one-subject degree, in particular by those who claim to possess 'private lines to something called "tradition" '.[57] It is notable how easily they slide into a canonical dogma, and it is therefore essential to insist that the Great Tradition can never legitimately become the Authorized Version. Sensibility is a fine thing and it ought to be cultivated, but it can never establish substantive criticism nor acquire the status of revelation. Or of legitimate orthodoxy: no two prophets of the Great Tradition agree on the canon, nor do any two generations. Dr Arnold could not bring himself to read Aristophanes until he was forty, and Juvenal was no better; yet both now rank high among the 'best classical authors' to whom the contemporary classical curriculum dedicates itself.

One claim requires further examination. 'The study of literature', we are told, 'is concerned with the results of the most far-reaching and subtle investigations that have been made into man's mind and passions and his life in society';[58] or that *A Passage to India* 'is a work of art concerned with the total human situation in the modern world'.[59] A large anthology of such assertions is easily compiled, but reiteration does not establish truth. A poet, a dramatist, a novelist probes individual experience and the meaning of that experience; no matter how much social detail he introduces, he cannot possibly concern himself with 'the total human situation'. Nor is he conducting an investigation, in any normal sense of that word. Poets and novelists are not systematic, disciplined thinkers, either in psychology or in sociology, either in ethics or in institutional behaviour. They strike resonances, they invite reflection and passion, they may even be said to 'teach', but they do not provide a sufficient education and surely not authority.[60] To claim that for them is to revive in another guise the ancient claims of myth, to replace the *Iliad* and *Odyssey*, the tales about Zeus, Apollo and Hercules by the plays of Shakespeare, the novels of Jane Austen and D. H. Lawrence.

For in antiquity myth was educative in the same way as poetry and literature today. Education is not merely the acquisition of facts and skills; the learning process creates and shapes attitudes and values as well. Even in the most mechanical kind of pedagogy the learner is not wholly passive: it is still necessary for him 'to relate the new material to relevant, established ideas in his own cognitive structure'.[61] The issue is therefore one of the range and variety of new material available to him which will enlarge his cultural capital and increase his potential for independent, rational judgments in the large area of behaviour that lies outside his technical and vocational interests; an issue, I shall say once again, made acute by the loss of common agreement on ethical and theological matters (in Eliot's phrasing), by the vastly increased amount of leisure (free time) in the lives of those who, by ancient standards, are still *ascholē*, lacking the leisure that comes of freedom from economic concerns, by the multiplicity of milieux represented among those now sharing a common pedagogy.

Rather than have physical science 'the principal thing in my son's mind', Dr Arnold wrote to a medical student in 1836, 'I would gladly have him think that the sun went round the earth, and that the stars were so many spangles set in the bright blue firmament'.[62] Quoted out of context, as I have seen it done, that remark sounds like an extreme know-nothing reaction of entrenched classicism and theology to modern science. But Thomas Arnold was not a fool, and he explained himself in the same letter when he wrote, 'The philosophy of medicine, I imagine, is almost at zero', and again, 'I might . . . wish that my children might be well versed in physical science, but in due subordination to the fulness and freshness of their knowledge on moral subjects'. The much vaunted neutrality of science *qua* science means that one must turn elsewhere for one's social and moral values; so too the claim (which I do not accept) that social science can also be value-free. And even the scientist *qua* scientist must, in the nature of things, work on projects which have moral implications, his form of the market research which appears to be the chief expression of 'value-free' social science.

To be sure, Dr Arnold's choice, under contemporary conditions, slides easily into mandarinism. 'The life of humanistic wisdom and enjoyment demands . . . both security and leisure.'[63] How many times have we read that in programmatic statements by academics who have pseudo-*scholē*, leisure that comes from their being paid to devote themselves to humanistic pursuits? How many books and articles are published annually that are consciously designed *not* to be read outside the small circle of the mandarins? To judge from reviews in the learned journals, the absence of footnotes is a moral fault; any attempt to communicate is damned with the faint praise, in French naturally, of *haute vulgarisation*. The mandarins should perhaps be reminded that at the University of Berlin the patron saint of twentieth-century classical scholarship, Ulrich von Wilamowitz-Moellendorf, gave two-hour public lectures every week which were events in the life of the city. 'Philology', he once wrote, 'is for philologists; whatever is immortal in Hellenism is for every man who wishes to come, to see and to grasp.'[64] And finally there is the mandarinism of the laments for the lost 'culture of the common people', in reality a culture of poverty and misery, of lack of education and of hierarchical values.

High culture *does* matter, more today than ever. The difference between high culture, humanistic study of literature and philosophy and history, on the one hand, and mass culture is not merely one of taste (and taste, as we all know, is not discussable–*de gustibus non disputandum*).[65] Man at play, *homo ludens*, is not to be neglected, as I said earlier, but the culture of play, in all its forms, is magical or rhetorical, not reflective; when, as with so much contemporary pop music, for example, it appears to have an element of social protest, it invariably lacks the essential element of criticism.[66] Contemporary mass culture may not give one the feeling, as E. M. Forster once said of Eliot's essays, 'that the Muses are connected not so much with Apollo as with the oldest county families';[67] it rather gives the feeling that the Muses are fleeing from both the gods and social reality.

That they should flee from mandarinism is neither surprising nor reprehensible. The spirit of Isocrates, of Dean Gaisford, has long since lost its legitimacy in the social order. However, dissatisfaction with, even sharp rejection of, certain important aspects of the cultural, social and political heritage is not to be confused with a complete break from the past, an impossible notion. We are all inextricably locked into the past, and the choice is between imprisoning oneself in the past and taking rational, innovatory steps into the future.

The implications for general education on the higher level are, then, not difficult to summarize, and, indeed, they have been more or less explicit throughout my discourse. First, the range and variety of experience, literary, philosophical, historical, scientific, which schooling contributes to the equipment of the student must be enlarged and correlated so as to be adequate to life in a democratic society of great technical complexity, improving material satisfaction and increasing free time. Second, that enlargement is possible only by extending the learning period beyond the present cut-off age into the early years of intellectual, emotional and social maturity. Third, the past must be deconsecrated, freed from cult, and converted into a living past, into–dare I use the word?–a relevant past. High culture must be anchored again, in new ways, to the search for, and the preservation of, values of the present and for the future. That requires abandonment of spurious, restrictive canons of eternal greatness and eternal truth: we must have the historical sense and the moral courage of the German classicist who said, addressing students at the Free University of Berlin in 1962, 'We are experiencing the collapse of a lie, the humanist lie of the identity of the true, the beautiful and the good.'[68] And we must recognize and accept in a positive way the new reality of the student population, with its heterogeneous background and therefore its very uneven cultural endowment, and with the most diverse occupational futures. The resulting burden on education may be much greater; it remains no less essential to retain the highest quality.

NOTES

Notes to Chapter 1

MYTH, MEMORY AND HISTORY

1. Humphry House, *Aristotle's Poetics* (London 1956) p. 11.

2. See generally on this distinction G. H. Nadel, 'Philosophy of History before Historicism', *History and Theory* 3 (1964) 291–315, esp. pp. 292–304. This is of course not the sense of 'paradigm' developed in T. S. Kuhn's influential *The Structure of Scientific Revolutions* (2nd edn, Chicago 1970), on which see e.g. D. A. Hollinger, 'T. S. Kuhn's Theory of Science and Its Implications for History', *American Historical Review* 78 (1973) 370–93.

3. See Gert Avenarius, *Lukians Schrift zur Geschichtsschreibung* Mciscnhcim/Glan 1956).

4. See F. W. Walbank, *Polybius* (Berkeley, Los Angeles, London 1972) pp. 34–40, with bibliography.

5. On the modern extensions of myth, see e.g. B. Halpern, ' "Myth" and "Ideology" in Modern Usage', *History and Theory* 1 (1961) 129–49.

6. The point is well brought out in the opening pages of P. Munz, 'History and Myth', *Philosophical Quarterly* 6 (1956) 1–16.

7. *Lectures on the Religion of the Semites* (new edn, London 1907) pp. 16–17.

8. Even more striking is the way Thucydides (3.104.5) accepts lines 165–78 of the 'Homeric' Hymn to Apollo as an autobiographical bit by Homer. See F. Hampl, 'Die Ilias ist kein Geschichtsbuch', in *Serta Philologica Aenipontana* [*Innsbrucker Beiträge zur Kulturwissenschaft* VII–VIII (1962)] pp. 37–63.

9. See I. Meyerson, 'Le temps, la mémoire, l'histoire', *Journal de psychologie* 53 (1956) 333–54.

10. H. Fränkel, *Wege und Formen frühgriechischen Denkens* (2nd edn, Munich 1960) p. 2.

11. *The Humour of Homer and Other Essays*, ed. R. A. Streatfeild (London 1913) p. 77. Perhaps I should say that I have not the slightest doubt that in this lecture, delivered in 1892, Butler was speaking in earnest.

12. See J.-P. Vernant, *Mythe et pensée chez les Grecs* (Paris 1965) pp. 19–47; 'Le mythe hésiodique des races', *Revue de philologie*, 3rd ser., 40 (1966) 247–76.

13. *Works and Days* 156–71. I use the translation by H. G. Evelyn-White in the *Loeb Classical Library*. Vernant, *op. cit.*, has ingeniously argued that the whole Hesiodic structure is a coherent one. Even if he should be right, my central argument stands, for the structure of the myth he finds is architectonic, not chronological.

14. O. Gigon, *Der Ursprung der griechischen Philosophie* . . . (Basel 1945) pp. 22–23. Gigon is talking about the *Theogony*, but the remark seems equally relevant to the opening of the *Works and Days*.

15. See W. den Boer, 'Herdot und die Systeme der Chronologie', *Mnemosyne*, 4th ser., 20 (1967) 30–60.

16. See P. Vidal-Naquet, 'Temps des dieux et temps des hommes', *Revue de l'histoire des religions* 157 (1960) 55–80, at pp. 65–69.

17. R. M. Cook, 'Thucydides as Archaeologist', *Annual of the British School at Athens* 50 (1955) 266–70. Note that Herodotus (2.125) thought that iron tools were used in building the pyramids.

18. Translated by Denys Page in *The Listener* for 15 January 1959, pp. 109–110.

19. It must be understood that no pre-fifth-century Greek historical writing ever existed (eventually the chronographers 'annalized' myths, which is another matter). All arguments to the contrary have been completely destroyed by the work of Felix Jacoby; see particularly his *Atthis* (Oxford 1949).

20. The more common variation is perhaps this: 'Western man has always been historically minded'–the opening words of J. R. Strayer's introduction to the English translation of Marc Bloch, *The Historian's Craft* (New York 1953).

21. On all this see Hans Meyerhoff, *Time in Literature* (Berkeley 1955); cf. e.g. P. Bohannan, 'Concepts of Time among the Tiv of Nigeria', *Southwestern Journal of Anthropology* 9 (1953) 251–62.

22. *Crossing the Line* (London 1958) p. 155.

23. See Hampl (cited in note 8 above) and my article initiating a discussion of the historicity of the Trojan War, in *Journal of Hellenic Studies* 84 (1964) 1–9.

24. 'Clothed in terms of a sober, pseudo-scientific "history" ' is S. F. Nadel's phrase for the analogous accounts of the distant past among the Nupe of Nigeria: *A Black Byzantium* (London 1942) p. 72.

25. 'The myth as it stands, and as it is treasured by the people of Nupe, is . . . the typical "mythical charter" [Malinowski's term] of the kingdom, and its common knowledge constitutes the first and foremost of these common beliefs and forms of cultural "commonness" which supply the background of political unity': *ibid.*, pp. 75–76.

26. On the foregoing pages, see e.g. Jack Goody and Ian Watt, 'The Consequences of Literacy', *Comparative Studies in Society and History* 5 (1963) 304–45, reprinted in *Literacy in Traditional Societies*, ed. Goody (Cambridge

1968) pp. 27–68; Ruth Finnegan, 'A Note on Oral Tradition and Historical Evidence', *History and Theory* 9 (1970) 195–201; R. C. C. Law, 'The Heritage of Oduduwa: Traditional History and Political Propaganda among the Yoruba', *Journal of African History* 14 (1973) 207–22.

27. See Jacoby, *Atthis* pp. 152–68.

28. See L. Pearson, 'Political Allusions in the Attic Orators', *Classical Philology* 36 (1941) 209–29; S. Perlman, 'The Historical Example, Its Use and Importance as Political Propaganda in the Attic Orators', *Scripta Hierosolymitana* 7 (1961) 150–66.

29. 'The conversion of legend-writing into the science of history was not native to the Greek mind, it was a fifth-century invention, and Herodotus was the man who invented it': R. G. Collingwood, *The Idea of History* (Oxford 1946) p. 19.

30. See J. G. A. Pocock, 'The Origins of Study of the Past: A Comparative Approach', *Comparative Studies in Society and History* 4 (1962) 209–46.

31. *Op. cit.*, pp. 26–27; cf. A. Momigliano, *Studies in Historiography* (London 1966) ch. 8 and 11.

32. (London 1953) pp. 10–11.

33. *Time in Literature* p. 109.

Notes to Chapter 2

THE ANCESTRAL CONSTITUTION

1. Quoted from J. W. Gough, *Fundamental Law in English Constitutional History* (Oxford 1955) p. 1.

2. Quoted from C. Rossiter, *Conservatism in America* (London 1955) p. 146.

3. F. M. Cornford, *Microcosmographia Academica* (4th edn, Cambridge 1949) p. 15.

4. The brief quotations are from L. Benson, 'An Approach to the Scientific Study of Past Public Opinion', *Public Opinion Quarterly* 31 (1967) 522–67, at p. 543, and W. G. Runciman, 'Sociological Evidence in Political Theory', in *Philosophy, Politics and Society*, 2nd ser., ed. P. Laslett and W. G. Runciman (Oxford 1962) p. 39, respectively.

5. Quoted by Aristotle, *Constitution of Athens* 29.3.

6. See *ibid.*, 34.3; Aristophanes, *Frogs* 967.

7. Fragment 1, ed. Diels-Kranz.

8. See A. Fuks, *The Ancestral Constitution* (London 1953) pp. 34–35. S. A. Cecchin, Πάτριος πολιτεία: *Un tentativo propagandistico durante la guerre del Peloponneso* (Turin 1969), who appreciates that the 'ancestral constitution' was defined by each faction to suit its political aims, nevertheless makes heavy weather of the terminology (and of other aspects of the debate) because he attributes too much precision and schematism to the arguments.

9. Antiphon 3.1.1. On the use of *nomos* to include *psephismata*, see Xenophon, *Hellenica* 1.7.21–25; cf. H. J. Wolff, ' "Normenkontrolle" und Gesetzesbegriff in der attischen Demokratie', *Sitzungesberichte d. Heidelberger Akademie der Wissenschaften, Phil.-hist. Kl.*, Abh. 2 (1970) p. 50, who is surely right to argue (pp. 38–41) that any attempt to distinguish between *nomos* and *psephisma* had as a necessary condition the legislative procedure known as *nomothesia*, introduced in 403/2 B.C.

10. This point should have been effectively settled by F. Jacoby, *Atthis* (Oxford 1949) p. 333, note 21, yet the anachronism persists, extremely in E. Ruschenbusch, 'Πάτριος πολιτεία. Theseus, Drakon, Solon und Kleisthenes im Publizistik und Geschichtschreibung des 5. und 4. Jahrhunderts v. Chr.', *Historia* 7 (1958) 398–424, whose analysis is vitiated by his failure to grasp this simple fact in the history of Greek (and later) political discussion (and by his attempts to apply statistical methods to evidence that does not lend itself to them).

11. See R. S. Stroud, *Drakon's Law on Homicide* [*Univ. of California Publications: Classical Philology* 3 (1968)] pp. 20–29, with full bibliographical references.

12. Aristotle, *Constitution of Athens* 34.3.

13. Quoted by Andocides 1.83.

14. Attempts, e.g. by Fuks, *Ancestral Constitution* pp. 38–40, Ruschenbusch, *op. cit.*, p. 408, to argue that the wording of the decree distinguishes between the laws of Draco and Solon and a constitution, not by Draco or Solon, rests on the fundamental error I have already discussed. Nor are they supported linguistically in the Greek. In *Phaedrus* 278C, Plato refers to Σόλωνι καὶ ὅστις ἐν πολιτικοῖς λόγοις νόμους ὀνομάζων συγγράματα ἔγραψεν. Aristotle, *Constitution of Athens* 7.1., has no objection to writing, with reference to Solon, πολιτείαν δὲ κατέστησε καὶ νόμους ἔθηκεν ἄλλους. Whoever introduced ch. 4 into that work uses πολιτεία, νόμοι and θεσμοί synonymously with reference to the 'Draconic constitution'. And Xenophon, *Hellenica* 2.4.42, has Thrasybulus, leader of the democratic restoration, speak of the ἀρχαῖοι νόμοι.

15. See Stroud, *Drakon's Law*; on the fictitious constitution of Draco, apparently an early fourth-century B.C. invention, see Fuks, *op. cit.*, ch. 4.

16. See Jacoby, *Atthis* pp. 154–55.

17. Plutarch, *Life of Phocion* 27.3.

18. J. G. A. Pocock, *The Ancient Constitution and the Feudal Law* (Cambridge 1957) p. 46.

19. *Ibid.*, pp. 42–45.

20. *Ibid.*, p. 44.

21. D. C. Douglas, *English Scholars 1660–1730* (2nd edn, London 1951) p. 53.

22. F. W. Maitland, 'The Laws of the Anglo-Saxons', originally published

in the *Quarterly Review* for 1904, reprinted in his *Collected Papers*, ed. H. A. L. Fisher, vol. 3 (Cambridge 1931) pp. 447–73, at p. 453.

23. Epistle Dedicatory to the *Maxims of the Law*, in *Works*, ed. J. Spedding *et al.*, VII (London 1859) p. 314 (I owe this reference to Gough, *Fundamental Law* p. 51). Cf. Matthew Hale, *The History of the Common Law of England* (published posthumously in 1713) p. 45: The common law 'is singularly accommodated to the Frame of the *English* Government'; it has 'in a manner become the Complexion and Constitution of the *English* Commonwealth'.

24. See H. Butterfield, *The Englishman and His History* (Cambridge 1944) pp. 31–38.

25. Strafford at his trial in 1641, quoted from M. A. Judson, *The Crisis of the Constitution* (New Brunswick 1949) p. 138.

26. Quoted from C. Hill, 'The Norman Yoke', in his *Puritanism and Revolution* (London 1958) ch. 3, at pp. 78 (Norwood) and 81 (Lilburne); cf. briefly Pocock, *Ancient Constitution* pp. 124–27.

27. See the admirable account by Hill, 'Norman Yoke'.

28. *Ibid.*, p. 90.

29. See I. Kramnick, 'Augustan Politics and English Historiography. The Debate on the English Past, 1730–35', *History and Theory* 6 (1967) 33–56, subsequently incorporated into his *Bolingbroke and His Circle* (Cambridge, Mass., 1968), with the unfortunate subtitle, *The Politics of Nostalgia in the Age of Walpole.*

30. Quoted in the opening sentence of D. W. Brogan, 'The Ghost of Jefferson', *The Fortnightly*, n.s. 140 (1936) 88–92.

31. *The Papers of Thomas Jefferson*, ed. J. P. Boyd, vol. 8 (Princeton 1953) p. 426.

32. See Kramnick, 'Augustan Politics'.

33. Full documentation will be found, without sufficient analysis, in M. D. Peterson, *The Jefferson Image in the American Mind* (New York 1960) ch. 7.

34. G. Chinard, *The Commonplace Book of Thomas Jefferson* pp. 64–65, quoted from Hill, 'Norman Yoke' p. 94.

35. Professor Dumas Malone, in an article published soon after Roosevelt entered the White House, 'Jefferson and the New Deal', *Scribner's Magazine* 93 (1933) 356–59, suggested that 'Jefferson would bestow his symbolic blessing on Franklin D. Roosevelt, as the new President buckles on his Hamiltonian sword', whereas Hamilton's 'philosophy and practice of class-rule', and 'his contempt for the stupidity of the lesser orders of mankind, would in our day lead straight to Fascism'.

36. Brogan, 'Ghost' p. 92; cf. the *New York Times* columnist who wrote on 14 April 1936: 'This is a very prosperous year for Thomas Jefferson. . . . Every political party and faction in the land calls him father' (quoted by Peterson, *Jefferson* p. 363).

37. Dr D. E. D. Beales has called my attention to an interesting, little

known instance from Belgium in 1787. Joseph II of Austria had suddenly decreed a radical change in the traditional administrative and judicial organization, but was forced by widespread protests to withdraw the new measure. Flanders was not satisfied; on 5 June the Flemish Estates-General memorialized the Governor-General: 'the Flemish nation . . . has noted with sadness that the declaration . . . promises only to restore matters to the state they were in before the innovations', and not 'that everything should be put back to the base on which it had rested two hundred years ago'. There followed a festive mood, says the chronicler, as if 'the nation had taken seriously the legend of the *Good Old Days*'. See P. A. F. Gérard, *F. Rapedius de Berg: Mémoires et documents pour servir à l'histoire de la révolution Brabançonne* I (Brussels 1842) 228–29.

38. Quoted from Brogan, 'Ghost' p. 88.

39. See Wolff, 'Normenkontrolle' p. 69.

40. It is a flaw in Pocock's argument, both in the *Ancient Constitution* and in 'Burke and the Ancient Constitution–A Problem in the History of Ideas', *Historical Journal* 3 (1960) 128–34, reprinted in his *Politics, Language and Time* (London 1972) ch. 6 (to which I shall refer), that he underplays this point when he does not ignore it. In view of my disagreement with some of his conclusions, I should like to record my indebtedness, like that of anyone else writing in this field, to Pocock's work.

41. See Hill, 'Norman Yoke' pp. 96–99.

42. Benson, 'An Approach' p. 543.

43. *Works* VII (London 1899) 264–65; see further note 78 below.

44. 'Historical Past and Existential Present', in *The Dissenting Academy*, ed. T. Roszak (London 1969) pp. 92–109, at p. 108. For a practical demonstration of 'vigorous criticism of the historical consensus' by New Left historians, see *Towards a New Past. Dissenting Essays in American History*, ed. B. J. Bernstein (New York 1968, London 1970).

45. J. H. Plumb, *The Death of the Past* (London 1969) p. 40.

46. Douglas, *Scholars* p. 14.

47. L. M. Hacker, *Alexander Hamilton in the American Tradition* (New York 1957) pp. v–vi. Despite the title, this is a personal reappraisal of Hamilton, with little about the later image of the man.

48. F. E. Manuel, 'The Use and Abuse of Psychology in History', *Daedalus* 100 (1971) 187–213, at p. 194. This sympathetically critical review, with a strong bent towards neo-Freudianism, provides a good recent statement of the situation. It has been reprinted in *Historical Studies Today*, ed. F. Gilbert and S. R. Graubard (New York 1972) pp. 211–37.

49. Hill, 'Norman Yoke' pp. 68–69.

50. Malone, 'Jefferson' p. 358. Cf. G. E. Mowry, 'The Uses of History by Recent Presidents', *Journal of American History* 53 (1966) 5–18, at p. 16, writing about Roosevelt and Kennedy: 'their inferences, on the whole', were 'within the bounds of arguable truth'.

51. 'Norman Yoke' p. 69.

52. For an account of how a materially prosperous upper class turned to the distant past for solace, see E. L. Bowie, 'Greeks and Their Past in the Second Sophistic', *Past and Present*, no. 46 (1970) 3–41, reprinted in *Studies in Ancient Society*, ed. M. I. Finley (London 1974) ch. 8. Optimistic believers in the idea of progress, however defined, of course turn to the past for a different kind of sanction, one which expects its transcendence.

53. See Paul Fraisse, *The Psychology of Time*, trans. by Jennifer Leith (London 1964), Index *s.v.* Pathology, with full bibliography.

54. *Time in Literature* (Berkeley and Los Angeles 1952) p. 52.

55. The significance of the *oikos* in Greek tragedy has been fully examined by John Jones, *On Aristotle and Greek Tragedy* (London 1962). Perhaps I should say explicitly that my stress on the family side of Oedipus has no connection with the Freudian complex; see J.-P. Vernant, 'Oedipe sans complexe', in Vernant and P. Vidal-Naquet, *Mythe et tragédie en Grèce ancienne* (Paris 1972) ch. 4.

56. See above all Jacoby, *Atthis*, esp. ch. 3, sect. 2.

57. See J. R. Goody, *Death, Property and the Ancestors* (London 1962), esp. pt. IV and the review of the literature, pp. 13–30; cf. Goody and Ian Watt, 'The Consequences of Literacy', in *Literacy in Traditional Societies*, ed. Goody (Cambridge 1968) pp. 27–68, at pp. 30–34.

58. The basic analysis was made by Erwin Rohde in 1893; see his *Psyche*, trans. from the 8th edn by W. B. Hillis (reprint, London 1950) pt. 1, ch. 4; cf. B. A. Van Groningen, *In the Grip of the Past* (Leiden 1953) ch. 3; A. Brelich, *Gli eroi greci. Un problema storico-religioso* (Rome 1958) pp. 129–51.

59. See Jacoby, *Atthis* p. 223.

60. *Death* p. 382, note 1.

61. *Reflections on the Revolution in France*, ed. Conor Cruise O'Brien (Pelican Classics 1968) pp. 119–21; cf. the final paragraph of *An Appeal from the New to the Old Whigs*, in his *Works* IV 214–15.

62. The opening essay in *The Search for a Usable Past* (New York 1967).

63. This point is touched on briefly, though from other concerns, by Manuel, 'Use and Abuse' pp. 199–200.

64. The Isocratean passages on the *patrios politeia* are conveniently assembled by K. Jost, *Das Beispiel und Vorbild der Vorfahren bei den attischen Rednern und Geschichtsschreibern bis Demosthenes* [*Rhetorische Studien* 19 (Paderborn 1936)] pp. 140–45; Fuks, *Ancestral Constitution* pp. 7–13.

65. Both Draco and Cleisthenes are mentioned in the miserable spurious dialogue, *Axiochos* 365D.

66. Plato, *The Statesman*, trans. and ed. by J. B. Skemp (London 1952) p. 205, note 3 (in paperback edn, 1961). If this analysis is correct, it removes the chronological basis of Ruschenbusch's argument (see above notes 10 and 14). Several times in the passage Plato refers to 'written or unwritten laws'; I take this to be yet another way of saying that it does not matter

whether you employ the current Athenian law-code, which forbade any reference to 'unwritten laws' (i.e. those not incorporated into the code), or the older laws. As a further example of the deliberate dropping of clues in the *Statesman*, note 296B: if a doctor changed his mind as a result of circumstances and gave his unwilling patient a new prescription, would we call that action παρὰ τὴν τέχνην? The sneer about the *graphe paronomon* (on which see Wolff, 'Normenkontrolle') is unmistakable.

67. W. K. C. Guthrie, *In the Beginning* (London 1957) p. 99.

68. On 'paradigmatic history' see ch. 1 at note 2. It is true that Aristotle believed that there has been enough experience to test most possible ethical ideas and norms, and that therefore some traditional ethical norms must be accepted as valid, provided that they do not contradict rationally established norms (e.g. *Politics* 1264a1–5, 68b25–69a28), but that does not contradict the position I have taken. Nor does the fact that he and his school produced studies of 158 'constitutions'. As Jacoby, *Atthis* p. 210, correctly said of the Athenian study, 'Aristotle intends to write not an historical or antiquarian treatise, but a description of one among many forms of constitution the accounts of which were to serve as the material for a philosophical (in the ancient sense) study of the State generally'.

69. *The English Works*, ed. Sir William Molesworth (London 1839–45) VI 259, quoted from Q. Skinner, 'History and Ideology in the English Revolution', *Historical Journal* 8 (1965) 151–78, at p. 161.

70. A recent attempt to make a systematic thinker of him–B. T. Wilkins, *The Problem of Burke's Political Philosophy* (Oxford 1967)–is not convincing.

71. John Dunn, 'The Identity of the History of Ideas', *Philosophy* 43 (1968) 85–104, at p. 87.

72. The relevant volume of the *Correspondence* is VI, ed. A. Cobban and R. A. Smith (Cambridge 1967). On the way Burke's response to the French Revolution evolved, see C. B. Cone, *Burke and the Nature of Politics* (2 vols., Univ. of Kentucky Press 1957–64) II chs. 13–14.

73. On Burke's attitude to France, see *ibid.*, Index *s.v.* Burke, Edmund: and French Revolution.

74. See e.g. *Correspondence* VI 26–27, 37, 44, 81, 91–95, 125ff., 141.

75. See e.g. the opening pages of Pocock, 'Burke'.

76. *Time* pp. 212–13 and 229, respectively. Not all readers of the article seem to have paid sufficient attention to the modesty of Pocock's claim, clearly stated in the final paragraph. The changes in nuance in his thinking about problems of traditionalism in political and historical thought, reflected in his later article, 'Time, Institutions and Action: An Essay on Traditions and Their Understanding', in *Politics and Experience, Essays Presented to Professor Michael Oakeshott*, ed. P. King and B. C. Parekh (Cambridge 1968) pp. 209–37 (reprinted in his *Time*, ch. 7), should also be noted.

77. Some of the best passages are quoted by R. Schlatter, *Private Property. The History of an Idea* (London 1951) pp. 178–81. Schlatter makes the just comment, 'His defence of the English political structure was a theory of

property as well as a theory of politics', though the 'theory' label is contestable.

78. I see nothing to support the notion that Burke ever took back the severe criticism of the common law to be found in his *Abridgement* (*op. cit.* in note 43). That Burke neither completed nor published that work is explained by reasons having nothing to do with our problem; see Cone, *Burke* I 30–33; *Correspondence* I, ed. T. W. Copeland (Cambridge 1958) p. 124, note 5, p. 164, note 1. I also doubt that Burke ever identified tradition and custom so closely with the common law as Pocock would have it.

79. This is of course not everyone's view. When Paul Veyne, e.g., in *Comment on écrit l'histoire. Essai d'epistémologie* (Paris 1971), dismisses the rise of historiography as a 'purely philological problem without interest for the philosophy of history' (p. 98), that rests on a prior decision that history is no more than 'an intellectual activity which serves the ends of simple curiosity' (p. 103). The suggestion that history is linked in the first instance with group identity is dismissed, in characteristic fashion, in four words: 'Quel esprit de sérieux!' (p. 97). In a different way, C. G. Starr, *The Awakening of the Greek Historical Spirit* (New York 1968), takes 'historical spirit' too broadly, with an 'awakening' over two and a half centuries culminating in Herodotus.

80. For what follows about the chronicles, the indispensable work is Jacoby, *Atthis*, and the introduction and notes to his edition, *Fragmente der griechischen Historiker*, 3B Suppl. (2 vols., Leiden 1954).

81. Too much can be made of the inadequacy of the Greek calendar and Greek archives as hindrances. Early in the third century B.C. Timaeus overcame the chronological difficulty by resorting to Olympiads for dating; Solon's laws were still available for direct scrutiny; even poor archives can be examined.

82. I do not underestimate the great antiquarians of any age, but I hold firmly to the view that their critical role was largely restricted to the establishment and publication of source material, and that they were therefore not historians in the sense I have tried to specify. Kurt von Fritz, *Die griechische Geschichteschreibung*, vol. 1 (Berlin 1967), washes the distinction away, and underestimates the Greek historians as well, when he says in his introduction (*allgemeine Grundlagen*) that their 'critical spirit' was 'directed to the facts'. He then tries to rescue himself with such vague notions as *geschichtliche Lebendigkeit* (p. 4).

83. *Atthis* p. 205.

84. For all this, see Douglas, *Scholars*. I do not forget John Selden, but he seems to me to have stood outside this whole discussion.

85. See above all A. Momigliano, 'Pagan and Christian Historiography in the Fourth Century A.D.', in *The Conflict between Paganism and Christianity in the Fourth Century*, ed. Momigliano (Oxford 1963) pp. 79–99, reprinted in his *Terzo Contributo alla storia degli studi classici . . .* (2 vols., Rome 1966) pp. 87–109; cf. his 'Popular Religious Beliefs and the Late Roman

Historians', in *Studies in Church History*, vol. 8, ed. G. J. Cuming and D. Baker (Cambridge 1971) pp. 1–18.

86. See the opening sentence of the last chapter of *The English Constitution*, reaffirmed in a footnote to the 2nd edn (1872).

87. *Collected Papers* III 451.

88. Skinner, 'History and Ideology' p. 177.

89. On this passage see Jacoby, *Atthis* pp. 158–64; A. Momigliano, 'L'*excursus* di Tucidide in VI, 54–59', in *Studi . . . in memoria di Leonardo Ferrero* (Turin 1971) pp. 31–35, with full bibliography.

90. L. Pearson, 'Historical Allusions in the Attic Orators', *Classical Philology* 36 (1941) 209–29, at p. 217; cf. Jost, *Beispiel* ch. 5, and for the ancient world generally, the opening pages of H. Strasburger, *Die Wesensbestimmung der Geschichte durch die antike Geschichtsschreibung* [*Sitzungsberichte d. Wiss. Gesellschaft . . . Frankfurt/Main*, V 3 (1966)].

91. The phrase in inverted commas is that of R. B. Perry, *General Theory of Value* (Cambridge, Mass., 1926) p. 486.

92. H. Butterfield, *The Englishman and His History* (Cambridge 1944) p. 6.

93. *Ibid.*

94. J. A. Barnes, 'The Collection of Genealogies', *Rhodes-Livingstone Journal* 5 (1947) 48–55; cf. Goody and Watt, 'Literacy' pp. 57–60.

95. Is it irrelevant to call attention to E. Durkheim's argument that 'free inquiry' in religion increases the risk of what he called 'egoistic suicide': *Suicide*, trans. by J. A. Spaulding and G. Simpson (London 1954) pp. 156–70?

96. *The Historian's Craft*, trans. by P. Putnam (Manchester 1954) p. 30.

97. Meyerhoff, *Time* p. 105. It is a fiction fondly believed to be true by English historians that neither Spengler nor Toynbee has been taken seriously by professionals. Although this is possibly correct in England, it is not the case elsewhere. In the first 18 volumes (1950–67) of *Saeculum*, subtitled *Jahrbuch für Universalgeschichte*, there are seven articles about Toynbee, six about Goethe (five by the same author), four on Marx, two each on Engels, Huizinga, Jaspers and Mommsen, no more than one about anyone else.

98. The necessary references will be found in W. H. Walsh's judicious critique, 'The Practical and the Historical Past', in *Politics and Experience* (*op. cit.* in note 76 above) pp. 5–18.

99. *The Practice of History* (Fontana Library edn, London 1960) pp. 67–68.

100. *The Myth of the State* (Doubleday Anchor Book edn, New York 1955) p. 373.

101. *Practice* p. 67.

102. *Inaugural Lecture on the Study of History* (London 1895), reprinted in his *Essays on Freedom and Power*, ed. G. Himmelfarb (London 1956) p. 29.

Notes to Chapter 3

GENERALIZATIONS IN ANCIENT HISTORY

1. (London 1955).

2. Recently Starr has returned to the problem, now in the form of a question whether a historian should or should not pass judgment (or can avoid doing so) on the institutions and behaviour of ancient societies, and he explicitly links his discussion with his older essay on generalization: 'The Roman Place in History', in *Aufstieg und Niedergang der römischen Welt*, ed. H. Temporini, vol. I i (Berlin and New York 1972) pp. 3–11.

3. 'Die Sklaverei in der griechisch-römischen Welt', in *Rapports* of the XIth Intl. Congress of Historical Sciences, vol. 2 (Uppsala 1960) pp. 71–97, at p. 81; reprinted in *Gymnasium* 68 (1961) 370–95.

4. See my 'The Servile Statuses of Ancient Greece', *Revue internationale des droits de l'antiquité*, 3rd ser., 7 (1960) 165–89; 'Between Slavery and Freedom', *Comparative Studies in Society and History* 6 (1964) 233–49.

5. I quote from the 2nd edn (Cambridge 1952). There is now a 3rd edn (1972), so thoroughly revised by Barry Nicholas that 'there are few pages which have remained altogether unaltered'. In the chapter I am considering, Nicholas has removed one flaw in the periodization by removing Jolowicz's period 1 and regrouping 2–4. One of my objections to Jolowicz's scheme is therefore obsolete. However, all my other quotations from the chapter (and its title) have survived the revision, and I have therefore allowed my original comments to stand in full, on a book on which generations of law students have been brought up for thirty-five years.

6. (Oxford 1946) p. 101.

7. M. Mandelbaum, 'A Note on History as Narrative', *History and Theory* 6 (1967) 413–19, at p. 417.

8. 'Some Observations on Causes of War in Ancient Historiography', most conveniently available in his *Studies in Historiography* (London 1966) ch. 7.

9. Exception must now be made for Y. Garlan, *La guerre dans l'antiquité* (Paris 1972), of which an abridged English translation is in preparation.

10. See my 'Aristotle and Economic Analysis', *Past and Present*, no. 47 (1970) 3–25, reprinted in *Studies in Ancient Society*, ed. Finley (London 1974) ch. 2.

11. 'Traders and Manufacturers in Greece', in his *Essays in Greek History and Literature* (Oxford 1937) pp. 42–66.

12. On all this see my *The Ancient Economy* (London, Berkeley, Los Angeles 1973).

13. (Berkeley and Los Angeles 1951) p. viii.

14. J. V. A. Fine, *Horoi, Studies in Mortgage, Real Security and Land Tenure* [*Hesperia*, Suppl. 9 (1951)] pp. v–vi.

15. *The Slave Systems of Greek and Roman Antiquity* (Philadelphia 1955) p. 18. In a clever *tour de force* P. F. Lazarsfeld said all that needs saying about common sense, in the opening pages of 'The American Soldier–an Expository Review', *Public Opinion Quarterly* 13 (1949) 377–404.

Notes to Chapter 4

THE HISTORICAL TRADITION

1. (Turin 1931, reprinted Amsterdam 1968).

2. In this context, see for example his review of Syme's *Tacitus* (III 739–744), the 'Marginal Notes on the History of Classical Philology' (I 379–87), or the complaint (I 343) on the lack of information about Rostovtzeff's Russian years.

3. *Science and Society* 10 (1946) 361–91.

4. Bradford Welles, who must have been aware of Reinhold's article, omitted it from the bibliographical note appended to the third and longest of his appreciations of Rostovtzeff, in *Architects and Craftsmen in History. Festschrift für A. P. Usher* (Tübingen 1956) p. 57, note 6.

5. *Journal of Hellenic Studies* 88 (1958) 156.

6. Attention should be called to the important book, much influenced by Momigliano, of B. Bravo, *Philologie, histoire, philosophie d'histoire. Etude sur J. G. Droysen, historien de l'antiquité* (Wroclaw, Warsaw, Cracow 1968).

7. See the review of Th. Boman, *Das hebräische Denken im Vergleich mit dem griechischen* (III 759–64), or 'Time in Ancient Historiography' (IV 13–41).

8. H. Langerbeck, in *Gnomon* 34 (1962) 101.

9. *Paideia: the Ideals of Greek Culture*, vol. 1, trans. from the 2nd edn by G. Highet (Oxford 1939) pp. xvii, xviii. The preface to the first German edition is dated October 1933, to the second, July 1935. Cf. W. Schadewaldt, 'Lebenswerte des Griechischen', in *Der Lebenswert des Griechischen*, ed. H. Gehrig [*Veröffentlichungen der Katholischen Akademie der Erzdiözese Freiburg*, no. 29 (1973)] pp. 65–75, which reads, unintentionally of course, like one long parody of D. H. Lawrence on the Etruscans.

10. See the 'Chiarimento' following the Berve review, published in *Athenaeum*, n.s. 43 (1965) 441–43, mentioned but not reprinted in the *Terzo Contributo*.

11. The one in English is reprinted (I 361–54), not the Italian one, *Rivista storica italiana* 65 (1953) 481–95, which covers the same ground but is not merely a translation.

Notes to Chapter 5

ARCHAEOLOGY AND HISTORY

1. *Studies in Historiography* (London 1966) p. 91.

2. L. R. and S. R. Binford, *New Perspectives in Archaeology* (Chicago 1968); cf. the review-article, 'Renouveau des méthodes et théorie d'archéologie', by S. Cleuziou and others, *Annales: Economies, Sociétés, Civilisations* 28 (1973) 35–51.

3. *Ancient Europe* (Edinburgh 1965) pp. 4–5.

4. *Dawn of the Gods* (London 1968) p. 6.

5. It is perhaps worth noting that Miss Hawkes is one of the most energetic defenders of the romance of archaeology against hard doctrine and the rapidly increasing employment of a battery of scientific tests; see her article, 'The Proper Study of Mankind', *Antiquity* 42 (1968) 255–62. But she is by no means the only one: see, for example, the regret expressed by R. Wauchope, in his introduction to *They Found the Buried Cities* (Chicago 1965), that 'in their published reports, few archaeologists reveal their hardships and adventures, or even their thoughts and emotions'.

6. *Anthropomorphic Figurines of Predynastic Egypt and Neolithic Crete . . .* (London 1968) pt. II.

7. *Analytical Archaeology* (London 1968) p. 17.

8. This point was made by C. Renfrew in opening his review of Ucko's book in *Man* 4 (1969) 297–8.

9. *Ibid.*

10. 'The Interpretation of Prehistoric Anthropomorphic Figurines', *Journal of the Royal Anthropological Institute* 92 (1962) 38–54.

11. *Op. cit.*, pp. 21–22.

12. A comparable argument, based on Malinowski's Trobriand material, will be found in M. A. Smith, 'The Limitation of Inference in Archaeology', *Archaeological News Letter* 6 (1955) 307, the most commonly cited statement of what I have been calling the pessimistic position.

13. *Op. cit.*, pp. 11, xiii, 3; cf. A. C. Spaulding, in Binford, *op. cit.*, p. 33: My 'argument turns on (1) the abandonment in effect by both groups [archaeologists and social anthropologists] of the notion of historical explanation as a valid category of intellectual activity and, even with more force, of scientific activity.'

14. Clarke, *op. cit.*, p. 13.

15. *Ibid.*, p. 22.

16. *Ibid.*, pp. 21–22.

17. *Ibid.*, p. 13.

18. See B. G. Trigger, 'Major Concepts of Archaeology in Historical

Perspective', *Man* 3 (1968) 527–41. This article and the books by Clarke and the Binfords provide full bibliographies on the new perspectives.

19. Clarke, *op. cit.*, pp. 112–13.

20. *Ibid.*, p. 392.

21. *Ibid.*, pp. 618–24. The original study is G. A. Fedorov-Davydov, 'On Dating Types of Artefacts from Burial Assemblages', *Sovetskaia Arkheologia*, no. 3 (1965) 50–65, reprinted in English in *Soviet Anthropology and Archaeology* 5, no. 2 (1966) 22–33.

22. Anyone who believes that it may be easy to draw safe inferences from certain types of objects, at least, will profit from P. J. Ucko, 'Penis Sheaths: a Comparative Study', *Proceedings of the Royal Anthropological Institute . . . for 1969*, pp. 27–67.

23. See, for example, M. I. Finley and others, 'The Trojan War', *Journal of Hellenic Studies* 84 (1964) 1–20.

24. See E. H. Warmington, ed., *Remains of Old Latin* III–IV, in the *Loeb Classical Library*.

25. Four volumes of E. Gjerstad's projected six on *Early Rome* have been published so far.

26. See A. Momigliano, *Terzo Contributo alla storia degli studi classici e del mondo antico* (2 vols., Rome 1966) pt. III, and *Quarto Contributo* . . . (Rome 1969) pt. III; E. Gjerstad, 'Discussions concerning Early Rome', *Historia* 16 (1967) 257–78.

27. It is fitting that the best general account has been written by an archaeologist: John Boardman, *The Greeks Overseas* (2nd edn, Penguin 1973).

28. Attention should be directed to the promising new inquiry now under way, based on the distribution in southern Italy and Sicily of imported Athenian pottery; see the brief report by G. Vallet, with discussion, in *La circolazione della moneta ateniese in Sicilia e in Magna Grecia* (published as a supplement to vols. 12–14 of the *Annali* of the Istituto italiano di numismatica, 1969) pp. 225–37. Cf. S. Dimitriu and P. Alexandrescu, 'L'importation de la céramique attique dans les colonies du Pont-Euxin avant les guerres médiques', *Revue archéologique*, n.s. (1973) no. i, pp. 23–38.

29. See my report on classical Greece in *Trade and Politics in the Ancient World*, vol. 1 of the *Proceedings* of the Second International Conference of Economic History, Aix-en-Provence 1962 (Paris and The Hague 1965) pp. 11–35.

30. Charles Singer and others, *A History of Technology* (Oxford 1954–58). I wrote a harsh review of vol. 2 in the *Economic History Review*, 2nd ser., 12 (1959) 120–25, and I have no reason to retreat in any way. Indeed, my objections are strengthened by the pernicious influence this work continues to exercise; the very recent *Technology in the Ancient World* (London 1970), a popular introduction by an acknowledged expert, H. Hodges, for which the 'two main sources' are the Singer volume and the late R. J. Forbes' multi-volume *Studies in Ancient Technology* (Leiden 1955–), reveals little

interest in non-archaeological evidence, and, it appears from the text, little acquaintance. Forbes, I hasten to add, did not belong to this school of thought.

31. See M. Renard, *Technique et agriculture en pays trévire et rémois* (Brussels 1959); J. Kolendo, 'La moissoneuse antique en Gaule romaine', *Annales: économies, sociétés, civilisations* (1960) 1099–1114, and *Postep techniczny sily roboczej w rolnictwie starozytnej Italii* (Polish Academy of Sciences 1968), with French summary, pp. 184–87, and in *Acta Poloniae Historica* 18 (1968) 51–62; K. D. White, *Agricultural Implements of the Roman World* (Cambridge 1967).

32. C. Renfrew and others, 'Obsidian in the Aegean', *Annual of the British School at Athens* 60 (1965) 225–47.

33. See C. Renfrew and J. S. Peacey, 'Aegean Marble: a Petrological Study', *ibid.*, 63 (1968) 45–66. One instance of how historical conclusions were drawn from a false guess about the provenance of a marble slab on which a decree had been inscribed is fully discussed by A. Georgiadès and W. K. Pritchett, 'The Koan Fragment of the Monetary Decree', *Bulletin de correspondence hellénique* 89 (1965) 400–40.

34. *Op. cit.*, p. 45.

35. *The Social and Economic History of the Hellenistic World* (3 vols., Oxford 1941) pp. 775–76.

36. It is only fair to add that the Rhodian catalogue may at last be in sight, thanks to the sustained efforts of Virginia Grace.

37. See P. Courbin in the introduction to a volume he edited, *Etudes archéologiques* (Paris 1963) pp. 14–16.

38. A. M. Snodgrass, 'Barbarian Europe and Early Iron Age Greece', *Proceedings of the Prehistoric Society* 31 (1965) 229–40. See now his *The Dark Age of Greece* (Edinburgh 1971) ch. 5.

39. The situation emerges clearly from M. Andronikos' fascicle, *Totenkult*, in *Archaeologia Homerica* (Göttingen 1968). Whereas his section on cremation and inhumation (pp. 51–76) permits a number of meaningful diachronic tabulations and formulations (though he has not made them himself, preferring the less revealing technique of continuous prose), the much briefer section on grave-goods (pp. 97–102) hardly advances our knowledge.

40. (London 1964).

41. For the Bronze Age an important step has been taken by W. A. McDonald and R. Hope Simpson in cataloguing sites in the Peloponnese; see *American Journal of Archaeology* 65 (1961) 221–60; 68 (1964) 229–45; 73 (1969) 123–77. Cf. Hope Simpson, *A Gazetteer and Atlas of Mycenaean Sites* [*Bulletin* of the London Institute of Classical Studies, Suppl. 16 (1965)].

42. See the details, chiefly for classical Greece, in S. C. Humphreys, 'Archaeology and the Social and Economic History of Classical Greece', *La Parola del Passato*, fasc. 116 (1967) 374–400.

43. F. M. Cornford, *Microcosmographia Academica* (4th edn, Cambridge 1949) p. 16.

44. See Courbin, *op. cit.*, p. 15: 'Working conditions [in archaeology] have very often destroyed the answers before the questions could be posed.... Why be surprised, under these conditions, that so many excavations turn out to be virtually useless for anything that is not art history?'

45. 'Die Bedeutung der bemahlten Keramik für den griechischen Handel', *Jahrbuch des deutschen archäologischen Instituts* 74 (1959) 114–23.

Notes to Chapter 6

ANTHROPOLOGY AND THE CLASSICS

1. The address is reprinted in the University Books edn of *Themis* (Hyde Park, N.Y., 1962).

2. Quoted from Clyde Kluckhohn, *Anthropology and the Classics* (Providence 1961) p. 20.

3. Gilbert Murray, *An Unfinished Biography*, ed. Jean Smith and Arnold Toynbee (London 1960) p. 140. Part II, from which this quotation is taken, consists of 'contributions by his friends'.

4. *The Greeks and the Irrational* (Berkeley and Los Angeles 1951) pp. 104 and 122 note 5.

5. *Myth: Its Meaning and Function in Ancient and Other Cultures* (Cambridge, Berkeley and Los Angeles 1970) p. 273.

6. Even Louis Gernet, the most tenaciously Durkheimian of all Hellenists, seems not to have been much involved with the anthropological studies pursued in North Africa during the thirty years he taught at the University of Algiers, from 1917 to 1947; see S. C. Humphreys, 'The Work of Louis Gernet', *History and Theory* 10 (1971) 172–96, at p. 176.

7. See briefly R. Ackerman, 'Jane Ellen Harrison: The Early Work', *Greek, Roman and Byzantine Studies* 13 (1972) 209–30.

8. Foreword to Thorne Deuel, *The Human Factor in the Behavior of Peoples* (Illinois State Museum, Springfield 1971) p. ix. Cf. A. L. Kroeber's introduction to the compendium he edited, *Anthropology Today* (Chicago 1953).

9. In *Man and Culture. An Evaluation of the Work of Bronislaw Malinowski*, ed. R. Firth (London 1957) p. 136.

10. *Op. cit.*, p. 22.

11. E. E. Evans-Pritchard, *Essays in Social Anthropology* (London 1962) p. 15.

12. Evans-Pritchard has said it elegantly, with respect to history generally: *ibid.*, ch. 1, 3.

13. 'Implications of Literacy in Traditional China and India', in *Literacy*

in Traditional Societies, ed. J. Goody (Cambridge 1968) pp. 70–84, at pp. 70–72.

14. The phrase is that of Philip Abrams, 'The Sense of the Past and the Origins of Sociology', *Past & Present*, no. 55 (1972) 18–32, at p. 20.

15. The two lectures are printed in his *Essays*. The sentence quoted appears on p. 46.

16. *History and Social Anthropology*, ed. I. M. Lewis (London 1968) p. xiv.

17. *Ibid.*, p. xxv.

18. A. G. Spaulding, in *New Perspectives in Archaeology*, ed. L. R. and S. R. Binford (Chicago 1968) p. 33. See generally ch. 5 above.

19. *Essays* p. 20.

20. Deuel, *op. cit.*, p. 148; cf. his next statement: 'People have to work to obtain food and other requirements.' C. Lévi-Strauss, *Structural Anthropology*, trans. C. Jacobson and B. G. Schoepf (London 1968) p. 13, quotes a number of statements by Malinowski on precisely this level of useless generality.

21. 'Some Problems of Methodology in the Social Sciences', reprinted in his *Race, Language and Culture* (New York 1940) pp. 260–9, at p. 268.

22. *Rethinking Anthropology* (London, corrected edn, 1966) ch. 1.

23. 'Sociology and History' (a review-article), *Past & Present*, no. 52 (1971) 118–25, at p. 122. Cf. W. G. Runciman's neat formulation, 'Sociology (together with history and anthropology) is a consumer of laws, not a producer of them': *Sociology in Its Place* (Cambridge 1970) p. 10.

24. Runciman, *op. cit.*, ch. 1, accepts the possibility of laws in a 'weak sense' in history, anthropology and sociology, but his distinction does not invalidate my contention.

25. J. A. Barnes, 'Time Flies like an Arrow', *Man*, n.s. 6 (1971) 537–52, at p. 541.

26. F. Boas, 'History and Science in Anthropology: a Reply', *American Anthropologist*, n.s. 38 (1936) 137–51, reprinted in his *Race, Language* pp. 305–11, at p. 305.

27. L. Rosen, 'Language, History, and the Logic of Inquiry in Lévi-Strauss and Sartre', *History and Theory* 10 (1971) 259–94, at p. 286.

28. *Ibid.*, p. 285. I trust that no one will object that I have quoted a commentator rather than the *ipsissima verba* of Lévi-Strauss.

29. I quote from the English translation (London 1966) p. 262. Cf. R. Nisbet, 'The Myth of the Renaissance', *Comparative Studies in Society and History* 15 (1973) 473–92.

30. In *Comparative Studies in Society and History* 13 (1971) 357.

31. *Op. cit.*, p. 545.

32. Cf. the opening sentences of Abrams, 'Sense of the Past': 'Sociology is an attempt to understand the direction of change. More completely, it is a science of social development.'

33. J. Piaget, *Structuralism*, trans. C. Maschler (London 1971) p. 12.

34. *Essays* p. 19.

35. Lewis, *op. cit.*, p. xi.

36. See Leach, *Rethinking Anthropology*, or, for that matter, the whole of his *Political Systems of Highland Burma* (London 1954).

37. 'Malinowski and the Study of Social Change', in Firth, *op. cit.*, pp. 229–244, at p. 243.

38. Leach, in Firth, *op. cit.*, p. 131, quoting Lienhardt's 'Modes of Thought', in E. E. Evans-Pritchard and others, *The Institutions of Primitive Society* (London 1954) pp. 95–107, at p. 97.

39. *Essays* pp. 16–17.

40. *Literacy* p. 28.

41. *Ibid.*, especially his introduction and the first chapter (by Goody and Ian Watt).

42. See Evans-Pritchard, *Essays* pp. 23–24; cf. Abrams, 'Sociology and History'.

43. Gough, *op. cit.*, provides a good example.

44. *Literacy* p. 2.

45. M. G. Smith, 'A Structural Approach to Comparative Politics', in *Varieties of Political Theory*, ed. David Easton (Englewood Cliffs, N.J., 1966) pp. 113–28, at pp. 114–15.

46. *Modern Revolutions* (Cambridge 1972) p. 242.

47. *African Political Systems*, ed. M. Fortes and E. E. Evans-Pritchard (London 1940) pp. xx–xxi.

48. *Political Anthropology*, trans. A. M. Sheridan Smith (Penguin edn, 1972) pp. vii–viii, 187, 195.

49. *Ibid.*, pp. 1, 23.

50. *Ibid.*, p. 149.

51. F. G. Bailey, *Stratagems and Spoils. A Social Anthropology of Politics* (Oxford 1969) pp. xiii, 1, ix. I am not frightened off by Bailey's prefatory threats (p. xi): 'To fasten upon the differences and use them to scale peoples into superior and inferior is scientifically unprofitable (because it blocks systematic inquiry) and it is also immoral.'

52. E. A. Winckler, 'Political Anthropology', in *Biennial Review of Anthropology 1969*, ed. B. J. Siegel (Stanford 1970) pp. 301–86, at pp. 305–6.

53. *Ibid.*, pp. 307–9, 303.

54. I. Schapera, *Government and Politics in Tribal Societies* (1956) pp. 61, 62, 205; and Lucy Mair, *Primitive Government* (Penguin edn, 1964) p. 111.

55. Mair, *ibid.*, p. 138.

56. *Op. cit.*, p. 13; cf. pp. 18 and 42 (Gluckman).

57. *Anthropologie de la Grèce ancienne*, ed. J.-P. Vernant (Paris 1968) pt. III.

58. The phrase quoted is Abrams', from the fuller quotation above, at note 23.

59. S. C. Humphreys, in *Man*, n.s. 5 (1970) 528.

60. See the collection of his essays, *Primitive, Archaic and Modern Economies*, ed. G. Dalton (Anchor Books 1968); cf. S. C. Humphreys, 'History, Economics, and Anthropology: The Work of Karl Polanyi', *History and Theory* 8 (1969) 165–212; my 'Aristotle and Economic Analysis', *Past & Present*, no. 47 (1970) 3–25, reprinted in *Studies in Ancient Society*, ed. Finley (London 1974) ch. 2; Dalton, 'Karl Polanyi's Analysis of Trade and His Wider Paradigm', in *Trade and Civilization*, ed. J. A. Sabloff and C. C. Lamberg-Karlovsky (forthcoming).

61. See Finley, *The Ancient Economy* (London, Berkeley and Los Angeles 1973).

62. See Runciman, *op. cit.*, chs. 1–2, most succinctly on pp. 16–17.

63. This point has been made sharply by Keith Hopkins, 'Classicists and Sociologists', *Times Literary Supplement*, 31 March 1972, pp. 355–56.

64. *Highland Burma* p. 16.

65. See E. Gellner, *Cause and Meaning in the Social Sciences*, ed. I. C. Jarvie and J. Agassi (London and Boston 1973) ch. 7.

Notes to Chapter 7

THE ANCIENT GREEKS AND THEIR NATION

1. *A History of Greece*, vol. 2 (London 1862) pp. 39–41.

2. There was another flurry among the world state (or 'one world') advocates immediately after the Second World War, e.g. Norman Cousins, *Modern Man Is Obsolete* (New York 1945).

3. One notable protest is that of H. Strasburger, 'Der Einzelne und die Gemeinschaft im Denken der Griechen', *Historische Zeitschrift* 177 (1954) 227–48, reprinted in *Zur griechischen Staatskunde*, ed. F. Gschnitzer (Darmstadt 1969) pp. 97–122 (I shall cite the original pagination). Another, tendentious one will be noted later: H. E. Stier, *Grundlagen und Sinn der griechischen Geschichte* (Stuttgart 1945).

4. Walbank, 'Nationality in Roman History' pp. 146–48. The Liddell-Scott-Jones Lexicon is similarly infected: for *patris*, originally a poetic feminine form of *patrios* (which we encountered in ch. 2) which then entered ordinary speech, the basic definition given is 'one's fatherland, country', then, as a secondary sense, 'native town or village'. The fact is that *patris* normally means 'fatherland, country' only in the particular sense of 'native town or village'; see Stier, *op. cit.*, pp. 117–19. Indeed, in Homer *patris* had the still narrower connotation of 'family estate': Strasburger, *op. cit.*, pp. 230–32.

5. John Stuart Mill, quoted from C. K. Ogden and I. A. Richards, *The Meaning of Meaning* (10th edn, London 1949) facing p. 1.

6. In a posthumously published easay, 'La nation', *L'Année sociologique*

(1953/4) 7–68, Marcel Mauss showed that the close conceptual link between nation and state underlines the notorious history of the difficulty in defining 'nation' satisfactorily. 'Nation', incidentally, cannot be translated into ancient Greek, and 'Hellas' was employed in a variety of senses, including 'old Greece' in the narrow sense of the Greek world before the great north-eastern and western expansion (e.g. Thucydides 1.2.1).

7. *Weltbürgertum und Nationalstaat. Studien zur Genesis des deutschen Nationalstaates* (Munich and Berlin 1908) p. 7. I have quoted only a portion of the prolonged (and mixed) biological metaphor, partly because such phrases as 'Selbstbestimmungsdrang der Nationen' are beyond my powers as a translator.

8. Stier, *op. cit.*, pp. 108–10, 167–70, criticizing Meinecke, denies this. The *polis*, he says, was a proper *Staatsnation*, but he disputes Meinecke entirely on the latter's terms, as is fitting for a historian closely associated intellectually with Spengler.

9. Walbank, 'Nationality in Roman History' p. 148. The further argument that the great dispersion of the Greeks precluded the political unification of the whole of Hellas is a red herring. Let us put aside Phasis or Sinope in Asia Minor, Marseilles in Gaul. There was no move to unite the Greek peninsula or Greek Sicily, where the conditions of contiguity and manageable size were fulfilled: each became a single Roman province before the end of the second century B.C.

10. Behind the ideology of common descent lay larger views of human and ethnic origins, which the Greeks manipulated in various ways to set themselves above and beyond the barbarians; see E. J. Bickerman, '*Origines Gentium*', *Classical Philology* 47 (1952) 65–81.

11. Xenophanes, frag. 11 and 15, Diels-Kranz ed.

12. Heraclitus, frag. 40 and 57, Diels-Kranz ed.

13. I have examined some of the implications in my *Democracy Ancient and Modern* (New Brunswick and London 1973).

14. Heraclitus, frag. 107. Epicurus held a similar view according to Clement of Alexandria, *Stromata* 1.15.67.1.

15. For a modest example of the discoveries made possible by such a quantitative analysis, see Helen H. Bacon, *Barbarians in Greek Tragedy* (New Haven 1961). I have refrained from using the technical term 'content analysis' employed in modern communication research because it appears to infuriate some, at any rate, among classical historians. Most of the current work seems to concentrate on the mass media, on propaganda and politics, or on psychotherapy, all in the contemporary world. For the historian, the most useful introduction is still B. Berelson, *Content Analysis in Communication Research* (1952, reissue New York 1971); cf. the introduction to part I, by K. Krippendorff, and the extensive bibliography in *The Analysis of Communication Content*, ed. G. Gerbner *et al.* (New York 1969). For an application of the techniques to a historical question, see e.g. G. Shapiro *et al.*, 'Quantitative Studies of the French Revolution', *History and Theory* 12 (1973) 163–91.

16. Translations of Hesiod are by H. G. Evelyn-White in the Loeb Classical Library.

17. I shall ignore the distinction suggested by R. K. Merton between 'groups' and 'categories', for, helpful though it is in certain analyses, it would introduce an unnecessary complication into the present discussion; see Merton and A. K. Rossi, 'Contribution to the Theory of Reference Group Behavior', in *Readings in Reference Group Theory and Research*, ed. H. H. Hyman and E. Singer (New York and London 1968) pp. 26–68, reprinted in part from Merton, *Social Theory and Social Structure* (rev. edn, Glencoe, Ill., 1957) pp. 225–75. Hellas is of course a category in this terminology. There were other categories, which I have not bothered to include in my list, such as Lacedaemonians and Ionians.

18. The best edition of Aeneas, with English translation and detailed commentary, is by L. W. Hunter, rev. by S. A. Handford (Oxford 1927). I have modified their translation slightly.

19. See L. P. Marinovitch, 'Greece in the Fourth Century B.C. Social Struggle and Mercenaries in the Work of Aeneas Tactieus', *Vestnik drevnei istorii* (1962) 49–77 (in Russian).

20. I take the definition from the only full-scale study of *stasis* known to me, the unpublished Cambridge dissertation of J. C. Octon, *Stasis in the Greek World . . . from the End of the Peloponnesian War to the Death of Alexander the Great* (1967) p. 7; cf. the Inaugural Lecture of D. Loenen, *Stasis* (Amsterdam 1953).

21. See the documentation for the fourth century B.C. in Octon, *op. cit.*, pp. 106–36.

22. Cf. the generalization that the formation of a self-conscious nation always 'starts with a relatively small social nucleus whose influence spreads strongly until it eventually reaches millions of people. . . . It originates with independent *individual leaders* in various realms of *cultural activity* . . .' (my italics): F. Znaniecki, *Modern Nationalities: A Sociological Study* (Urbana, Ill., 1952) p. 24.

23. I cannot enter into a discussion of Greek leagues, on which see J. A. O. Larsen, *Greek Federal States* (Oxford 1968), and his earlier *Representative Government in Greek and Roman History* (Berkeley and Los Angeles 1955). Some were in reality miniature empires, in which one *polis* sought to dominate another. Others were more genuine attempts at voluntary federation in limited areas, and the striking fact is that these arose in precisely the more backward regions, notably Aetolia and Achaea, in which the *polis* was little developed. They were anyway no more immune from *stasis* than their component cities.

24. See the documentation in Walbank, 'Nationality in Roman History' p. 147.

25. The fundamental study is A. Aymard, 'Le protocole royal grec et son évolution', *Revue des études anciennes* 1 (1943) 232–63, reprinted in his *Etudes d'histoire ancienne* (Paris 1967) pp. 73–99. The sole and infrequent exception

to what I have just said, the 'tribal' monarchy (hence 'king of the Macedonians'), is irrelevant here.

26. Diogenes Laertius, *Lives of the Philosophers* 6.63. Cf. Marcus Aurelius, *Meditations* 4.23.

27. In Ptolemaic Egypt, a Greek's 'city' continued for a long time to be, in many cases, the city from which he or his forebears had emigrated to Egypt, and therefore had no juridical significance: see E. Bickermann, 'Der Heimatsvermark und die staatsrechtliche Stellung der Hellenen im potolemäischen Ägypten', *Archiv für Papyrusforschung* 8 (1927) 216–39; D. Nörr, 'Origo. Studien zur Orts-, Stadts-, und Reichszugehörigkeit in der Antike', *Tijdschrift voor Rechtsgeschiedenis* 31 (1963) 525–600, at pp. 539–49.

28. See the subtle distinction, in the city-*ethnos* sphere, uncovered by J. Roy, 'Arcadian Nationality as Seen in Xenophon's *Anabasis*', *Mnemosyne*, 4th ser., 25 (1972) 129–36.

Notes to Chapter 8

THE PROBLEM OF THE UNITY OF GREEK LAW

1. (Leipzig 1891, reissue 1963) pp. 61–62.

2. H. L. A. Hart, *The Concept of Law* (Oxford 1961) p. 171.

3. The plausible suggestion has been made that what Strabo (3.3.7) had in mind about the Lusitanians was a contrast with the Baleares, among whom, according to Diodorus (5.18.1), it was the custom for the groom's kinsmen to have intercourse with the bride first.

4. The best edition will be found in *Inscriptiones Graecae Siciliae . . .*, ed. V. Arangio-Ruiz and A. Olivieri (Milan 1925).

5. H. J. Wolff, in *Seminar* 3 (1945) 104, a review-article (of Calhoun, *Introduction to Greek Legal Science*) reprinted in German in his *Beiträge zur Rechtsgeschichte Altgriechenlands . . .* (Weimar 1961) pp. 243–58.

6. This is well stated by L. Gernet in the concluding pages (cciii–ccvi) of his introduction in volume 1 of the Budé edition of the *Laws* (Paris 1951).

7. M. I. Finley, 'Marriage, Sale and Gift in the Homeric World', *Revue internationale des droits de l'antiquité*, 3rd ser., 2 (1955) 167–94.

8. H. J. Wolff, 'Die Grundlagen des griechischen Eherechts', *Tijdschrift voor Rechtsgeschiedenis* 20 (1952) 1–29, 157–81.

9. *Ibid.*, p. 160.

10. The citizenship of different kinds of *nothoi* is not entirely clear; see generally A. R. W. Harrison, *The Law of Athens: the Family and Property* (Oxford 1958) pp. 61–70.

11. 'Eherecht' p. 167. I do not find convincing a recent attempt to interpret the document of 311 B.C. as remaining strictly within 'the Greek tradition of marriage by *engyesis*': C. Vatin, *Recherches sur le mariage et la condition de la femme mariée à l'époque hellénistique* (Paris 1970) pp. 165–67.

12. Wolff, 'Eherecht' pp. 159, 162. Contrast the conclusion drawn from the same evidence by U. E. Paoli, 'Diritto attico e diritto greco', in *Scritti . . . in onore di Contardo Ferrini* (Milan 1946) pp. 571–93.

13. *Elephantine-Papyri*, ed. O. Rubinsohn (Berlin 1907) no. 1, reprinted in L. Mitteis and U. Wilcken, *Grundzüge und Chrestomathie der Papyruskunde* (Leipzig and Berlin 1912) II no. 283.

14. The document is a 'double' one. In the first copy the scribe carelessly omitted the name of the groom's city, Temnos in Asia Minor, which appears in the second copy. The original editor called attention to the fact, but it was overlooked by Mitteis-Wilcken and by scholars ever since, myself included, despite a protest by J. Bingen in *Chronique d'Egypte* 41 (1966) 403. Obviously there is no reason to turn to the bride's city, rather than the groom's, for a model, and the Coan parallel falls on that ground alone. I have nevertheless retained my original text because the type of reasoning I am criticizing cannot be met by the elimination of one single text.

15. *Sammlung der griechischen Dialektinschriften* no. 3624.

16. In *Beiträge* p. 221, Wolff compares this passage with the phrase in Demosthenes 57.53, 'were I a *nothos* or a *xenos*'. The two passages together prove that *nothoi* were not *xenoi*, not members of another community, which is unarguable but not very illuminating.

17. *The Definition of Law*, ed. A. H. Campbell (Cambridge 1958) p. 4.

18. See E. Rabel, 'Nachgeformte Rechtsgeschäfte', *Zeitschrift der Savigny-Stiftung für Rechtgeschichte, Romanistische Abteilung* 27 (1906) 290–335; 28 (1907) 311–79, reprinted in his *Gesammelte Aufsätze*, vol. 4, ed. H. J. Wolff (Tübingen 1971) pp. 9–104.

19. See F. Bömer, *Untersuchungen über die Religion der Sklaven in Griechenland und Rom* 2 [Akademie der Wissenschaften und der Literatur, Mainz, *Abhandlungen der geistes- und sozialwissenschaftlichen Klasse* (1960) no. 1] pp. 29–49.

20. *Inscriptiones Graecae* XII Supp., no. 347, lines 1–2.

21. See J. Modrzejewski, 'La règle de droit dans l'Egypte ptolémaïque', *American Studies in Papyrology* 1 (1966) 125–73.

22. There was failure of diffusion even in this field; see briefly my *Ancient Economy* pp. 162–63 on the Athenian commercial courts (*dikai emporikai*).

23. See W. Kamps, 'Les origines de la fondation cultuelle dans la Grèce ancienne', *Archives d'histoire du droit oriental* 1 (1937) 145–79.

Notes to Chapter 9

THE ALIENABILITY OF LAND IN ANCIENT GREECE

1. For a full presentation of the sources and bibliography see D. Asheri, *Distribuzioni di terre nell'antica Grecia* [*Memoria dell'Accademia delle Scienze di Torino, Classe di Scienze Morali . . .*, 4th ser. (1966) no. 10], supplemented

by his 'Supplementi coloniari e condizione giuridica della terra nel mondo greco', *Rivista storica dell'antichità* 1 (1971) 77–91. A useful summary and critique will be found in F. Cassola, 'Sull'alienabilità del suolo nel mondo greco', *Labeo* 11 (1965) 206–19. Whereas the discussion had previously concentrated on the archaic period, a new turn was given to it by the argument, which has received some support, that in Athens land remained inalienable until late in the fifth century B.C.: J. V. A. Fine, *Horoi* [*Hesperia*, Suppl. 9 (1951)] ch. 8.

2. See W. Kamps, 'La fiducie dans le droit de Grande-Grèce et l'origine de la *mancipatio familiae*', *Revue historique de droit français*, 4th ser., 15 (1936) 142–55. The texts are published in *Inscriptiones Graecae Siciliae* . . ., ed. V. Arangio-Ruiz and A. Olivieri (Milan 1925) nos. 18–20. For the dating see L. H. Jeffrey, *The Local Scripts of Archaic Greece* (Oxford 1961) pp. 258–59.

3. *Sylloge inscriptionum graecarum*, 3rd edn, no. 141, *Inschriften von Milet* I 3, no. 333e, and *Sylloge* no. 490, respectively.

4. *Sylloge* no. 1106 B 43–46. See generally W. Kamps, 'Les origines de la fondation cultuelle dans la Grèce ancienne', *Archives d'histoire du droit oriental* 1 (1937) 145–79.

5. Attempts to alter the position by asserting that the word *chremata* excludes real property are lexically indefensible, as should be obvious from two passages in the Code, II 48–50 and VIII 42–53, and from the way *chremata* is qualified by *epipolaia* in V 41 when it is desired to specify 'movable goods'. It is further demonstrable that *chremata* can never be assigned a more precise meaning than 'possessions' or 'wealth' without help from the context; see briefly A. Kränzlein, *Eigentum und Besitz im griechischen Recht* (Berlin 1963) pp. 23–24. This is also the place to protest the injection of etymologically stimulated overtones into the word *kleros* whenever it is used. The employment of the English word 'lot' in present-day land registers ought to provide a sufficient antidote.

6. Athens: Lysias 19.37; Thera: *Inscriptiones Graecae* XII 3, 330 B 29–33.

7. Gortyn: VI 31–36; Tegea: *Sylloge* 306, sects. 2, 7 (324 B.C.).

8. *Distribuzioni* p. 21.

9. The story appears in Athenaeus IV 167D.

10. See Fine, cited in note 1.

11. L. Gernet, 'Droit et prédroit en Grèce ancienne', *L'Année sociologique* (1948–49) 21–119, reprinted in his *Anthropologie de la Grèce antique* (Paris 1968) pp. 175–260.

Notes to Chapter 10

SPARTA

1. In 'The Credibility of Early Spartan History', *Historia* 14 (1965) 257–72, C. G. Starr defined the situation succinctly (p. 258): 'We are, I

fear, sometimes in danger of becoming Hellenistic rumour-mongering historians.' Anyone who cares can find the whole exhausting bibliography in the footnotes in F. Kiechle, *Lakonien und Sparta* (Munich and Berlin 1963), but not one sentence to explain how so much accurate ancient information was transmitted to Pindar, who then assembled it in a sort of *Burke's Peerage*, not to mention the *Erinnerungen* of Stephanus of Byzantium.

2. J. Boardman, 'Artemis Orthia and Chronology', *Annual of the British School at Athens* 58 (1963) 1–7.

3. Cf. now Claude Mossé, 'Sparte archaïque', *Parola del Passato* 28 (1973) 7–20.

4. The so-called Great Rhetra, if authentic, was a brief, almost gnomic, early enactment about government, particularly about legislative procedure. No agreement exists among historians even about the date, but most place it earlier than the 'sixth-century revolution', as do I without any hesitation.

5. On the various rites, see W. den Boer, *Laconian Studies* (Amsterdam 1954) pt. III.

6. *Eunomia* became an ambiguous term: 'good order' slid into 'stable government' and *eunomia* became a catchword of propagandists against political change, in particular change to democracy. Herodotus was surely thinking of the primary sense. See A. Andrewes, 'Eunomia', *Classical Quarterly* 32 (1938) 89–102; V. Ehrenberg, *Polis und Imperium* (Zurich and Stuttgart 1965) pp. 139–58.

7. The fact that *homoioi* first appears as a 'technical term' in Xenophon, or that Xenophon alone speaks of *hypomeiones*, Inferiors, does not impress me as having any significance. Spartan social terminology was filled with common nouns and participles assigned a technical meaning, such as *tresantes* (tremblers), *agathoergoi* (well-doers), *neodamodeis* (those newly enfranchised).

8. L. Moretti, 'Olympionikai, i vincitori negli antichi agoni olimpici', *Memorie* of the Accademia nazionale dei Lincei, Classe di scienze morali, 8th ser., 8 (1959) 55–198.

9. On the whole I follow the interpretation of the *krypteia* by H. Jeanmaire, *Couroi et Courètes* (Lille 1939) pp. 540–69. Aristotle, according to Plutarch, *Lycurgus* 28, tied it entirely to policing the helots, but that this is too narrow seems a legitimate inference from Xenophon's carefully veiled generalities (4.4), from the few details we have about the suppression of Cinadon's revolt, and, if it is to be trusted, from the reference to the *krypteia* in Plutarch, *Cleomenes* 28.3. On the other hand, I do not believe that the silence in Plato, *Laws* 633B–C (and in the scholia on the passage), entitles us to reject the Aristotelian tradition as a pure invention reflecting the outside world's image of Spartan brutality to the helots.

10. Xenophon 11.2, 13.11; cf. his *Agesilaus* 1.26; Thucydides 4.80.5. Pierre Vidal-Naquet reminded me that the Athenian state provided each ephebe with a shield and spear, at least in the fourth century B.C. (Aristotle, *Constitution of Athens* 42.4). This comparison reinforces my preference.

11. The main passages in Herodotus are 3.148, 5.51, 6.50, 6.72, 6.82, 8.5.

12. The inscription is reprinted in E. Schwyzer, ed., *Dialectorum Graecarum exempla . . .*, no. 12.

13. See Aristotle, *Politics* 1334a35–39.

14. See A. Andrewes, 'The Government of Classical Sparta', in *Ancient Society and Institutions. Studies Presented to Victor Ehrenberg*, ed. E. Badian (Oxford 1966) pp. 1–20.

15. Thucydides 5.15.1 (however one prefers to heal the corrupt text), 5.34.2.

16. See G. E. M. de Ste. Croix, *The Origins of the Peloponnesian War* (London 1972) pp. 94–101.

17. *The History of Militarism* (New York 1937) pp. 11, 13.

18. Isocrates 6.81; Plato *Laws* 666E.

19. Translated by Richmond Lattimore (Chicago 1947).

20. E.g. E. Kirsten, 'Ein politisches Programm in Pindars ersten pythischen Gedicht', *Rheinisches Museum*, n.F. 90 (1941) 58–71.

21. The fragment is no. 1 in Schroeder's edition; see E. Will, *Doriens et Ioniens* (Paris 1956) p. 59.

22. Translation by C. M. Bowra, *Pindar* (Oxford 1964) p. 152, of fragment 189 in his edition.

23. Jeanmaire, *Couroi* pp. 463–65.

Notes to Chapter 11

UTOPIANISM ANCIENT AND MODERN

1. Translated in Ernest Barker, *From Alexander to Constantine* (Oxford 1959) pp. 58–59.

2. F. E. Manuel, 'Toward a Psychological History of Utopia', *Daedalus* 94 (1965) 293–322, at p. 293.

3. See Ernst Bloch, *Das Prinzip Hoffnung* (Frankfurt 1950) p. 549.

4. 'Varieties of Literary Utopias', *Daedalus* 94 (1965) 323–47, at pp. 330, 339.

5. This is not said in criticism of the fundamental work of Erwin Rohde, *Der griechische Roman und seine Vorläufer* (reprint, Darmstadt 1960) pt. II.

6. This distinction has been formulated as one between a 'utopia d'evasione' and a 'utopia di ricostruzione' by A. Giannini, 'Mito e utopia nella letteratura greca prima di Platone', *Rendiconti* of the Istituto Lombardo, Classe di Lettere, 101 (1967) 101–32. The objection raised by Braunert in his Kiel rectoral address, that the distinction has no ancient textual authority, has no force: H. Braunert, *Utopia* [*Veröffentlichungen der schleswig-holsteinischen Universitätsgesellschaft*, n.F. 51 (1969)] p. 7.

7. See J.-P. Vernant, *Mythe et pensée chez les grecs* (Paris 1965) ch. 1.

8. Quoted in Diogenes Laertius 6.85.

9. On Euhemerus see especially Diodorus 5.41.4–56.7; on Iambulus, Diodorus 2.55.1–60.1.

10. See Bodo Gatz, *Weltalter, goldene Zeit und sinnverwandte Vorstellungen* (Hildesheim 1967) pp. 114–28.

11. See F. Bömer, *Untersuchungen über die Religion der Sklaven in Griechenland und Rom* III [Akademie der Wissenschaften und der Literatur, Mainz, *Abhandlungen der geistes- und sozialwissenschaftliche Klasse* (1961) no. 4] pp. 173–95.

12. *Oracula sibyllina* 3.743–50, translated in A. O. Lovejoy and G. Boas, *A Documentary History of Primitivism and Related Ideas in Antiquity* (Baltimore 1935) p. 86.

13. See I. Hahn, 'Die soziale Utopie der Spätantike', *Wissenschaftliche Zeitschrift . . . Halle, Gesellschafts- und sprachwissenschaftliche Klasse* 11 (1962) 1357–61. This view is peremptorily dismissed by Alan Cameron, *Claudian* (Oxford 1970) p. 369: 'But these are empty clichés. Claudian was deceiving no one–least of all himself.' Elsewhere (p. 46) he insists on the 'crucial distinction between mere flattery and actual propaganda', a distinction I do not find useful.

14. Diodorus 2.59.7.

15. For a summary of the story and a survey of the bibliography, see Ed. Will, *Histoire politique du monde hellénistique* II (Nancy 1967) pp. 350–56, to which add now Cl. Mossé, 'Les utopies égalitaires à l'époque hellénistique', *Revue historique* 241 (1969) 297–308.

16. See Norman Cohn, *The Pursuit of the Millennium* (reprint, Harper Torchbooks 1961); E. J. Hobsbawm, *Primitive Rebels* (Manchester 1959) chs. 4–6.

17. See J. Vogt, 'Zur Struktur der antiken Sklavenkriege', in his *Sklaverei und Humanität* [*Historia*, Einzelschrift 8 (1965)] pp. 20–60; Finley, *Ancient Sicily* (London and New York 1969) ch. 11; E. A. Thompson, 'Peasant Revolts in Late Roman Gaul and Spain', *Past & Present*, no. 2 (1952) 11–23, reprinted in *Studies in Ancient Society*, ed. Finley (London and Boston 1974) ch. 14.

18. In *Millennial Dreams in Action*, ed. S. L. Thrupp [*Comparative Studies in Society and History*, Suppl. 2 (1962)] p. 215.

19. J. H. Hexter, *More's Utopia* (reprint, Harper Torchbooks 1965) pp. 70–71.

20. The attempt by Braunert, *Utopia* pp. 15–16, to challenge this statement has been answered by B. Kytzler, 'Utopisches Denken und Handeln in der klassischen Antike', in *Der utopische Roman*, ed. R. Villgradter and F. Krey (Darmstadt 1973) pp. 45–68, at pp. 66–68.

21. Lewis Mumford, 'Utopia, the City and the Machine', *Daedalus* 94 (1965) 271–92, at p. 277; cf. J. Vogt, 'Die Sklaven im utopischen Denken der Griechen', *Rivista storica dell'antichità* 1 (1971) 19–32.

22. See the quotations preserved in Athenaeus 6.94–98 (267E–270B).

23. Attempts to put right the confusions in Diodorus do not in the least alter my point; see e.g. H. Braunert, 'Die Heilige Insel des Euhemeros in der Diodor-Ueberlieferung', *Rheinisches Museum für Philologie*, n.F. 108 (1965) 255–68.

24. See R. J. Buck, 'Communalism in the Lipari Islands', *Classical Philology* 54 (1959) 33–39.

25. J. H. Hexter, in his introduction to the edition of *Utopia* by E. Surtz and himself (New Haven and London 1965) p. cxxiii. More's egalitarianism was not quite complete: there were the Siphograuntes with their 'perpetual license from labour to learning', also the criminals and war prisoners who were reduced to quasi-slavery. However, it is a travesty to challenge More's essential, seminal radicalism and egalitarianism on the basis of such flaws in the system, as in the extraordinary assault by S. Avineri, 'War and Slavery in More's *Utopia*', *International Review of Social History* 7 (1972) 260–90; see the review-article by Quentin Skinner in *Past & Present*, no. 38 (1967) 153–68.

26. Frye, 'Literary Utopias' p. 327.

27. Chad Walsh, *From Utopia to Nightmare* (London 1962).

28. *Ibid.*, p. 11.

29. H. Marcuse, *One-Dimensional Man* (Boston and London 1964) p. x.

Notes to Chapter 12

THE HERITAGE OF ISOCRATES

1. E. R. Curtius, *Kritische Essays zur europäischen Literatur* (Bern 1950) pp. 313, 322.

2. A. R. Evans, Jr., in *On Four Modern Humanists*, ed. Evans (Princeton 1970) p. 144.

3. That is the title of the English translation by W. R. Trask (New York 1953), which I shall cite.

4. *Essays* p. 433.

5. *European Literature* p. x (from the author's foreword to the English translation).

6. *Deutscher Geist in Gefahr* (Stuttgart and Berlin 1932) p. 126, reprinted, in the slightly abridged version I have quoted, in the first draft of the introduction to *European Literature*, which had been published in the journal *Die Wandlung* in 1945, was replaced in the book itself by another introduction, and was then reprinted as an appendix to *Essays*, where the passage quoted appears on p. 432.

7. *Education & the University* (London 1943) p. 48. Dr Leavis still clings fast to his early principles: see his *Nor Shall My Sword* (London 1972).

8. *European Literature* p. 580, an appendix (in the English edn only) reproducing his address at the Goethe Bicentennial Convocation in Aspen in 1949. In *Deutscher Geist* he calls Scheler 'the last universal thinker in Germany' (p. 54); Toynbee also gains admission to the golden circle in some oblique and mysterious way: *European Literature* pp. 4–7, *Essays* pp. 347–79.

9. *European Literature* p. 589.

10. *Education* pp. 41–42.

11. *Ibid.*, pp. 24–25.

12. The quotation comes from E. Mikkola, '"Schole" bei Aristoteles', *Arctos*, n.s. 2 (1958) 68–87.

13. See M. K. Hopkins, 'Social Mobility in the Later Roman Empire: the Evidence of Ausonius', *Classical Quarterly*, n.s. 11 (1961) 239–49.

14. On this strain, see R. Joly, *La thème philosophique des genres de vie dans l'antiquité classique* [*Mémoires* of the Académie Royale de Belgique, Classe des lettres . . ., 51 no. 3 (1956)]; A. Grilli, *Il problemo della vita contemplativa* . . . (Milan 1953).

15. R. L. Nettleship, *The Theory of Education in Plato's Republic* (1880, reprint Oxford 1935) p. 27.

16. G. Ryle, in a review in *Mind* 56 (1947) 167–72, at pp. 169–70, reprinted in *Plato, Popper and Politics*, ed. R. Bambrough (Cambridge and New York 1967) pp. 85–90. On Plato's logical difficulties with his soul-society parallel, see B. A. O. Williams, 'The Analogy of City and Soul in Plato's *Republic*', in *Exegesis and Argument* [*Phronesis*, Suppl. 1 (1973)] pp. 196–206.

17. Pseudo-Plutarch, *Lives of the Ten Orators* (in Plutarch, *Moralia*) 838C.

18. E. Mikkola, *Isokrates* (Helsinki 1954). I have quoted Mikkola because his is the most serious (but not persuasive) effort to acquit Isocrates of this accusation and to see him as a political, and even philosophical, thinker of some stature.

19. See F. Kühnert, *Allgemeinbildung und Fachbildung in der Antike* [*Schriften der Sektion für Altertumswissenschaft*, Deutsche Akademie der Wissenschaften zu Berlin, no. 30 (1961)].

20. Trans. by E. S. Haldane and F. H. Simpson (1894, reprint London 1955) II 242.

21. For what follows, see M. Fuhrmann, *Das systematische Lehrbuch. Ein Beitrag zur Geschichte der Wissenschaften in der Antike* (Göttingen 1960).

22. This is the work that eventually crept into the corpus of Aristotle's writings, under the title (in Latin), *Rhetor ad Alexandrum.*

23. H.-I. Marrou, *Histoire de l'éducation dans l'antiquité* (6th edn, Paris 1965) p. 297.

24. See Kühnert, *Allgemeinbildung* pp. 22–25.

25. *Ibid.*, pp. 3–4.

26. I have compiled these figures from R. A. Pack, *The Greek and Latin Literary Texts from Greco-Roman Egypt* (2nd edn, Ann Arbor 1965). Not all

the identifications are secure, so that some of my figures may be a little too high.

27. R. A. Nisbet, 'Sociology in the Academy', in *Sociology and Contemporary Education*, ed. C. H. Page (New York 1964) p. 65.

28. Much the best and fullest account of the situation known to me is John Hajnal, *The Student Trap* (Penguin 1972), to which I am much indebted.

29. A convenient, and rather bleak, summary will be found in the *Report of the Consultative Committee on Secondary Education*, commonly known as the Spens Report (H.M.S.O. 1938), Appendices IV–V.

30. R. Borger and A. E. M. Seaborne, *The Psychology of Learning* (Penguin 1966) p. 144.

31. E. L. Kelly, 'Transfer of Training: an Analytic Study', in *Psychological Concepts in Education*, ed. B. P. Komisar and C. B. Macmillan (Chicago 1967) pp. 30–50, at p. 37.

32. 'Roughly speaking, direct training is from 3 to 20 times as efficacious [as indirect training], according to the nature of the task': C. Burt, 'Transfer of Training', *Educational Review* 12 (1960) 77–93, at p. 80.

33. R. V. Jones, in the Joseph Payne Memorial Lecture, 1963–64, of the College of Preceptors, p. 41, quoted from Hajnal, *Student Trap* p. 149.

34. Hajnal, *Student Trap* pp. 163–64.

35. L. Hudson, 'Selection and the Problem of Conformity', *British Journal of Psychology* 51 (1960) 67–73, reprinted in *Genetic and Environmental Factors in Human Ability*, ed. J. E. Meade and A. S. Parkes (Edinburgh and London 1966) pp. 90–99.

36. Note should be taken of a related error in narrowing the concepts of education and learning. One 'consequence of the growth of knowledge is that children must learn more . . . the sheer bulk facing the child increases year by year': Michael Young, *Innovation and Research in Education* (London 1965) p. 5. The fallacy is quickly exposed by Borger and Seaborne, *Learning* pp. 230–31.

37. R. M. Cook, *Greek Art* (London 1972) p. 181.

38. Leavis, *Education*, *passim*.

39. C. Segal, 'Ancient Texts and Modern Literary Criticism', *Arethusa* 1 (1968) 1–25, at pp. 8–9.

40. *Essays* p. 300.

41. R. Wellek, 'Literary Criticism and Philosophy', *Scrutiny* 5 (1937) 375–83. Leavis's reply was published in vol. 6 (1937) 59–70, reprinted in his *The Common Pursuit* (Penguin edn, 1962) pp. 211–22.

42. *Education* p. 18.

43. Liam Hudson, *Frames of Mind* (Penguin edn, 1970) p. 16.

44. P. Marris, *The Experience of Higher Education* (London 1964) p. 49.

45. Hudson, *Frames of Mind* p. 29.

46. E. Durkheim, *Education and Sociology*, trans. S. D. Fox (New York and London 1956).

47. M. Furhmann, *Die Antike und ihre Vermittler* [*Konstanzer Universitätsreden*, no. 9 (1969)] p. 20; cf. U. Hölscher, *Die Chance des Unbehagens* (Göttingen 1965) pp. 68–80. It is, of course, equally illogical to argue the demerits of such an education from the German experience, or to claim, with Leavis, that English is superior to classics because Robert Bridges disapproved of Gerard Manley Hopkins and because other classically trained critics enjoyed *A Shropshire Lad*, P. G. Wodehouse, Thornton Wilder and Charles Morgan: *Education* pp. 39, 135.

48. Hajnal, *Student Trap* p. 147 and *passim.*

49. See P. Bourdieu, 'L'école conservatrice. Les inégalités devant l'école et devant la culture', *Revue française de sociologie* 7 (1966) 325–47. Totals are what matter in this context, not percentages.

50. *Education and Sociology* p. 67.

51. P. Bourdieu, 'Systems of Education and Systems of Thought', *International Social Science Journal* 19 (1967) 338–58, at pp. 341–42. Bourdieu's work is fundamental on this point; see especially Bourdieu and J.-C. Passeron, *Les héritiers. Les étudiants et la culture* (Paris 1964). I have been unable to find any account in English of comparable importance and sophistication.

52. Z. Bauman, 'Some Problems in Contemporary Education', *International Social Science Journal* 19 (1967) 324–37, especially pp. 325–29.

53. *The Times* for 16 September 1972, p. 16.

54. *Essays* p. 8.

55. 'A Definition of the Humanities', in *The Meaning of the Humanities*, ed. T. M. Greene (Princeton 1940) pp. 1–42, at p. 37. I do not know whether or not Perry had Curtius specifically in mind, but the comment applies to all such 'returns to the past'.

56. 'Religion and Literature', in his *Essays Ancient and Modern* (London 1936) p. 93.

57. Ernest Gellner, *Thought and Change* (London 1964) p. 212, note 1.

58. Conor Cruise O'Brien, *The Suspecting Glance* (London 1972) pp. 90–91.

59. Q. D. Leavis, *Fiction and the Reading Public* (1932, reprint London 1965) p. 265.

60. For a case-study of the absurdities which these claims may reach, see L. Lowenthal, 'Die Auffassung Dostojewski im Vorkriegsdeutschland', *Zeitschrift für Sozialforschung* 3 (1934) 343–81.

61. D. P. Ausubel, in *School Learning*, ed. Ausubel and F. G. Robinson (London 1971) p. 9.

62. Quoted in A. P. Stanley, *The Life and Correspondence of Thomas Arnold* (12th edn, London 1881) II 32.

63. T. M. Greene, in *Meaning of the Humanities*, ed. Greene, p. xv.

64. Quoted from Hölscher, *Chance des Unbehagens* p. 24.

65. That in effect is the argument of H. J. Gans, 'Popular Culture in America: Social Problem in a Mass Society or Social Asset in a Pluralist Society?', in *Social Problems, a Modern Approach*, ed. H. S. Becker (New York 1966) ch. 11. One of his main targets remains unmarked by the cannonade: Leo Lowenthal, *Literature, Popular Culture and Society* (1961, Pacific Books edn, 1968).

66. Cf. E. Chinoy, 'Popular Sociology', in Page, *Sociology and Education* ch. 5.

67. *Abinger Harvest* (Pocket edn, London 1953) p. 111.

68. Hölscher, *Chance des Unbehagens* p. 64.

INDEX

INDEX